D0386927

THE FORGOTTEN FIRST

Also by Bob Glauber

Guts and Genius: The Story of Three Unlikely Coaches Who Came to Dominate the NFL in the '80s

Also by Keyshawn Johnson

Just Give Me the Damn Ball!: The Fast Times and Hard Knocks of an NFL Rookie

THE FORGOTTEN FIRST

Kenny Washington, Woody Strode, Marion Motley, Bill Willis, and the Breaking of the NFL Color Barrier

By Keyshawn Johnson and Bob Glauber

GRAND CENTRAL PUBLISHING

NEW YORK BOSTON

Grand Central Publishing

Hachette Book Group

1290 Avenue of the Americas, New York, NY 10104

grandcentralpublishing.com

twitter.com/grandcentralpub

First Edition: September 2021

Grand Central Publishing is a division of Hachette Book Group, Inc. The Grand Central Publishing name and logo is a trademark of Hachette Book Group, Inc.

The publisher is not responsible for websites (or their content) that are not owned by the publisher.

The Hachette Speakers Bureau provides a wide range of authors for speaking events. To find out more, go to www.hachettespeakersbureau.com or call (866) 376-6591.

Print book interior design by Jeff Stiefel

Library of Congress Cataloging-in-Publication Data has been applied for.

ISBNs: 978-1-5387-0548-3 (hardcover), 978-1-5387-0547-6 (ebook)

Printed in the United States of America

LSC-C

Printing 1, 2021

In remembrance of the four men on whose shoulders generations of NFL players now stand: Kenny Washington, Woody Strode, Bill Willis and Marion Motley.

CONTENTS

INTRODUCTION

The clock stopped with fifteen seconds left in the fourth quarter—the first undefeated season in UCLA history now assured—and Kenny Washington was called to the sidelines by coach Babe Horrell.

More than 103,000 fans had packed into the Los Angeles Memorial Coliseum on a sun-splashed afternoon on December 9, 1939, to watch the USC-UCLA game. The outcome would decide which team went to the Rose Bowl and be in position to win the national championship. As Washington made his way to the bench, the crowd stood and roared. Even USC fans understood the magnitude of the moment and paid tribute to the player whose dashing runs and powerful arm had built the Bruins into a national contender.

Washington had produced one of the greatest seasons in college football history, playing almost every minute of every game in leading UCLA to a 6-0-4 record and nearly conquering a USC team that had more talent, more swagger, and more history than the upstart Bruins.

The game would end in a 0–0 tie—maybe the most impactful scoreless game in football history, given the circumstances and the stakes. And while the result might represent a failure by today's standards, given how easy it has become to score points, this was an epic game—

up to and including the dramatic 71-yard drive Washington engineered in the fourth quarter that nearly resulted in one of the biggest upsets of the season.

Washington played at the left halfback position, giving him primary responsibilities in both the passing and the running game. He led the Bruins on a thirteen-play drive alongside teammate Jackie Robinson—yes, that Jackie Robinson—and his best friend, renowned end Woody Strode, getting the team inside the USC 5-yard line with a mix of his passing and running.

USC stood up to the Bruins near the goal line, stopping UCLA on three straight inside runs, setting up a dramatic fourth-down play. This was an era when coach-to-player communication was prohibited from the sidelines, meaning that the players had to decide whether to go for the game-winning field goal—which might have seemed like a no-brainer but was complicated by the fact that UCLA had missed its last five extra-point kicks over the previous two games.

A vote was taken in the UCLA huddle to decide their fate. Five players wanted to go for the touchdown. Five wanted to kick the field goal. Ned Matthews, ultimately responsible for the play calling, broke the deadlock. The Bruins would go for six points.

Washington walked to the line of scrimmage and surveyed the USC defense. Crouching down low behind the center, he took the snap and faded back to pass. End Don MacPherson, lined up to the right of the formation, sprinted into the end zone and quickly cut to his right. Washington delivered the pass, but Trojans defender Bobby Robertson stepped in front of MacPherson to swat the ball away.

The game would end in a scoreless tie, USC would get the Rose Bowl berth and eventually earn the national title with a win over Tennessee. But Washington's impact was unmistakable against 14-point favorite the Trojans. Washington played all but a few seconds of the entire season—halfback on offense, where he was the leading rusher *and* passer, and safety on defense. He'd become the first player in Bruin history to win All-America honors and was considered among the best—if not the best—college players in the country.

Now it was time for his curtain call.

As he walked to the sidelines, the applause grew. It quickly reached a level almost never heard before in the stadium.

Strode couldn't believe how loud it got.

"It was the most soul-stirring event I have ever seen in sports," he later said. "As Kenny left the field and headed up to the tunnel, the ovation followed him in huge waves. It was like the Pope of Rome had come out."

As his eyes welled with tears at the emotion of his farewell to college football, Washington couldn't have known then that the next time he walked onto this same field years later, he'd make history and open the doors of opportunity for thousands of players after him. Nor could Strode, his closest friend and teammate.

* * *

While Washington left to a thunderous ovation that afternoon, the NFL was in the midst of its annual college draft for the 1940 season. On a cold, overcast day in Milwaukee, representatives from the league's ten teams gathered in the ballroom of the stately Schroeder Hotel.

The draft would last twenty-two rounds, with each team taking twenty players. In all, two hundred players were selected, starting with Tennessee fullback George Cafego going first and five halfbacks among the first ten selections.

Kenny Washington's name was not called that day.

Nor was Strode's.

All two hundred players selected were white.

* * *

Cleveland coach Paul Brown didn't tell Marion Motley and Bill Willis why he wasn't taking them to Miami. He just handed them their weekly salary and told them they wouldn't be traveling with the Browns for their December 3, 1946, game against the Miami Seahawks.

It was the next-to-last game of the inaugural season of the All-America Football Conference, and the Browns were dominating the eight-team league with a 10-2 record. Motley and Willis were two of Brown's most indispensable players—Motley, the bruising fullback who teamed with quarterback Otto Graham to form one of the greatest backfields in pro football history; and Willis, the cat-quick defensive lineman and reliable offensive lineman who'd played for Brown at Ohio State and now was part of Brown's team in the fledgling pro league.

The letters came a few days before the game, and Brown was mortified. Yet he chose to withhold the information from Motley and Willis, the only two African-American players in the league. He didn't tell them of the plot to murder them.

"Paul decided he wasn't going to let them travel to Miami to let them play," said Willis's son, Bill Willis Jr. "He just gave them $500 apiece to stay home. Paul did not say to them, 'I don't want you to go because they're going to kill you.'"

Instead, the coach kept the information to himself and decided not to take any chances.

"They were not aware of the death threats until much later," Willis said. "It would have been terribly upsetting if he'd told them at the time."

* * *

The construction crew arrived at RFK Stadium in Washington, DC, early the morning of June 19, 2020. Workers carefully slipped heavy-duty straps around the ten-foot high monument of George Preston Marshall, founder of the then–Washington Redskins. The night before, the words "Change the Name" had been spray-painted on it in bold letters. Once the statue was secured, it was hoisted off its moorings by a giant crane and taken away from the place it had stood since Marshall had moved the team from Griffith Stadium in 1961.

That the statue was removed on this particular day was not a coincidence. June 19—Juneteenth—is the holiday celebrating the official end of slavery. Also called Liberation Day and Emancipation Day, it commemorates the date of June 19, 1865, when Union Army general Gordon Granger announced slavery's end in Galveston, Texas.

Marshall owned the team from 1932, when he purchased the Boston Braves and then moved the franchise to Washington a year later, until his death in 1969. Marshall, who was behind an unwritten agreement preventing African-American players from joining the NFL from 1933 to 1945, was the last NFL owner to integrate his team. And he only did it in 1962, long after every other team, and only because then–attorney general Robert F. Kennedy and Secretary of the Interior Stewart Udall threatened to prevent the team from playing at the stadium because it was on federally owned land.

"This symbol of a person who didn't believe all men and women were created equal and who had actually worked against integration is counter to all that we as people, a city, and nation represent," read a statement by Events DC, which operates the stadium. "We believe that injustice and inequality of all forms is reprehensible and we are firmly committed to confronting unequal treatment and working together toward healing our city and country."

That same day, the statue of another former sports owner with ties to Washington and a racist past—Calvin Griffith, who moved the Senators to Minnesota in 1960—was taken down at newly built Target Field in Minneapolis.

In a 1978 speech he made in Waseca, Minnesota, in 1978, Griffith said, "I'll tell you why we came to Minnesota. It was when we found out you only had 15,000 Blacks here.... We came here because you've got good, hard-working white people here."

Both statues were removed during a national reckoning following the death of George Floyd, who was killed in Minneapolis on May 25 while in police custody. The forty-six-year-old African-American man died during an arrest after he had allegedly passed a counterfeit $20 bill in Minneapolis. Police officer Derek Chauvin knelt on Floyd's neck for nine minutes and twenty-nine seconds, and he was later pronounced dead at a local hospital.

The event was captured on video and led to monthslong protests around the country. Chauvin would be found guilty of second-degree unintentional murder, third-degree murder, and second-degree manslaughter.

* * *

The Forgotten First is the largely untold story of integration in pro football, a painful chapter in the country's most popular spectator sport. It is the story of the first group of players to break the color barrier, the people who helped them get there—and the people who tried to block them.

A year before Jackie Robinson became the first African-American to play in the major leagues, Washington, Strode, Motley, and Willis helped pave the way for the players to come after. While Robinson's transformative story is an iconic piece of sports history and American culture, the first year of integration in pro football is mostly overlooked and doesn't carry nearly the same impact as Robinson's journey.

Each year on April 15, every Major League Baseball player celebrates Jackie Robinson Day by wearing his No. 42 jersey to commemorate the day he played his first game for the Brooklyn Dodgers at Ebbets Field in 1947. It was the first time a Black man had played in the big leagues in more than fifty years.

Even the most casual sports fan knows it was Robinson who broke baseball's color barrier.

Yet chances are even the most diehard football fan can't tell you the first African-American to be signed by an NFL team. It was Kenny Washington with the Los Angeles Rams on March 21, 1946, followed by his teammate Woody Strode a few weeks after that. Bill Willis was invited by Brown for a tryout with the Browns that summer, and he and Marion Motley soon made their own history by integrating the AAFC.

Washington, who played alongside Robinson in football and baseball at UCLA, made history against the wishes of the league owners, and only after public pressure was brought to bear on then–Rams owner Dan Reeves when he moved the team from Cleveland to Los Angeles.

The impact of Paul Brown's actions on integrating pro football was much more closely aligned with that of Dodgers general manager Branch Rickey in Major League Baseball in terms of intentionally bringing Willis and Motley to the Browns. It was Rickey who made the bold decision to sign Robinson to a minor league contract in 1945 that led to his Major League career two years later, even though Rickey knew there would be harsh blowback from fans and opposing players, and even some of Robinson's teammates. Rickey felt the combination of Robinson's talent and character would live up to the moment, as he once told Robinson he wanted a man who "had guts enough not to fight back."

Brown, however, was reluctant to attach the kind of racial significance that Rickey acknowledged. Even so, Willis and Motley knew the sacrifice made by their coach and the ramifications it carried, and they were grateful he would stand up for them and give them a chance.

Motley and Willis would go on to produce Hall of Fame careers along with Brown, one of the most innovative coaches in sports history, who has a place in Canton alongside two of his greatest players.

"This story needs to be told over and over and over, so our young people see how all of this led them to where they are now," said former Browns Pro Bowl guard John Wooten, the longtime executive director of the Fritz Pollard Alliance, an organization dedicated to promoting coaching and executive diversity in the NFL. "That's the history. That history is not told enough, in my opinion."

Wooten is right. Not enough people know the story of these men, and I—Keyshawn—speak from experience.

I grew up in the same city as Kenny Washington and Woody Strode, played high school football twelve miles from Lincoln High School, where Washington was a legend. I played my USC home games at the Los Angeles Memorial Coliseum, walked off the same field one last time, just like Washington did to those roars of more than 103,000 people on that December afternoon in 1939.

But I'd never heard of Washington or Strode, never realized what Motley and Willis had to go through to blaze the trail for the players, like me and so many others, who came after them.

Yes, the story of these men—the forgotten first of the NFL—really does need to be told. They need to be remembered for who they were, for what they did, and for what they meant.

THE FORGOTTEN FIRST

Chapter 1

INTO HIS UNCLE'S ARMS

The signs of neglect simply couldn't be ignored any longer.

Kenny Washington needed help—even if he was too young to understand what was happening. Uncle Rocky knew he had to rescue his nephew. He knew he had to step in and be the father his brother couldn't.

Edgar "Blue" Washington didn't argue with his brother when Rocky insisted on taking Kenny into his home to raise him. After all, Blue had time to pursue his passion for baseball—he pitched in the Negro Leagues for the Chicago American Giants and Los Angeles White Sox and also played first base for the Kansas City Monarchs. And he loved to act, playing small roles in films like *King Kong, Tarzan's Magic Fountain,* and *Haunted Gold,* starring John Wayne.

He'd been given the nickname "Blue" by childhood friend Frank Capra, who grew up to be a renowned movie director; his 1946 classic *It's a Wonderful Life* is seen by millions every year around Christmas.

What Blue didn't have enough time for was fatherhood.

From the time Kenneth Stanley Washington was born on August 1, 1918, Blue was rarely home. Kenny's teenage mother, Marion, struggled to provide a stable upbringing for her son. After she discovered that Blue had developed a relationship with another woman, she left.

Rocky, who lived in the largely Italian and Irish neighborhood of Lincoln Heights in Los Angeles, knew this couldn't go on, that he had to save his nephew before things got worse. All this happened before Kenny had even turned four years old.

Rocky and Hazel Washington, along with Rocky's mother, Susie, brought Kenny into their home.

Finally in a stable environment and under the watchful and protective eye of Uncle Rocky—the first African-American lieutenant watch commander on the Los Angeles police force—Kenny could lead a normal life with a man who treated his nephew as if he were his son.

"Kenny's uncle Rocky was really the father," Strode recalled. "Kenny made no bones about it. He'd tell people it was between Grandma Susie and Uncle Rocky that accounted for his success."

Kenny loved to ride his bike around the neighborhood, and the streets were mostly traffic free in those days, before the population in and around Los Angeles started booming in the 1930s.

Lincoln Heights was one of the oldest neighborhoods near downtown Los Angeles, an early suburb once known as East Los Angeles and a place considered one of the area's most appealing neighborhoods. The eventual commercialization of the area made it less appealing to wealthier Angelenos, and by the time Kenny Washington joined his uncle, the area was predominantly Italian-American.

Kenny, in fact, spoke more Italian than English as a child, and his friends were often amused by Washington's unique accent that wasn't fully Italian but wasn't entirely English either.

He was a quiet but friendly child who began to thrive around the people who took him in. Kenny grew close to his aunt Hazel and uncle and was deeply attached to his grandmother. Susie was the custodian at the Avenue 19 Grammar School, and she was a mother figure of sorts, adored by the young students for her kindness or concern.

Kenny would often run errands for his grandmother, and also do favors for friends of the family. One day, as he was running one of those errands on his bike, he got into an accident and fell to the street. He'd suffered fractures in both knees, and cartilage damage as well. The convalescence took months, and Washington eventually regained his strength, but not without complications in his knees that would flare throughout his life.

He'd also suffered from a case of rickets as a young child. Brought on by a severe vitamin D deficiency, symptoms of the disease can include bowed legs and knock-knees—both of which Kenny developed.

"At one point, he was malnourished," said Marvel Washington, Kenny's daughter-in-law. "Rocky and Susie fed him, gave him milk because of the rickets, and got him healthy again."

"Rocky nursed him back to being able to function the right way," said Kenny's grandson, Kraig, who lives in Los Angeles. "He was like a father to him."

Once Kenny did recover from his various knee ailments, particularly after the bike accident, sports became his passion, and he'd spend hours at the Downey Avenue Playground two blocks from his home. It was a place where neighborhood kids gathered, but also older residents who played baseball and football. A semipro baseball team called the Lincoln Heights Merchants played there, and Washington was drawn to the games, having become interested in baseball because of his father's career. Even though Blue and his son didn't see one another very often, Kenny had gravitated toward the sport.

The coach of the team was a man named Paul Schultz, known to everyone as "Dutch." He took a liking to Kenny and allowed him to shag flies with the players; eventually, Kenny became one of the team's mascots. "Kenny showed me a team picture with him sitting on the ground in front of the players," Strode recalled. "It was quite cute, this little Black kid with this white baseball team."

By the time Washington enrolled at Lincoln High School in 1933, he'd established quite a reputation among the locals for his athletic skills. It was baseball and football he gravitated to the most, and the school would soon reap the benefits.

Lincoln football coach Jim Tunney knew he had someone special.

"I was six years old when I first met Kenny," said Tunney's son, Jim, the longtime NFL referee whose dad was also a teacher at Lincoln. "I have a picture of my dad and Kenny, and I had no clue who he was or what he did. But my dad loved him. He was a wonderful ball player, and a wonderful human being. He and his family were great people."

As was the custom for football players at the time, Washington played both offense and defense, but his strength was on offense, where he excelled in running and throwing. His arm strength was incredible, and he could throw the ball more than 60 yards.

He'd also developed a unique running style that was both impressive and awkward—almost physically impossible, actually. He'd had such a severe case of knock-knees that the bottoms of his legs would flare out with each step, making it look as if he were almost running sideways.

But make no mistake: Washington could run faster than anyone on the team, and Tunney knew he had a coach's dream.

Washington did not disappoint. He was a one-man show during his junior and senior seasons, leading his team to a city championship as a senior before helping the school's baseball team win the title the following spring. Washington dominated like few other players in the country. He ran. He threw. He played defense.

As a junior against Beverly Hills High, Washington led an 80-yard drive and finished it off with a one-yard dive into the end zone in the final minutes to produce a 13–12 victory upset. A week later, Washington was a one-man machine in a 40–0 rout of Franklin High. He had two first-quarter touchdowns and single-handedly scored 24 points, which included a spectacular individual effort.

"The third quarter found Washington sneaking through a small opening at left tackle and snake-hipping his way for 70 yards to again score," said a dispatch in Lincoln High's yearbook.

As a senior, Washington was even better.

He led the Tigers to an unbeaten season and a city championship for a team affectionately referred to as the Tunneymen in honor of their coach. But Tunney could thank his star quarterback for that memorable run, because Washington was the Tigers' star player in every game, up to and including Lincoln's 13–9 win over Fremont to win the city title.

On November 25, 1935, Washington prevailed in a defensive struggle that was decided by his second-half heroics.

"Early in the third quarter, Washington snatched a pass thrown by the pass-frenzied [Fremont quarterback] Dennis Francis, and hula hipped his way to the 17-yard stripe where, after a series of plays, he ploughed through for the initial score," an article in the school's 1936 yearbook read.

Washington scored the eventual winning touchdown later in the quarter. On the two-point conversion, fullback Joe Garofalo completed a pass to Washington in the end zone.

"Lincoln rooters went wild as the signal gun sounded at the end of the fourth quarter and the Tigers trotted off the Coliseum greensward undisputed city champions," another 1936 yearbook dispatch read.

Washington would walk off that same field twice more at the end of two more chapters of his football career, to even bigger ovations as Los Angeles's favorite son, carving out his unique place in history both times.

Chapter 2

FROM "BEANPOLE" TO BRUIN

Woody Strode could never have imagined he'd lead a life filled with an assortment of experiences so different, so diverse, so groundbreaking, and so filled with love. That he'd become a professional athlete who was part of a historic breakthrough...a football champion who celebrated by riding a horse inside a hotel lobby...a professional wrestler who would make enough money to buy a ranch in Glendora...an actor who helped blaze a trail for African-Americans who'd been shunned from the movie industry altogether or been given work as extras with racially stereotyped roles.

No, when Strode grew up in southeast Los Angeles, he had no idea what awaited him. The son of a bricklayer whose family had moved to Los Angeles from Washington, Louisiana, in 1900, Woodrow Wilson Woolwine Strode was born on July 25, 1914. Named after the United States president and Thomas Lee Woolwine, the Los Angeles district attorney who earned a reputation for fighting against public corruption and once ran for governor in California, Strode was known simply as "Woody."

The Strode family lived in a three-bedroom house near Fifty-First Street and Holmes Avenue in an area called the Furlong Tract

Community, one of the first Black neighborhoods in Los Angeles, which also attracted German, Italian, and Mexican immigrants. Today, the area is South Central Los Angeles.

Like his father, Strode was physically strong and gravitated toward sports at an early age. As a teenager, he was tall but so thin that schoolmates called him "Beanpole," a deeply hurtful nickname, he confided to his son many years later.

"When he was in school and he wanted to play football, everybody told him he couldn't because he had shot up so quickly but he hadn't fleshed out," said Pamela Larson Strode, the widow of Woody's son, Kalai. "He was teased about it, 'You're a beanpole,' they'd tell him. His fellow students said no way are you going to be successful, and he wasn't fond of that. But he ignored them and kept pursuing it."

Strode would eventually blossom into a physical specimen, growing to six foot four, 210 pounds, with a chiseled physique and athleticism that were the foundation of his versatile talents. Football was his favorite sport, but he also became a track-and-field enthusiast and would become one of the country's top all-around athletes.

Strode didn't find out until his teen years about his Native American heritage and was surprised when his father told him about his ancestors. Strode discovered that his great-grandfather was a slave who'd been captured in Africa and went to work on a sugarcane plantation in the South. He eventually escaped and was taken in by a tribe of Creek Indians. Woody Strode's grandfather eventually married a woman from the Blackfoot tribe and moved to New Orleans.

Strode said his father, Baylous Strode Sr., moved to Los Angeles in 1900 to get away from the discrimination he and his family had experienced in Louisiana. His father earned his high school diploma at Thomas Jefferson High School, where Woody attended. Woody would have been happy to take after his father and become a mason, but his father and mother, Rose, who'd been college educated in New Orleans, wanted Woody and his older brother, Baylous Jr., to focus on school and church.

Not a problem for Baylous, who took after his mother and read constantly. Easier said than done for Woody—at least on the education front.

Strode struggled with his schoolwork, preferring instead to play sports. It wasn't until he was noticed by football coaches at UCLA that he realized he needed to focus on his academics to be eligible to play sports there.

Woody was an affable child, but he had a temper that flared when he sensed danger. Once, his brother, who'd been reading a book in the park, was surrounded by a group of kids poking fun at him. Woody ran over and got into an argument, hitting one of his brother's tormentors with a baseball bat.

"I laid him out, completely unconscious," Strode later recalled. "The playground director came and carried me away, but I was exonerated because I was defending my brother. That's when Mama pulled me into church to try to teach me some rules."

Strode couldn't get enough of sports, and after school and at lunchtime at the Holmes Avenue Grammar School and later at McKinley Junior High School, he grew to love football, baseball, and basketball. But football was what he loved most, even if his gangly build suggested he couldn't stand up to the physical rigors of the sport.

At sixteen, he stood six foot one and weighed 135 pounds. "I looked like a toothpick," he said. Jefferson coach Harry Edelson, a terrific halfback at USC whose teams were 27-3-2 when he played for the Trojans, assigned Strode to be a backup end (what they called receiver in those days). A few games into his first year on the team, Strode went into the lineup after the starting end was injured. A switch went off once Strode started playing, and he became enraptured by the competition. "I was like a wild man, hitting anything that came my way," Strode said.

"When I got off the field, Harry said, 'My God, Woody, I thought you were going to be broke in half.'... Harry Edelson taught me everything about playing the end. I played that position the rest of my career."

Strode went on to earn all-city honors in football, and he was an all-state athlete in track-and-field, where his versatility shone as a hurdler, high jumper, and shot putter. He could high-jump more than six feet, could throw a 16-pound shot fifty feet, and was the best high school hurdler in Los Angeles. In the 1933 city state championships at the Coliseum, Strode attempted what was termed "an odd double" in the low hurdles and shot put, finishing second in the shot put and third in the hurdles.

By his senior season, Strode had filled out, gained forty pounds, and was widely recognized as one of California's premier athletes. Had it not been for sports, Strode was prepared to become a bricklayer like his father. At Jefferson, there was an emphasis on learning a trade—carpentry, industrial math, and printing were stressed.

Strode's athletic ability attracted colleges, although many of the premier programs in the country—specifically nearby USC and Notre Dame—did not have integrated sports programs at the time. It was UCLA, which was more liberal in accepting Black students and athletes, that Strode gravitated toward.

"USC and Notre Dame didn't give Black athletes a chance to play," Strode said, "so I ended up at UCLA, and that turned out to be one of the best things that ever happened to me."

Chapter 3

THE BIG KID FROM CANTON

Shakeful and Blanche Motley didn't see a future for their family in Leesburg, Georgia, in the early 1920s, and word of a jobs boom in Ohio convinced them it was time to seek a better life.

That was a sentence that could have been written about thousands of African-American families in the South at that time, families that felt the restrictive and prejudiced attitudes that impacted their everyday lives and forced them to seek opportunity elsewhere. It was an environment that led to what historians call the Great Migration.

When World War I began in Europe and the United States later joined the conflict, industrialized areas—particularly in the North and the Midwest—needed workers during the manufacturing boom. Drawn by the promise of middle-class jobs, hundreds of thousands of African-Americans from the South moved to major cities including New York, Chicago, Philadelphia, Detroit, and Cleveland.

The Motleys came to the Akron, Ohio, suburb of Canton, where they moved when Marion was two. Shakeful Motley got a job as a foundry moulder, and they made a home in the small town.

It wasn't long before Marion grew to be one of the biggest kids in town, and he eventually gravitated toward football.

Motley was so much bigger than his classmates when he first went out for the junior high team, he wasn't given the proper equipment, including pads, before practices started.

"When I first went to junior high school, they wouldn't give me a uniform," he said. "I had an uncle who was in World War I, and he had these khaki pants with these laced boots. I took these khaki pants, rolled them up, and went out for the team."

Motley was so physical on the first day of drills that his teammates implored the equipment manager to outfit him with pads so his hits wouldn't hurt quite so much.

McKinley coach Johnny Reed had built a strong program, and lost only one game in 1936, Motley's sophomore year. But Reed hadn't yet realized then that Motley's greatest gifts would be as a running back, so the coach initially had Motley play right guard.

A year later, Reed put Motley at fullback, and it became immediately apparent that this was where the young athlete would flourish. In his first two games in 1937, Motley scored 4 touchdowns in his first two games and then ran for a whopping 239 yards and 2 touchdowns on just 20 carries against Cleveland Collinwood. Motley also threw touchdown passes of 63 and 36 yards, and McKinley reeled off eight straight wins.

That set up a battle against the unbeaten Massillon Washington High School Tigers, coached by Paul Brown, who had built his team into a legendary Ohio powerhouse. With nearly thirteen thousand spectators packing the stands at Massillon on a frigid afternoon on November 20, 1937, Brown's team dominated the game, thanks to some ingenious tactical maneuvers by Brown and one gigantic misstep by Reed.

Brown had secretly installed a new offensive alignment during the week, incorporating misdirection plays in the running game that would fool the McKinley defenders.

The Tigers went on to a 19–6 win, outgaining McKinley 252–51 on the ground and limiting the visitors to just 8 first downs.

Reed made a fatal mistake with Motley that might have cost him the game and a state championship. Instead of keeping Motley at fullback, he had him move back to guard to allow Tip Lockard, who was back from an injury, to play fullback. It doomed McKinley's chances.

Years later, when Brown and Reed appeared at a football banquet, the former Massillon coach wouldn't let Reed forget that mistake. Especially after Reed had been fired at McKinley, in large measure because of his inability to beat Brown's Tigers.

"You know, John, anyone who would play Motley at guard should get fired," Brown said. He and Reed shared a laugh, but that one hurt. And carried some truth to it.

By his senior season, Motley was a bruising six foot one, 220 pounds, and was a machine in the running game. He ran for 264 yards and 4 touchdowns on just 11 carries against Canton Lehman in the opener. He had 223 yards and 4 touchdowns on just a dozen carries and also threw a touchdown pass against Alliance. And then 223 more yards and a pair of touchdowns on 15 attempts against Steubenville. Oh, and he threw for two more scores and had 3 interceptions while playing on defense.

Once again, Motley's unbeaten season came down to a matchup against Brown's Tigers. And once again, it was a loss—this time by a 12–0 margin to end his high school career. This time, his game ended prematurely after being injured on a tackle by Lin Houston. Three years, three losses—all to Brown.

Motley finished with 1,228 yards on just 69 carries as a senior—an astonishing 17.8-yard average—and threw for 454 yards and 7 touchdowns.

"Many people dispute his rushing average, but it's totally legitimate," McKinley football historian Charles Bowersox said in a 1999 interview in the *Akron Beacon Journal*. "He was just so much bigger and faster than everybody he played against. He could run, pass and kick, and he was a great tackler as a linebacker. I would have to say he's definitely the greatest player in McKinley's history."

"I did the math myself," said Larry Phillips, managing editor of *Richland Source* in north central Ohio. Phillips's book, *Ohio's Autumn Legends*, includes a chapter on Motley. "When they reported the yards and attempts, they added up."

But Motley's accomplishments weren't recognized as they should have been, and Phillips can only conclude there was one reason behind the snub.

"He played for one of the state's powerhouse teams, but he did not make first-team All-Ohio," Phillips said. "I can only pin that on racism. If you look at his statistics, they're almost jaw-dropping."

Neither Motley nor Brown knew it at the time, but they would eventually reconnect after embarking on their uniquely different football journeys in the years ahead.

When they did, they made history.

Chapter 4

OUT FROM HIS BROTHER'S SHADOW

Claude "Deacon" Willis was a legend at Columbus East High School, an All-City and All-State fullback who thoroughly dominated his opponents.

He got into his younger brother's head, too.

When it came time for Bill Willis to play, his natural position would have been the same as his brother, who was six years older.

"Until his dying day, whenever we'd talk about football, he would always mention how much better a football player his older brother was," Willis's son, Clem, said.

It was to the point that Bill refused to follow in his brother's footsteps. He simply didn't think he could live up to the legacy left behind by Claude.

"One day, some of my friends were playing in the park throwing a ball back and forth when one of the people shouted, 'Let's see if you are as good as your brother!'" Willis recalled in a later interview with former Ohio State teammate Don Steinberg. "The ball came sailing through the air, I jumped to catch it, and I dropped it. 'Well, you ain't no Deacon Willis, that's for sure.'"

Bill told Coach Ralph Webster before the 1938 season he'd rather play along the offensive and defensive lines. Webster preferred the younger Willis to be a running back, because Bill had such speed and agility that he'd be a natural.

Willis refused.

So they settled on this: Bill would play tackle and end (receiver) on offense, and be a down lineman on defense.

It worked out perfectly. Within a year, Willis had carved out his own niche for the Tigers, using his catlike quickness, especially on defense, to help revive the school's fortunes. In a game against Findlay, Gene Fekete, who would become Willis's teammate in college and the pros, summed up Willis's performance like this:

"The only recollection I have of that game is that we had a fifth man in our backfield," Fekete said. "It was him."

Football was a terrific outlet for the Willis brothers, who didn't have it easy growing up without their father, Clement, who died when Bill was just four. Clement and his wife, Williana "Anna" Willis, had moved to Columbus from Georgia in 1922. Like Marion Motley's parents, they were part of the Great Migration and traveled north.

"What brought [Clement Willis] north to Ohio was the railroad," Bill Willis Jr. said. "During the Great Migration, a lot of jobs were available because of the railroad."

The family lived at first in the "Flytown" section of Columbus.

"It was a destination for new migrants to Columbus," Willis Jr. said.

Why the nickname?

"They had meatpacking and other industries that attracted flies," he said. "Or, people would stay thirty days and 'fly' up to another place. It was a hardscrabble place, and it was hard to get steady employment. Uncle Claude used to say you didn't tell people that you were new to Columbus, because that meant you didn't have friends to back you up. If they know you don't have friends, you get picked on because the kids perceive you to be the weakest link."

Clem's death rocked the family.

"This tragedy left my mother to rear two sons [and three daughters] in dire poverty during the Depression of the Thirties," Willis said. "[My mother] did housework in homes in Columbus to support her children and was ever mindful of the necessity to educate her sons."

After Clem's death, the family eventually moved to the east side of town, and by then, members of Willis's extended family had moved to the area to help with raising the children—it was Bill and Claude and three sisters. Claude welcomed the role of big brother.

"Uncle Jim and Claude helped teach my dad to swim," Bill Willis Jr. said, laughing at the memory of the story told by his dad. "They took him to a little puddle of water somewhere, and said, 'We're going to teach you how to swim. You lay in the puddle, you wiggle your feet and you flail your arms.'"

Bill was helpful around the home, excelled in school, and was well-liked by his teammates in sports; in addition to football, he also played basketball and was on the track team. While he was intimidated by his older brother's athletic prowess, it was somewhat ironic in light of the fact that Bill was every bit as fast as Claude—maybe even faster.

The Willis brothers were known around the neighborhood for their athletic talents, not to mention their friendly demeanors as two of the nicest people in the area. They spent summers playing pickup games, and even crossed paths with a young man who came down with his family from their home in Cleveland to visit with relatives in the Columbus area.

"Jesse Owens used to come down in the summers when he was a kid," Clem Willis said. "They'd play pickup games on the west side. It was a small universe of people who were making their way. Jesse was more around Claude's age, but they all knew each other."

Owens, of course, would go on to become a world-famous athlete, winning four gold medals for the United States Olympic Team in the 1936 Berlin Olympics. The United States had seriously considered boycotting the Games because of the vile behavior of the German leader, Adolf Hitler. But Owens became an important symbol to combat the vicious racial and ethnic stereotypes being propagated during these years.

Bill Willis would also enjoy a solid track career, but nothing close to Owens. Football was what he did best, and while he helped a struggling Columbus East program improve its fortunes in his junior and senior seasons, the Tigers didn't have enough around Willis to compete against the city's better teams. Still, Willis was recognized for his talents, earning Honorable Mention All-City recognition as a senior.

It was during his senior year that he encountered racism for the first time. After a 1940 game against Toledo DeVilbiss, Willis and two Black teammates went to get sandwiches before heading back on the bus.

"The proprietor made the sandwiches, which we paid for, and then he said, 'We don't allow you boys to eat in the restaurant.'"

Willis and his teammates were incensed.

"We sat at one of the tables discussing what to do," he said. "First, we thought we could just leave the sandwiches uneaten, but then decided to open the sandwiches and then throw them on the floor as we left the restaurant. This we did, and raced back to the bus and hid under the seats until it was time to leave for home."

Bill became further disillusioned when Claude was passed over by Ohio State coach Francis Schmidt. His unique talents would certainly have helped the Buckeyes' program, but there were no Black players at Ohio State, and Schmidt recommended that Claude look to play at an all-Black school. He did just that, attending Claflin University in Orangeburg, South Carolina.

"When my uncle [Claude] was in high school, some folks from Ohio State said, 'Let us know when you graduate,'" said Bill Willis Jr., referring to the potential of a scholarship offer that school officials had hinted might be available for the Columbus schoolboy star. "Well, when he graduated, he reached out, but they said, 'We"re fresh out of scholarships.'"

Webster, the Columbus East coach who was convinced Bill Willis could play at a big-time program, encouraged him to attend Illinois, his alma mater. Willis declined.

But Webster remained in touch with him, and after Paul Brown was hired at Ohio State in 1941, Webster arranged a meeting between the two.

Neither man's life would ever be quite the same afterward.

Chapter 5

UCLA BECKONS FOR WASHINGTON AND STRODE

Kenny Washington was the best high school football player in Los Angeles and had his sights set on a college career after two brilliant seasons at Lincoln under Coach Tunney. With Uncle Rocky continuing to serve as the dominant influence in his life, Washington dreamed of playing for the most storied college program in the country: Notre Dame.

By 1936, the legend of the Fighting Irish had already been well established. During Knute Rockne's tenure from 1918 to 1930, the team had amassed 105 wins, three national championships, five unbeaten seasons, and a Rose Bowl victory in 1925. The famed backfield of the 1924 team—Harry Stuhldreher, Don Miller, Jim Crowley, and Elmer Layden—were forever transformed into football lore after sportswriter Grantland Rice assigned the nickname to the group: "The Four Horsemen." Four years later, Knute Rockne had delivered his famous "Win one for the Gipper" in honor of the late All-America halfback/quarterback George Gipp at halftime over previously unbeaten Army.

Washington wanted to add his name to the Notre Dame mythology so that he, too, might capture the imagination of the nation's college football fans.

But Notre Dame did not want Washington.

The school's football team wasn't integrated until 1953, when Wayne Edmonds and Dick Washington became the first Black players to appear in a game.

Washington needed to look elsewhere to pursue his football dreams, and he didn't have to go far to see where his next step would take him.

USC had expressed interest, but there were suspicions the Trojans weren't as committed to him as they let on.

"They were interested in sitting him on the bench so none of the other schools could have him," Strode said.

Tunney, Washington's high school coach who had great interest in making sure his player had the best opportunity to succeed in college, was under pressure from his alma mater at Loyola University in Los Angeles to get Washington to play there. But Tunney knew Washington couldn't create a high profile at the smaller, private Jesuit school, no matter how well he played.

"Loyola is my school and they want me to get you to go there," Tunney told Washington. "But look, go to a big school so that when you graduate, you can get national recognition. At a small school, who cares if you ran 100 yards against Pomona? But at a big school, you can get national recognition and capitalize on that."

UCLA already had a keen interest in Washington. Bill Ackerman, a former UCLA student who became the team's tennis coach and also took on the role as head of Associated Students UCLA, and Bruins head football coach Bill Spaulding, who came to the school in 1925 from the University of Minnesota, saw Washington's final high school game at the Coliseum. They knew then he could help vault the program into national prominence.

With Notre Dame out of the picture and USC and Loyola having limitations for different reasons, Washington settled on UCLA.

* * *

Woody Strode, meanwhile, took a more circuitous route to UCLA, one that required more time after his high school days had ended because of an admitted lack of desire to focus on his studies. He'd really hoped to go to USC, especially after the Trojans' 1931 upset win over Notre Dame at South Bend made an indelible impression.

Notre Dame was headed for what appeared to be an easy win, building a 14–0 lead. But the Trojans came back to win it, 16–14, on Johnny Baker's 33-yard field goal with a minute left in the game. "Johnny Baker's 10 little toes and three BIG points" was how sportswriter Maxwell Stiles called it.

Strode marveled at what came next, when more than three hundred thousand fans gathered in Los Angeles to celebrate the win over Notre Dame, which had a twenty-six-game unbeaten streak broken and was USC's first win ever in South Bend.

"When the Trojans got home, the city gave them a ticker tape parade downtown," Strode wrote. "USC was the biggest, richest, most popular school."

It was also the school that gave Strode and other Black players hope. At least initially.

Guard Brice Taylor was a star on the 1925 team and became the school's first All-American football player. He was also one of the first Black players in Trojans history. (Taylor's accomplishments were not fully recognized until much later; it wasn't until the 1950s when influential African-American sportswriter Brad Pye Jr. successfully lobbied to have Taylor's name added to the USC media guide that listed All-Americans.)

Admittedly, Strode wasn't good enough as a player to be recruited by USC, so eventually he gravitated toward UCLA. But not before having to resort to some creative tactics. Because he didn't have the grades to immediately matriculate at UCLA, Strode had to take classes to try and meet the school's requirements.

He also followed up on the advice of a friend to keep UCLA's attention on him. Cliff Simpson suggested that Strode enter a 1934 AAU track meet in San Diego to "compete against somebody with a reputation and get yourself a headline." Jesse Owens was among the headline athletes at the event, but it was the high jump event that gave Strode an opening.

Discus thrower Ken Carpenter befriended Strode at the event and suggested he try the high jump. Strode didn't have the proper footwear, so Carpenter lent him a pair of shoes. Strode leaped over the bar at six feet two inches, but broke the shoes. When they moved the bar up to six feet four, Strode cleared it—barefoot—to win the event.

There was his headline.

"That's how bad I wanted to go to UCLA," he said.

It was also around this time that Strode had attracted the attention of the infamous German filmmaker Leni Riefenstahl, whose movies were a key part of the Nazi propaganda machine.

Why would she have gravitated toward Strode?

Well, since his high school days, the onetime Beanpole had developed into a powerful athlete with a chiseled physique. He'd dabbled in some professional modeling. Unbeknownst to Strode, in the run-up to the 1936 Berlin Olympics, he had somehow caught the attention of German authorities. Even Hitler himself.

"The Nazis were interested in me because I was a mixed breed," Strode wrote, referencing his African-American and Native American heritage. "Somewhere they saw a photograph of me, and they came over to do some paintings for their Olympic Art Show."

Strode was contacted by Riefenstahl, who came to LA to do a photo shoot with Strode and have the Art Show paintings made. She brought him to a club in the Wilshire District of Los Angeles, where they went into a room with an artist. She had him remove his clothes down to his underwear so the artist could take some measurements. The artist did two paintings—one of Strode doing the shot put and another doing the discus.

"When Hitler saw my pictures, he couldn't believe how I looked," Strode said. "He sent Leni Riefenstahl back here to shoot some film on me."

Strode was willing to go, but by then, some friends had told him more about Riefenstahl.

"People started whispering, 'Don't you know who she is? Don't you know what's happening over there in Europe?' "

Strode called and told her he couldn't make it.

"I was a goddamned innocent," Strode wrote. "I've often thought that if Hitler had won the war, they would have picked me up and either bred me or dissected me."

Strode did hope to compete in the 1936 Olympics, but passed up a chance to attend the U.S. Olympic trials to make up some course work for entrance requirements at UCLA.

* * *

Strode and Washington developed a friendship quickly during their early days at UCLA. The two had plenty in common. Though they didn't know each other growing up, despite their high schools being just seven miles apart, they'd been two of the city's finest athletes. More important, they were the only two African-American players on the team.

Their personalities also contributed to their friendship; Washington was mostly serious and reserved, while Strode was more outgoing and gregarious. It was a perfect fit.

While UCLA was known for its more progressive attitudes on race relations, things weren't always smooth for Washington and Strode during their early college days. As freshmen, they'd heard some grumbling about a varsity player who would refuse to play on the same team as African-Americans. Strode recalled that it was a tackle from Oklahoma named Celestine Moses Wyrick—nicknamed "Slats"—who would refuse to play with them.

While the freshmen couldn't play with the varsity, Strode knew there'd be a problem the next year.

Spaulding would put Strode into the lineup at left end—next to Wyrick—and Slats would walk off the field. After it happened a few more times, Spaulding told Wyrick he had to stay on the field. But he kept walking off.

"He said, 'I can't play next to a n—r because my folks would disown me.'"

Spaulding decided to line Strode up on defense instead—right across from Wyrick.

"The whistle blew, the scrimmage started, I threw a block and Slats went down," Strode recalled. "He said, 'You Black son of a bitch.'"

The two exchanged punches before coaches and teammates broke up the fight.

But out of that exchange grew an unlikely friendship and a defining moment for the team.

"He didn't know what kind of guts we had," Strode said. "He had no respect for Negroes, but I stood up for myself and he respected that."

When the Bruins played Oklahoma later that season, Strode said Wyrick went up to some Oklahoma players he knew and told them, "Kenny Washington and Woody Strode are my friends. They may whip you, but you'd better respect them for the good players that they are."

It was Washington who exploded onto the scene in his first game on the varsity, leading the Bruins to a resounding win over Oregon on September 24, 1937, at the Coliseum. United Press International reporter Ronald Wagoner described the performance as follows:

> The University of California at Los Angeles placed on display a sensational sophomore halfback here tonight and opened the 1937 Pacific Coast Conference football season with a 26–13 victory over the University of Oregon.
>
> Sparked by Kenneth Washington, a 200-pound negro left half who defied the superstitions of his race and wore a huge golden "13" on his purple jersey, UCLA played a wide open game to turn back a fighting club from the great northwest before 35,000 fans.

Wagoner went on to write that "Washington was virtually the whole show for UCLA. The big negro's first effort in the opening quarter was a 57-yard run for a touchdown through the entire Oregon team."

Washington and Strode had begun to attract attention, in large part because they were the only Black players on the UCLA team—and among the only African-Americans to play big-time college football in the country. But their brilliance on the field created a passionate following. *Los Angeles Examiner* sportswriter Bob Hunter dubbed them the "Gold Dust Twins," which later morphed into the "Goal Dust Twins."

Hunter might have meant well with his nickname, but it actually had racist overtones because of the advertisement from which it was taken. There was a popular soap product called "Fairbank's Gold Dust," which featured two young African-American children playfully cleaning up in a bathtub.

The Gold Dust Twins was also the name of a popular radio show in the 1920s, which was sponsored by the maker of the soap product. The name was phased out in the 1950s, when it became more obvious to the sponsor that the racial stereotypes of the images were inappropriate.

At the time, though, Washington and Strode thought nothing of the nickname. Just as Washington hadn't minded being called "Kingfish" when he was becoming a football and baseball legend at Lincoln

High. "Kingfish" was a character on a radio—and later television—comedy series called *Amos 'n' Andy*. The creators of the show, Freeman Gosden and Charles Carrell, were both white, but the characters they played were two Black men from the South who moved to Chicago to seek their fortune. George "Kingfish" Stevens was a character who tried attracting them to get-rich-quick schemes. Protests from within the African-American community about the show's racial stereotyping began in late 1930 and continued until the show's cancellation nearly two decades later.

The rest of Washington's 1937 season was unremarkable record-wise; the Bruins were winless in seven of their next eight games to finish 2-6-1 and next to last in the PCC. But there was two transformative events late in the season—the first when the Bruins were scheduled to host Southern Methodist University on November 20.

There had been discussion before the game about whether SMU would even take the field against UCLA, because the school had never allowed its players to compete against a team with African-American players.

The Mustangs had won a share of the national championship in 1935 in a split decision among three voting bodies that separately had SMU, Minnesota, and Texas Christian University winning the title. (A year later, the Associated Press would settle on a single national champion.) UCLA was anxious to host the Mustangs, and SMU coach Madison "Matty" Bell wanted to make the trip to the Coliseum.

But only if Washington and Strode played.

It would be another thirty years before SMU's Jerry LeVias became the first Black player to be offered a scholarship by a Southwest Conference team, but Bell was adamant about playing against an integrated team. In what was considered a stunning interview with Wendell Smith, the renowned columnist at the *Pittsburgh Courier*, a leading Black newspaper that had national influence, Bell foretold of the eventual integration of sports in the south. He wasn't just years ahead of his time; he was decades ahead.

"I don't believe in drawing the color line in sports, because when you do, it takes something out of it," Bell said. "I think that every boy should have his chance to participate, regardless of his color.

"Someday, a Colored boy will make a good record in athletics in high school and some southern white school is going to take him in." Bell added, "Southern college must realize that they cannot keep on making such demands [to prohibit Black players]. It not only weakens teams when they must bench these Colored stars, but also creates a lot of ill feeling."

Bell paid tribute to Washington and Strode afterward.

"Kenny Washington is one of the best football players I have ever seen," he told Smith. "Why, that guy can do everything. He passes, runs, kicks and is a great defensive man. He sure had us worried in that game."

Bell said Strode "played a great game, too. He's a sweet end. He wasn't as great as Kenny, but believe me, he's a wonderful player."

The season ended with a matchup against USC at the Coliseum—a home game for USC that drew seventy-five thousand fans. It wasn't certain that Washington would even play in the game, because he'd taken such a pounding by playing both offense and defense.

"Kenny got so beat up he'd spend his weekends at the Hollywood Hospital getting glucose dripped into his arm," Strode recalled. "Before the USC game, Kenny told me, 'Boy, if we weren't playing USC, I wouldn't be playing. My ribs are really hurt. I haven't told anybody. Promise you won't tell anybody, Woody.' "

Strode kept the secret.

And Washington put on a show.

While it appeared through the early going that USC would cruise to an easy victory, building a 19–0 lead, Washington led a furious fourth-quarter comeback. First, he fired off a 44-yard touchdown pass to right halfback Hal Hirshon, with Walt Schell kicking the extra point to make it 19–7. On UCLA's next possession, Washington heaved the ball 65 yards in the air to Hirshon, who turned it into a 73-yard score to make it 19–13.

As the clock wound down late in the fourth quarter, Washington again drove the Bruins deep into USC territory. The Bruins were down to their final play—fourth and 13—one last chance to pull off one of the greatest upsets of the college football season.

Strode would be the intended target, as he ran a hook pattern to the 1-yard line. Strode broke free from his defender and was wide open as Washington delivered a perfectly thrown pass.

As the ball sailed toward him, Strode delighted in the possibility of completing the dramatic result.

It wasn't to be.

The ball went through his hands and fell incomplete, assuring USC the win.

"As I turned, I saw the ball coming at me like a bullet," he said, "and like a bullet, it went right through me."

The missed pass would bother Strode for years.

"Sorry Kenny," he told Washington after the game. "That potato was just too hot to handle."

"That's OK, buddy," Washington told him. "I knew it was hard, but I just had to open up on that one. Those Trojans were charging in too fast for me."

After the game, Spaulding went to the USC locker room to congratulate Coach Howard Jones. "It's all right to come out now," Spaulding yelled to Jones from outside the door. "Kenny's stopped passing."

Though the comeback fell short, it offered further proof that Washington's ascension into stardom was continuing. It was therefore no surprise that Washington, as well as his friend and reliable receiver

Strode, helped the Bruins achieve a breakthrough season in 1938. UCLA went 7-4-1 and began to take some of the attention away from USC as the unquestioned No. 1 football draw in Los Angeles.

The two stars helped the Bruins improve to 7-4-1, with victories over Iowa, Washington, Stanford, and Washington State highlighting a 5-2 start.

The rematch against USC was a letdown, however, as the Trojans were ready for whatever UCLA had and routed the Bruins 42–7.

The season ended with a three-week trip to Hawaii, as Spaulding brought his team via ocean liner to the island, first for a game against the Hawaiian All-Stars and then for a January 2 game against the University of Hawaii. UCLA won both by huge margins—46–0 against the All-Stars and 32–7 against Hawaii in the Poi Bowl at Honolulu Stadium.

The trip would be especially memorable for Strode, who met a woman named Princess Luukialuana Kalaeloa, a relation of the former Queen Lili'uokalani, the last monarch of the Hawaiian Kingdom. He didn't know it at the time, but he and Princess Luana—as she came to be known—would fall in love and soon be married.

The improved record and a first-ever bowl win weren't good enough for Spaulding, however, and he was fired after the season. Over the coming months, two critical decisions set the stage for a 1939 season that was one of the most celebrated in the school's history.

The first was the hiring of Babe Horrell as Spaulding's replacement.

The second was the successful recruiting of Pasadena Junior College star athlete Jackie Robinson.

Chapter 6

50 BUCKS AND GET OUTTA HERE

Years before his hometown became the epicenter of pro football greatness—and where he would one day achieve gridiron immorality—Marion Motley was the pride of Canton, Ohio. In 1938, Motley produced one of the most legendary seasons of any high school player in the state.

Or the nation, for that matter.

The bruising fullback rushed for 2,178 yards—with an incredible 17.2-yard average per carry—threw for 683 yards and accounted for 174 points. His teams were a combined 25-3 from 1936 to 1938, with the only losses coming each year at the hands of Paul Brown's Massillon teams.

"He was a great one," Canton McKinley historian Chuck Bowersox once said. "He had more long runs than the man in the moon."

In today's world, college football recruiters would be inundating Motley with offers, and surely Ohio State would do everything in its power to coax Motley to join the Buckeyes. But back then, there were no offers from the traditional football powerhouses for Black players. If Motley wanted to continue playing, it would have to be elsewhere.

Motley settled on South Carolina State University, an all-Black school that is now among the Historically Black Colleges and Universities (HBCUs). The team was coached by Oliver "Bull" Dawson, a legendary figure in South Carolina State history. Dawson coached five sports at the school from 1935 to 1976 and won championships in four of them. The team's football stadium, originally built in 1955, is called the Oliver C. Dawson Bulldog Stadium.

A commanding presence who was universally respected by his own players and opposing teams and coaches, Dawson seemed like a good fit for Motley. A disciplinarian who expected maximum effort from his players, Dawson could bring out the best in a uniquely talented player who was to play fullback on offense and linebacker on defense.

But Motley quickly grew homesick while living away from home for the first time. And while he experienced racism in and around Canton during his time growing up, living in the Jim Crow South was deeply uncomfortable for him.

Across the country at the University of Nevada, Motley's former Canton McKinley coach Jim Aiken was now coaching the Wolf Pack. Motley was being coaxed to transfer to Nevada.

The timing couldn't have been better for the Wolf Pack coach, who tried to convince Motley to play for him.

It didn't have to be a hard sell. The hard part for Motley was telling Dawson.

He need not have worried, though.

"Motley went to Oliver Dawson and said, 'Coach, the University of Nevada, they're offering me $50 a month to come and play,'" recalled Willie Jeffries, another renowned South Carolina State coach from 1973 to 1978. "Coach Dawson told him, 'You haven't gone yet? Well, get outta here!'"

Motley had his coach's blessing, and he made the move west the next year.

Nevada had its own issues with racial intolerance—it was referred to as the "Mississippi of the West" because of restrictions placed on African-Americans living there—but Aiken did not take kindly to bigotry.

Aiken was tested early. Before a game against Idaho in his first year there in 1940, the school said it would not play against Nevada if Motley took the field.

Aiken refused, called Idaho's bluff, and the game was played.

Motley never forgot it.

"When [the Idaho coach] told Jim I couldn't play, I had to grab Jim and pick him up around his waist and hold him off the ground," Motley said. "He was going to punch this guy in the mouth."

Something else happened that year that left an indelible mark on Motley.

On March 25, 1940, Motley and three passengers had driven to Fairfield, California, to visit a friend. Heading along U.S. 40 between Sacramento and San Francisco, Motley attempted to pass a vehicle but didn't give himself enough room to avoid an oncoming car.

Berkeley resident Tom Nobori and his wife were in the other car, and Nobori suffered a fractured skull. He later died.

Motley was initially charged with reckless driving, but after Nobori died, the charge was upgraded to negligent homicide. On October 29, just days after he ran for 131 yards and 2 touchdowns in a win over Eastern New Mexico, Motley was found guilty and sentenced to prison.

Similar cases allowed for guilty parties to pay a $1,000 fine and get probation, but Motley didn't have that kind of money. But the community around Reno rallied support, creating a Motley Fund campaign that asked for donations. The money was raised and taken to the courthouse in California. Among others, the Reno police chief expressed support for Motley, and he was given probation. The money was donated to Nobori's son.

"I cannot tell you in words how grateful I am for what you have done for me," Motley said in a statement to the *Nevada State Journal*. "I shall try to show it by the quality of school work I do and the service I can render on behalf of the University of Nevada and the people of this state."

Motley thrived at Nevada, where he was a physical education major, played on the varsity basketball team, and even boxed in a local Gold Gloves tournament. According to the Professional Football Researchers Association, Motley also pitched on two semipro baseball teams. One of those teams—the Reno Larks—had a three-game exhibition series in 1941 with the Kansas City Monarchs, one of the top Negro League teams. The Monarchs invited Motley to pitch a game against the Larks, and he walked three batters and struck out four, allowing just one run in six innings.

He was dominant on the football field, and quickly justified the faith Aiken had placed in him. There was a 105-yard kickoff return and a 67-yard touchdown run against San Jose State in 1941, and a 125-yard performance against the Cal Aggies in his final game in 1942. And so many other dominant games along the way.

But there was also a knee injury and family considerations that cut short Motley's collegiate career. He and Eula Coleman were married in 1943, and they soon had a family to raise. Motley decided he needed to forego his football career for now and return home to Canton to support his family.

"I spent three years at Nevada and hurt my knee, so I came home to Canton and got a job with Republic Steel," he said. "My knee was pretty bad, because the muscle around it had been torn."

Working in the mill actually helped.

"I was burning scrap iron with a torch, and it got awful hot where I was working," he said. "All that heat seemed to help the knee, and it healed up just fine."

At the same time Motley returned to Canton, World War II was raging in Europe and Asia, and while there were family considerations, he decided to enlist in the Navy. On Christmas Day, 1944, he signed up to do his part and was assigned to the Great Lakes Naval Station, the Navy's largest training installation that served as the boot camp for sailors and officers who would eventually be sent overseas. The sprawling facility, located just outside Chicago along Lake Michigan, would be Motley's home for most of the following year.

And it was there he would cross paths once again with Paul Brown, the only coach to ever beat Motley's teams at Canton McKinley. Only this time, the two would be on the same team, and they would be partners in what turned out to be a life-changing journey for both men.

Chapter 7

THE SCRAWNY QUARTERBACK TURNED COACHING LEGEND

Lester and Ida Brown didn't want their son playing football.

As a freshman at Washington High School in Massillon, Ohio, Paul Brown barely weighed 120 pounds and was no match for the players going out for Dave Stewart's team. When Paul begged his parents to pay the $10 fee for Stewart's preseason camp, they refused, convinced he'd get hurt playing against so many bigger, older players.

Paul could barely eat or sleep for two or three days, worrying his father, a railroad dispatcher who'd recently moved the family to Massillon from Norwalk, Ohio, midway between Cleveland and Toledo. His mother also was worried and preferred Paul might take up music as a younger child.

Finally, they relented, allowing their son to attend the camp.

"I'm told that my dad gave [Stewart] a big wink behind my back," Brown wrote in his autobiography, *PB: The Paul Brown Story*, "because Dave took one look at this skinny little kid and said, 'Well, Mr. Brown, I certainly hope he doesn't get hurt. We've got some big boys here, and they don't discriminate on who they hit or how hard they do it.'"

Stewart used Brown as his fifth- (and last-) string quarterback, figuring the kid would realize he wasn't ready to play at this level.

"Dave never actually thought I had a chance to make the team then, if at all," Brown said. "I certainly wasn't ready for varsity competition. It wasn't too long, however, before he sensed my obsession with football and became intrigued."

Brown got his chance during the sixth game that season, after Stewart's Tigers had built a big enough lead that the coach gave his backups some playing time. On his first pass, Brown threw a touchdown.

"I'm sure I was quite a sight," he said, "trotting off the field as if I had done this all my life. I didn't consider it anything special... though I know my parents almost fell out of their seats—first out of surprise at seeing me get into the game and then at watching me throw that touchdown pass on my first play."

And so began the legend of Paul Brown, who never did grow big enough to fulfill his dream of being the starter at Ohio State, but went on to become one of the most impactful coaches in football history. Brown would also become a critical figure in providing African-Americans the opportunity to play pro football when no one else would.

Like his first pass at Massillon, Brown didn't think it a big deal when he gave Bill Willis and Marion Motley a chance to play for the Cleveland Browns and break the color barrier in the All-America Football Conference in 1946. But deep down, Brown knew his role in history was an important one, even if he rarely admitted so publicly.

"Branch Rickey spoke on many occasions about breaking the color barrier in baseball, and he would take credit for his role in integrating Major League Baseball," Brown's son, Mike, who now owns the Bengals, said of the former Dodgers general manager. (Rickey had signed Jackie Robinson to play for the 1947 Brooklyn Dodgers.) "My father never said anything [publicly] about his role."

About the only time Paul Brown did open up about those experiences was on a car ride with his sons, Mike and Pete, nearly forty years after Willis and Motley joined the Browns.

"We were driving to the Scouting Combine in Indianapolis, and for some reason, on that drive, he got to reminiscing," Mike Brown said. "He came to talk about signing Bill and Marion. He never thought of himself as doing anything other than signing the best players. He didn't think of someone who merited credit as a civil rights leader. He did it just because he thought he was doing the right thing. They had the right to play, just like anyone else, and he wanted them to play because they were the best people for the jobs."

It was a credo Paul Brown lived by throughout his coaching career, from his formative days at Severn School—a prep school for the Naval Academy—to his legendary run at Massillon Washington High, then at Ohio State and the Great Lakes Naval Academy before his professional career began with the Browns.

Had he been physically capable, Brown would have preferred becoming an elite college quarterback and not a coach. At least not initially.

He became Stewart's starter at Massillon as a junior, and in two seasons with the Tigers produced a combined 15-3 record. He once threw five touchdown passes out of the single wing and ran for another, prompting the *Massillon Evening Independent* to call him "cool" and "heady," and "not the least bit inclined to get flustered and the type of [player] who never shoot their passes until they see a man out in the open."

Brown also played basketball and baseball and earned letters in track and field, where he did the pole vault and long jump. Football was his main love, though, and he desperately wanted to play at Ohio State, where he enrolled as a freshman in 1926. Unlike high school, where Stewart gave Brown a chance—albeit as his last-string quarterback—Brown didn't even get that far at Ohio State.

Homesickness quickly set in for Brown, but there was more to it than that.

"Being homesick wasn't as bad as not being allowed to try out for

Ohio State's freshman football team," he said. "I was too small for that caliber of football, they told me, and it was a mortal blow to my pride."

Brown eventually decided he wanted to transfer, and he settled on Miami University in Ohio, where he had visited before taking his father's advice to attend Ohio State. It took some convincing, but Lester Brown finally relented when his son told him he wanted to switch schools.

As was the case when Paul convinced his parents to let him play football at Massillon, his decision to transfer once again worked out. After a year of working with the freshman football team, he succeeded Weeb Ewbank as the starting quarterback. (Yes, that Weeb Ewbank, who led the New York Jets to their only Super Bowl title in a shocking upset of the Baltimore Colts after the 1968 season.)

Brown thrived at the smaller program, and led Miami to a 13-4 record in his two seasons as the starter. He earned second-team All-Ohio small-college honors from the Associated Press in 1928.

Brown also did something at Miami he could never have imagined while playing for Stewart at Massillon: He disobeyed his coach's orders.

Brown was supposed to be the backup, but a preseason injury to the starter forced Coach Chester Pittser to go with Brown as his starter. Yet Brown disagreed with much of Pittser's thinking, mostly because the coach was a conservative play caller and Brown preferred to take more chances with an aggressiveness that would eventually transform him into one of the most progressive coaches in football history.

It was therefore a salient moment when Brown first went against Pittser's instructions. When he did it again, he knew deep down that he had to play with the courage of his convictions. In a game against Denison, played in strong winds, Brown was victimized by his own stubbornness; he called for a quick kick that was botched to set up a

Denison touchdown. He later tried to throw into the wind and threw an interception that was returned for another touchdown. Miami lost, 14–7.

But Brown kept doing what he thought was best, even when it went against Pittser's orders.

"I was never afraid to throw the football because I was confident the pass would be completed—even when it wasn't," Brown said. "I carried the same philosophy into professional football."

In a game against Wittenberg, Brown was told to stay conservative early on, but Brown ignored his coach again. One of Brown's receivers was Jim Gordon, who went on to run the 400 meters for the 1932 U.S. Olympic team. Rather than keep it close to the vest as Pittser wanted, Brown had Gordon run a number of deep patterns, many of which were completed. Miami won, 18–0.

What Pittser didn't realize was that Brown had an advanced knowledge of defenses—much more than Pittser himself—and the young quarterback was willing to defy orders because he was convinced he was right.

"There were times when I'd see something in our opponent's defense that gave me the impulse to try something outside of Mr. Pittser's game plan," Brown said. "Even though more of them worked than didn't, it only made him madder than ever. I was living by Dave Stewart's principles, though, that football was supposed to be fun and you shouldn't be afraid to try different things."

Brown was a prelaw student at Miami and briefly toyed with the idea of studying history on a Rhodes Scholarship. But football still burned brightest, and a coaching career beckoned. He'd married his high school sweetheart, Katy, in 1929, and the couple moved to Maryland, where Paul got a teaching job at Severn School, the Naval Academy's prep school. The school also agreed to use Brown as an assistant football coach, thanks in part to a glowing recommendation from Stewart, who'd grown to respect Brown's football acumen during their time at Massillon.

Circumstances quickly changed, though, and Brown suddenly found himself in the role of head coach.

"When he showed up [at Severn], they asked him if he wanted to help out as an assistant," said Mike Brown, Paul's son. "The head coach took sick, and he couldn't go on, and that's how my father became a football coach."

Brown immediately embraced the coaching life, meticulously planning his practices and using the lessons he'd learned from Stewart, but also expanding his own knowledge of how to prepare players and teams for victory. Brown succeeded quickly at the prep school, going 7-0 in his first season to win the Maryland state championship. In his two years there, Brown was a combined 12-2-1, and he developed several fine players who went on to attend the Naval Academy.

One of those players was Slade Cutter, who achieved national prominence when his 18-yard field goal beat Army, 3–0, in 1934 to help Navy break Army's thirteen-game winning streak on a muddy Franklin Field before a packed house of seventy-nine thousand fans in Philadelphia. Press accounts afterward indicated that Cutter hadn't played football until he got to the Naval Academy, which made Brown chuckle. The coach had helped turn Cutter into a fine player in his two seasons at Severn.

"When they tell you Cutter never played football before he entered Annapolis, they are having a pipe dream," Brown said. "He was on my team at Severn for two years and what a great football player he was. He played fullback on offense and tackle on defense. He was a great kid and a mighty fine player."

"It took a heavyweight flute player who also goes in for boxing and field goal kicking to end Navy's losing streak in football against Army and cause the sea-going forces of Uncle Sam to celebrate, wherever they gather tonight, the first Annapolis triumph in 13 years," the *Baltimore Sun* said of Cutter's feat against Army.

Another of Brown's players at Severn who went on to a successful career at Navy was Dick Pratt, who played quarterback on the 1934 team that beat Army.

"Both were taught their football fundamentals by Paul Brown," Warner Murphy wrote in a letter to the editor to the Hartford *Daily Times* in 1934. "Brown gave Cutter and Pratt a lot of special attention and deserves credit for developing them, as he does for the development of other Navy stars who were at Severn before going to the academy."

Cutter and Pratt went on to become heroes in World War II, with Cutter being awarded four Navy Crosses and sinking the second-highest number of Japanese ships. Pratt earned two Navy Crosses, the Silver Star, and the Distinguished Service Medal.

(Bob here: Among the ships for which Pratt was commanding officer was the U.S.S. *Lansdowne* during World War II. My father, Marvin Glauber, was onboard when the Japanese surrendered in 1945.)

After two seasons at Severn, Brown grew despondent that more attention wasn't being paid to his football program, even if he understood the reasons why. The primary focus on the school was academics, and while he appreciated the value of a good education, he knew the school was far more interested in preparing the students for Naval Academy admittance.

But he did come away with the foundation of his football philosophy, based in part on what he saw as a unique system being used by Jimmy DeHart at Duke.

"I had watched Jimmy DeHart's Duke team mesmerize Navy with a version of the close double wingback formation, which used deceptive ball handling," he said. Brown also discovered that lacrosse, which was quite popular in Maryland, was an excellent way for football players to train in the off-season.

A stroke of good fortune came Brown's way after his second year at Severn, when the job at Massillon's Washington High—his alma mater—came open. His mentor, Dave Stewart, had departed several years earlier and the program had fallen on hard times. But thanks to a ringing endorsement from Stewart, Brown got the job and moved back home to begin one of the most celebrated high school coaching careers in football history.

Brown laid out a no-nonsense philosophy to his players right from the start:

> No smoking or drinking at any time during the year.
> No riding in motor vehicles.
> There would be nightly study sessions that must be monitored by parents.
> Players had to be at home by 9:30 p.m. and in bed by 10.

He made the players study plays—essentially creating the first playbook in football. No one—not college nor professional teams—had thought of creating playbooks, which are now central to every football program from high school up. Brown believed the mental part of football was just as important—if not more so—than the physical aspect. He used hand signals from the sidelines and shuttled in offensive plays with his guards, a system eventually adopted by other teams and leagues before the advent of electronic communications.

Pride was another essential element of Brown's program, which was reflected in the sign he'd put up in the Tigers' locker room that reflected his expectations:

"You represent the best football town in the United States," it read. "Never disappoint your people."

Success did not come overnight, but it did come quickly.

Brown inherited a team that had gone 2-6-2 the year before he got there, but the Tigers went 5-4-1 in his first season and then 8-2 a year later. In the final game of the season, though, Brown's Massillon team lost to rival Canton McKinley. A year later, the Tigers entered the Canton McKinley game with a 9-0 record but lost again.

And then came the first of Brown's unbeaten seasons. He lost only one game between 1935 and 1940, compiling an 80-8-2 record that featured a thirty-five-game winning streak. He won the Ohio state championship five times and the High School Football National Championships four times. The Tigers outscored their opponents by a combined 2,393–168 during that magical run, and Brown beat Canton McKinley six straight times—including the three games when Motley starred for the local rivals.

Brown used every tactical advantage at his disposal, including his appointment as Massillon's athletic director and eventually his position as the town's recreation director.

"We always knew who the best players were by the time they reached the ninth-grade level," he said, "and at that point, we began grooming some of them to meet our needs when they came to the varsity the next year."

Something else that separated Brown from his peers: Unlike many high school coaches of his day, he was not afraid to have African-American players on his teams. Though most of his players were white, Brown did not hesitate to invite Black players to participate with the Tigers. That included running back Fred "Pokey" Blunt and Horace Gillom, whom Brown once called "the greatest high school player I ever coached."

Brown knew of Gillom long before he suited up for Washington High.

"He proudly showed me at recess one day how he could punt a football," Brown said.

The coach was impressed, but noticed that Gillom's technique was raw. So Brown explained to Gillom how to hold the ball with his fingertips, turn the laces to the right and angle the ball so the front tip was slightly elevated.

Gillom went on to play for Brown almost everywhere the coach went—Massillon, Ohio State, and the Browns. "In my mind," Brown said, "there has never been a better punter than Horace."

Here's how much of an impact Gillom had on the Brown family: One day during Gillom's tenure as the Tigers' punter and end, Brown's son, Mike, had been horsing around at a neighbor's house, pretending to be a superhero, and jumped off the garage roof. He suffered a broken leg and was taken to the hospital.

Katy summoned her husband at football practice to meet her at the hospital. When Brown walked into his son's room, Mike was having a cast put on. As he saw his father walk in, Mike smiled and said, "Gee, Daddy, I'll bet you're glad it wasn't Horace."

The physician, Dr. H. W. Bell, who'd also been president of the school board and hired Brown at Massillon, looked at the coach. "PB, I'll bet that's true."

Gillom was captain of Brown's Massillon team in 1940, his final year at the school that featured one of the greatest high school teams ever. The Tigers outscored their opponents by a combined 477–6 to win their sixth straight state title.

"The best high school team I ever saw was our 1940 team," Brown said. "For the first half of the season, our starting eleven didn't even have to play after the first two quarters, and I seriously doubted my first team at Ohio State the following year could have beaten that team because it was so meticulously coached in our system and had far greater speed."

Before that season, the beginnings of World War II had started to cast an ominous shadow on the country, and there was certainly an uneasy feeling growing even in Massillon. The football season still took center stage and captivated the fans who flocked to see Brown's team. By then, there was a new stadium, triple the size of the dilapidated facility Brown inherited when he first got to the school. Tiger Stadium, which would subsequently be named after Brown himself, now held twenty-one thousand fans, and sellout crowds were routine.

Even before the season started, Brown knew he had a special team. In a spring scrimmage against Kent State, the Tigers won, 47–0, and Kent State, which had won eight of nine games during the regular season, canceled the remainder of the scrimmage despite several minutes remaining on the clock.

Brown's Tigers walloped Cleveland Latin, 64–0, the only game that team would lose all season. Brown beat West High School of Weirton, West Virginia, 48–0, and drubbed East High School from Erie, Pennsylvania, 74–0.

And there was the game against Warren Harding High when Coach Pierre Hill complained before the game that Massillon's brown uniforms were too close in color to the football, making it difficult for defenders to figure out who had the ball. Officials conferred before kickoff and gave Hill the option of playing the game with a white football. He declined.

The Tigers won, 59–0.

Another coach, Jack Mollenkopf of Toledo Waite, had disputed Brown's state title from the 1939 season. Brown was so incensed that he decided to settle the debate on the field. Toledo Waite wasn't originally on the Tigers' schedule that year, but Brown convinced Canton Lehman to take a buyout so he could face Toledo Waite instead.

More than twenty-one thousand fans showed up, with thousands more turned away, for a rain-soaked game. Brown's team won, 28–0, outgaining Waite in total yards, 353–54.

"Waite's 19-game win streak ended in pneumonia weather," Frank Buckley of the *Toledo Blade* wrote. "Massillon outclassed the Indians in as complete a style as any Toledo high school team has ever been beaten."

Brown ended the season with an easy win over McKinley, 34–6.

It was an incredible run, as Brown won all but one game between 1935 and 1940 to cap arguably the finest career in the history of high school coaching. And don't think that one loss didn't bother him. The Tigers were beaten by New Castle (Pennsylvania), 7–0, in 1937, mostly because his key players were sick with the flu. But even then, he had a chance to win, and were it not for a mental error by one of his substitutes, who failed to correctly react to a reverse play, the Tigers might have salvaged a win.

"Whatever the reason for our falling short," he said, "the record still says we lost, but I've always regretted there wasn't some way to note the circumstances. That game taught me one real lesson: The public is interested in only one thing—whether you win or lose."

Brown's strategic brilliance and development of talent were incomparable, and many of the methods he employed then have carried over into modern football. Case in point: In a game against Canton McKinley, Brown needed a big play to get his team going. He had his tailback take a direct snap from center, then run to the right for what appeared to be a sweep. But then he handed it off to the wingback coming in the opposite direction. And then the wingback lateraled to the end, who stopped and threw a long pass for a touchdown.

Thus was born the flea flicker, a play that is still in use today at every level of the game.

So brilliant was Brown's performance at Massillon, particularly after a 1940 season that ended with yet another state championship and the coach himself calling it the greatest team he'd ever seen, that Ohio State came calling.

The school that had once spurned the undersized Brown as a quarterback was now ready to welcome his genius as a coach to help turn the program around.

Chapter 8

BROWN AND WILLIS DOT THE I

Paul Brown welcomed Bill Willis and another recruit into his office at Ohio State a few months before Brown's debut season with the Buckeyes in 1941. The two prospective members of Brown's new team took a seat across from the coach's desk.

Willis got an invite after his high school coach at Columbus East, Ralph Webster, had contacted Brown to give his star defensive player a shot at joining the Buckeyes. Willis took Webster up on this recommendation to go to OSU after previously turning down the chance to play at Illinois, Webster's alma mater.

Even so, Willis remained somewhat skeptical because of the way Ohio State had passed over his older brother, Claude, years earlier. Claude Willis was told there were no scholarships available. Nor were there any Black players on the team, something Willis did not believe was a coincidence.

But Bill was willing to give it a chance this time. Only because Brown was the coach.

"When [Webster] got word that Paul Brown was being hired at Ohio State out of Massillon, it was widely known that Paul had worked with Black players on his teams," Bill Willis Jr. said. "So my dad went for his interview. Black players weren't allowed to live on campus back then, but he lived close enough to go to the school."

The interview didn't last long, but it was enough for Brown to make his decision. One of the players would stay. One would not.

"Paul decided to recruit my father and not the other guy," said Clem Willis, Bill's son.

Brown had known about Willis's talents from Webster, who lauded the stunning quickness of his defensive lineman and knew he could find a spot with the Buckeyes. So there wasn't much convincing to do. As for the other player...

"This fella had a pack of cigarettes in his pocket," Clem said. "Paul Brown was a disciplinarian. No cigarettes allowed. Those were his rules."

Brown quickly came to appreciate Willis's skill set, even though it would still be a year before he could coach him due to a restriction on freshmen best able to participate on the varsity.

"During my freshman year at Ohio State, one of the physical education departments was gauging the physical performances of entering freshmen," Willis said. "To the amazement of the examiners, most of my performance tests were off the chart compared to the other students."

Playing on the freshman team helped improve his technique and quickness, and Willis kept in shape the following spring by participating on the Buckeyes' track-and-field team.

Brown, meanwhile, picked up at Ohio State where he left off at Massillon, leading the Buckeyes to a 6-1-1 record and resurrecting the team's image. The only loss was a shocker, a 14–7 home defeat to Northwestern before a crowd of 71,896.

That loss would turn out to be significant for more reasons than the simple fact that it was Brown's first in thirty-seven games, going back to his days at Massillon. It featured Northwestern's star halfback, Otto

Graham, a former intramurals football player who'd come to the school on a basketball scholarship. Coach Lynn "Pappy" Waldorf had heard about Graham's strong arm and superb running ability—Graham had been an all-state runner at Waukegan High School—and offered him a tryout.

Brown never forgot the impression Graham left on him during that game.

"Otto was only a sophomore, playing as a single wing tailback, but against us, he looked like anything but a sophomore," Brown recalled. "Perhaps it is true you don't forget the players who beat you."

Brown finished the season with a 20–20 tie at rival Michigan—which almost felt like a win for Brown. After all, the Wolverines had destroyed Ohio State the year before, 40–0.

With a vastly improved rookie season for Brown now complete, the stage was set for what would be one of the finest seasons in Ohio State history.

Willis was ready to be a part of that team after spending his freshman year getting ready for a shot at the varsity. He would compete for a spot at tackle and along the defensive line. And despite being relatively undersized at six foot one, he and Don McCafferty shared time at tackle.

"There was so much talent on our line, along with the intensity of training under Paul Brown," Willis said. "The players who formed the line of the '42 team were almost to a man either to be selected as All-Americans or would have outstanding careers in playing or coaching in universities of the professional leagues."

Willis was the prototype player for Brown.

"Speed was our trademark," the coach said, "and Willis was as quick as a snake's fang."

Brown loved everything about Willis: great player, great attitude with a willingness to be coached, and leadership qualities few players possessed.

"As a human being, it was just his general nature that made it conducive to him being so well liked," Bill Willis Jr. said. "Even though a lot of people back then didn't associate with Black folks, they tended to gravitate toward him because of his personality. Plus, the fact that when the chips were down and the going got tough, he knew how to exercise restraint."

The season started with wins over Fort Knox (a nonconference game) and Indiana heading into a showdown against USC in Columbus. Ohio State won the game, 28–12, but not before Brown got into hot water over something he'd said—or actually didn't say—to USC coach Jeff Cravath at halftime.

There was a controversial ending to the half after Ohio State receiver Dante Lavelli was injured at the USC 1-yard line. The clock kept running to end the half, but after some debate, ten seconds were restored to give Ohio State another chance. The Buckeyes didn't score, but Cravath was livid and approached the officials.

Brown, still seething that his team couldn't score on the final play, said to the coach as he walked by on the way to the locker room, "If I were you, I'd settle for that."

Cravath heard something different, and after the game he told reporters Brown had threatened him.

"He said he'd settle with me for that," Cravath told reporters.

"Jeff had garbled my remark to mean that I was going to get him personally because I thought his team had deliberately injured Lavelli," Brown said. "John Bricker, the governor of Ohio, came to see me after the game and said, 'What's this I hear about you threatening Jeff Cravath?'

"Threatened him?" Brown said. "I simply said to him that if it were me, I'd settle for us not scoring from his 1-yard line, and I couldn't understand what he was beefing about."

Ohio State went on to beat Purdue and then Northwestern and

Otto Graham, to run their record to 5–0 and gain the No. 1 ranking in the AP poll heading into a Big Ten game at Wisconsin. The team normally chartered a train to road games, but because of the war effort, the military had sequestered all the first-class coaches in the area, leaving the team to travel in older cars that hadn't been used much in recent years.

The water tanks hadn't been cleaned and refilled, and many of the players drank what turned out to be contaminated water. Brown himself had taken a swig, detected a funny taste, and spit it out. Many of his players weren't so lucky.

Not only that, but because it was homecoming week for Wisconsin, the Buckeyes could only get a hotel downtown, not the kind of quiet environment Brown preferred for his team the night before a game. To compound matters, the elevator had broken down the night before, and some Wisconsin fans snuck into the hallway on the sixth floor where the team was staying, keeping the players awake.

The result: "Most of the team was stricken with diarrhea," Willis said.

Dubbed the "Bad Water Game," Wisconsin, led by Elroy "Crazy Legs" Hirsch, pulled off the 17–7 upset at Camp Randall Stadium.

The Buckeyes bounced back a week later by crushing Pitt, 59–19, and then beat Illinois, 44–20, in a game at Cleveland Stadium, where fans who'd watched Brown's teams at Massillon flocked to see the coach who had made good at Ohio State.

Little did Brown—or Willis—know they'd be back to play in this stadium many times in a future chapter of their careers.

Brown then conquered Michigan for the first time, 21–7, at home and closed out the season with a 41–12 win over Iowa Pre-Flight Seahawks, a Navy-affiliated team that played three seasons during World War II.

Ohio State was voted the top team in the land, and Brown was selected as the top coach—although he never accepted the award. The American Football Coaches Association had voted Brown as its winner, but the award went to Georgia Tech's Bill Alexander, who was ill, after Brown agreed to forego the honor.

Because he was only in his second season at Ohio State, the association convinced Brown that he'd have many more opportunities to win the award, while Alexander wouldn't.

Little did Brown know at the time he'd never be in a position to win it again.

Willis would continue to be a big part of Brown's life at Ohio State on the football field, but their relationship grew even stronger as the result of something that happened in the months after the Buckeyes' championship season.

Willis once again ran track the following spring, and attended the prestigious Penn Relays in Philadelphia. It was there that he was once again confronted by the harsh reality of racism. And knew to count on Brown to help him out.

"We traveled by train and were checking into the hotel the day before the track meet was to begin," Willis recounted. "As I came to the front desk to check in, I was told that the hotel did not allow Black people to register. Other arrangements were made for me to stay with a Black family in the city."

When the competition was over, Willis went back to the hotel to meet up with the rest of the team for the train ride back to Columbus. But he was told the team had already departed.

"Stranded in Philadelphia, I called Paul Brown, who arranged for the money and a ticket to get me back home."

Brown was furious about what had happened.

"You can be sure I let Ohio State's track coach know I didn't appreciate any of our football players being abandoned like that," Brown said.

With the war expanding in Europe and now the Pacific, college football in 1943 was significantly impacted, particularly at Ohio State, where many of Brown's players were drawn into the military. Willis himself was ready to serve in the war effort, and fully expected to be deployed after being drafted.

"I was drafted in the late summer of 1943," he said. "Expecting to be sent to basic training camp from Fort Hayes in Columbus, I put my toothbrush in my pocket and reported to the induction center."

It was there that Willis got a surprise.

"I was declared 4-F because of severe varicose veins," he said. "The induction officer told me that the Army had no provisions to correct this type of disability and to return after I had surgery. I had no money to have the surgery, so I returned to the university and fall practice for the 1943 season."

It would be a transformative season for both Willis and his coach, albeit for different reasons.

Willis would continue his football maturation process and develop into an All-American for the Buckeyes—the first Black All-American in school history—while Brown would struggle with a team that came to be nicknamed the "Baby Bucks."

Despite having won the national championship the year before, Brown's roster in 1943 looked nothing like that one that went 9-1 and had the makings of a potential college football dynasty. With the war effort now in full gear, Ohio State had partnered with the Army's ROTC (Reserve Officers' Training Corps) to train college students for service. As part of the Army's requirements, ROTC rules mandated that anyone in the program couldn't participate in varsity sports.

It was different with Ohio State's Big Ten rivals Michigan, Northwestern, and Purdue, who partnered with the Navy V-12 outfit. There were no such prohibitions against participating in varsity sports for the Navy ROTC programs, so those schools could bring back all their returning upperclassmen. Indiana and Iowa were also partnered with the Army's program, meaning they faced the same problems as Ohio State.

So, rather than going into the 1943 season with the defending championship team largely intact—minus graduating seniors—Brown brought back only five players. That included Willis, but only because he had been declared 4-F.

Because the team was made up mostly of freshmen, Ohio State was nicknamed the Baby Bucks.

And, as you can imagine, Brown struggled to compete against the teams who had their usual complement of older and more experienced players. Brown also had to face two military teams—Iowa Pre-Flight and Great Lakes Navy, which included some professional players—in addition to the regular Big Ten schedule.

"We had to play against teams who were loaded with professional players and outstanding college players," said Cecil Souders, who played end and tackle for the Buckeyes and was one of the few returning players on that team. "They were in the various military programs carried out on the college campuses. Almost all our players were freshmen with little football experience."

Willis was easily the most talented player on the team, and No. 99 began to assert himself through his play, to the point where he was now recognized as one of the country's top performers.

"The war shattered Paul's dream of a football dynasty," Willis said. "The enlistments and draft left few players with Big Ten experience to face other schools well entrenched with experienced collegiate or professional football players. I was the only first-string player from the previous season."

"The Baby Bucks" might have been a catchy nickname, but the season was anything but cute for Brown, who would go on to post a losing season for the first time in his career. The team lost five of its first six games, including a 30–7 blowout loss to Purdue, which would finish 9-0 that season to win a share of the Big Ten title.

"Well, gentlemen, the score was 30 to 7, and there's not much I can add to that," Brown told reporters after the game. "Our boys took a physical beating today. I couldn't do much substituting until we were hopelessly behind, because I don't have any capable replacements."

A week later, though, against No. 17 Northwestern and Graham, who had beaten Brown's Buckeyes two years earlier, the Baby Bucks fared much better. Yes, they lost, 13–0, but against a heavily favored Wildcats team, it was considered a moral victory.

"It was a doggone good football game in which the Bucks made the Wildcats work for everything they got," *Akron Beacon Journal* columnist Jim Schlemmer wrote. "And when it was over, there were many in the crowd of 37,243 who must have felt like the majority in the press coop: that with a little more luck here and there, the Bucks might actually have won it."

Willis had done his part from his left tackle and defensive line positions, helping to establish at least some semblance of a running game while limiting Graham from pouring it on against a hopelessly overmatched defense.

"With the material available to him, Paul built a very respectable team," Willis said of the Baby Bucks.

"We were a happy group, and as the season progressed, we got better and better," Souders said. "I think this team was an excellent example of the wonderful coaching ability of Paul Brown."

Brown finally got his second win against Pitt, which was also decimated because of ROTC rules, and he came away with a valuable tactical revelation in facing Clark Shaughnessy's team. Unlike many teams of his era, Shaughnessy went with a T-formation—where three running backs lined up behind the quarterbacks. It's also commonly referred to as a "full house" backfield. But it's something Brown took note of and used with his teams in Cleveland.

The most memorable game of that otherwise dismal season came in the next-to-last game against Illinois at Ohio Stadium. With the score tied at 26–26 on the final play of regulation, Ohio State attempted a pass that fell incomplete, and the teams left the field thinking the game was over. But an official had called a defensive penalty on the Illini, and a few minutes after the teams were in their respective locker rooms, Brown and Illinois coach Ray Eliot had the situation explained by the referee. Brown was given the option of running one more play, and he chose to do so.

Going for a touchdown at the Illinois 18-yard line was a low percentage option, so Brown turned to his freshman kicker, Johnny Stungis, who was just seventeen years old. Though Brown risked a field goal block that could have been returned for a touchdown, he went with his gut feeling and turned to Stungis.

The coach tried to loosen his kicker up as they returned to the field.

"John, I never missed a field goal in my life," Brown told Stungis.

"No kidding, Coach," Stungis replied. "Did you kick many?"

"No," Brown said. "I never even tried to kick one."

The two cracked up. Moments later, Stungis's kick just managed to clear the crossbar.

Ohio State won, 29–26. The kick came in what was dubbed the "fifth quarter" of the game.

Years later, Eliot recalled the knock on the locker room door by the referee who came to resume the game.

"I would have never let him in the dressing room to talk to us," he said.

The season ended with another painful reminder for both Brown and Willis of the challenges facing the Baby Bucks. Michigan routed Ohio State, 45–7, in Ann Arbor.

It would be Brown's last game as the Buckeyes' coach, but the beginning of another unusual journey in which he'd be reunited with Willis and also join forces with Motley. After his first losing season as a coach, Brown was commissioned as a naval officer and sent to the Great Lakes

Naval Training Center. It was a move that proved pivotal not only for the coach but, as they would soon find out, for Motley as well.

Willis, meanwhile, had one more year at Ohio State, and he made the most of it. With Brown off to Great Lakes, one of his longtime assistants, Carroll Widdoes, who had previously coached under Brown at Massillon and then Ohio State, took over as the Buckeyes' head coach.

The team got a huge break when Les Horvath, who'd been a talented halfback on the 1942 national championship team but graduated and went to dental school the following year, had another year of college eligibility due to a change in the rules. Horvath returned to play quarterback, and the team left behind by Brown, which featured Willis and guard Bill Hackett, enjoyed a renaissance season. It helped, too, that the Army had loosened its restrictions for the ROTC program and allowed underclassmen and not just freshmen to play.

Widdoes went 9-0, earned coach of the year honors, and Horvath became the first player in Ohio State history to win the Heisman Trophy. Among the wins Widdoes produced: a 26–6 decision over Brown's Great Lakes team in Columbus.

"It was an emotional wrench for me because my heart was not in it," Brown said. "I did not want to go back to Ohio State as an adversary."

There were mixed emotions in Brown's family, too.

"My son, Mike, who was eight, told me flat out a couple of days before the game, 'You might as well know, Daddy, I'm rooting for Ohio State.'"

Willis had mixed feelings about facing his old coach, but that didn't stop him from having a terrific game bottling up the Great Lakes offense from his spot on the interior defensive line. Brown singled out Willis and his fellow linemen afterward for a fine performance.

"They dominated the Great Lakes players and put such a pass

rush on [quarterback] Jim Youell that our passing game became totally ineffective," Brown said.

Willis's exploits were again noticed nationally, and for the second year in a row, he won All-America recognition. Horvath starred for the team, but Willis was a major contributor as well. Among his signature plays: a touchdown-saving tackle from behind on one of college football's fastest players. In a 26–12 win over Illinois, Buddy Young was headed for what appeared to be a sure touchdown, but Willis, who had sprinter's speed, tracked him down. Young finished with just 61 rushing yards.

* * *

On November 3, 2007, just three weeks before Willis died at age eighty-six, his No. 99 was retired at halftime of Ohio State's game against Wisconsin.

"Bill Willis is the ultimate Buckeye," athletic director Gene Smith said. "His record of accomplishment on the field and the class and dignity he exudes exemplify the qualities of Ohio State... Recognizing his career and legacy as an athletics pioneer by retiring his jersey number is a way to salute not just the Willis family, but the Buckeye program overall."

Then–Ohio State coach Jim Tressel called Willis "an inspiration to all Buckeye fans and football fans in general. His career was unparalleled and the class he has always demonstrated is extraordinary."

Former Ohio State running back and two-time Heisman Trophy winner Archie Griffin, who also had his number (45) retired at the school, called Willis "an icon, and his achievements have been a pinnacle at all levels of football. The recognition is very deserving."

Willis was the first lineman and defensive player to have his jersey retired at the school.

Chapter 9

BLACK PLAYERS NOT WANTED

The physical reminders are now gone.

All of them.

The monument that had stood outside RFK Stadium for decades came down on June 19, 2020—not coincidentally, on Juneteenth, the day that commemorates the official end of slavery.

His name was removed from the seating area at FedEx Field.

His place in the team's Ring of Fame, where he'd stood alongside the most fabled players and coaches in franchise history, was no more.

The team's nickname he had created in 1933, which for years had been criticized as an affront to Native Americans, was removed.

George Preston Marshall had literally been erased from the Washington Football Team.

But the scars he left behind can never be truly forgotten, nor his legacy as part of one of the darkest chapters in NFL history.

Marshall was widely recognized to be at the forefront of a movement to keep African-American players out of the league. In 1933, two Black players—running back Joe Lillard of the Chicago Cardinals and tackle Ray Kemp of the Pittsburgh Pirates (which eventually became the Steelers)—were on NFL rosters. But by season's end, both were gone under questionable circumstances. For the next twelve seasons, there would be no African-American players in the league.

The ban on Black players was never official. There were no documents from league meetings declaring that they were prohibited from playing in the league. There are no records of direct conversations involving owners. There is only this fact: From 1934 through 1945, no Black players participated in an NFL game.

"The key figure here is George Preston Marshall," said Rob Ruck, professor of sport history at the University of Pittsburgh. "He comes from Boston and ends up in Washington, he's in commercial laundry and he's a real showman and he's got a great position in the DC market and the South. And that market, that clientele, he does not believe, will look favorably on a Black player."

Marshall himself once said while under public pressure to integrate his team, "We'll start signing Negroes when the Harlem Globetrotters start signing whites."

And once the NFL did reintegrate, starting in 1946 with the signings of Washington and Strode in Los Angeles, Marshall was the last owner to do so. He didn't have a Black player on his roster until 1962, and only then due to a campaign by the Kennedy administration as a prerequisite to having a stadium built in Washington, DC, on publicly owned land.

"I didn't know the government had the right to tell the showman how to cast the play," Marshall told *Washington Post* sportswriter Dave Brady after he received a letter from Secretary of the Interior Stewart Udall. "I'd like to debate the president. I could handle him with words. I used to be able to handle his old man," a reference to John F. Kennedy's father, Joseph. Marshall said he knew the Kennedy family patriarch from their days together in Boston, where Kennedy was a leading businessman and politician and Marshall ran the Boston Braves football team before renaming it and moving the franchise to Washington in 1937.

While Marshall was certainly the most outspoken proponent of keeping Blacks out of the NFL, his fellow owners were complicit in going along with him.

"[Marshall] basically said you can't play in Washington with Black players," said Jim Rooney, the grandson of Steelers founder and owner Art Rooney. "My grandfather, new in the league, sort of followed the rule there, which he has admitted was the biggest mistake in his life. [Art Rooney] lived the life he lived and pushed hard in his own way, but he had a personality that was accommodating to a certain degree."

The early 1930s was a time of great challenges for the NFL, which faced severe financial hardships brought on by the Great Depression and underwent a significant transformation. The league's early days, beginning with the 1920 formation of the American Professional Football Association—it was renamed the National Football League in 1922—featured as many as 21 teams in 1921 and 22 clubs in 1926. But by 1930, there were only 11 teams and just 8 teams by 1932.

Marshall, who was born in rural West Virginia and moved to Washington, DC, after his father began operating a laundromat, had grown the laundry business into a highly successful franchise that made him one of the wealthiest men in the city. He invested in the Washington Palace Five professional basketball team, which folded in 1928, but not before Marshall had met another owner, George Halas, an NFL founder who owned the Chicago Bears. The two had kept in touch over the years, and Halas had urged Marshall, who had a flair for showmanship and promotion he'd rarely seen, to join the NFL.

Marshall attended a Giants-Bears game at the Polo Grounds in 1931, after which he attended a dinner that included New York investment banker Jay O'Brien, among others. By the end of the night, Marshall had made his decision.

"My worst nature got the best of me," he wrote in a *Saturday Evening Post* story about his involvement with the NFL in 1938. He bought into the franchise as a shareholder, and eventually became the principal owner of the Boston Braves.

Marshall renamed his team the Boston Redskins to differentiate it from the Boston Braves baseball team, but after five seasons with only limited success, he moved the team to Washington, DC.

From the NFL's earliest days until 1933, a handful of Black players dotted the league's rosters, and it wasn't entirely uncommon to see Native Americans play professionally. Jim Thorpe, who won two Olympic gold medals in 1912, played for seven professional teams, and was the NFL's first president in 1920–21. He was the most well-known Native American in NFL history.

Charles Follis is thought to be the first African-American professional football player—he played for the Shelby Blues in the early 1900s—while Frederick Douglas Pollard, nicknamed Fritz, was the most accomplished Black player of his time. As a halfback for the Akron Pros, he led that team to the first NFL title in 1920 and became the team's player-coach in 1921. There would not be another African-American coach in the NFL until 1989, when Art Shell was named coach of the Raiders.

Pollard was subject to racist taunts and physical intimidation during his time in the NFL. Often stepped on by opposing players after he was tackled, Pollard said he learned to "ball up" to protect himself. During his college career at Brown University, where he led the 1916 team to the Rose Bowl, there were other challenges.

"When they took the train to play in the Rose Bowl, he goes to the train station and they didn't want to let him stay in the Pullman car, because the guys working in the Pullmans were Black," said Pollard's grandson, Fritz Pollard III. "The whole team was going to get off the train. They served his white teammates, and his teammates gave him the food. Then they get to California, and they didn't want to let him stay in the hotel."

His coaches and teammates again backed up Pollard.

"[They said,] 'Well, I guess there's not going to be a Rose Bowl game and we'll go back to the train station and we'll leave,'" Pollard III said in recounting the story he was told. "So, they let him stay in the hotel, but he couldn't come into the lobby."

It was not an easy transition for Pollard at Brown. His older brother, Leslie, starred at Dartmouth, but Leslie recommended Pollard play elsewhere and he settled on Brown.

"Back in those days, Brown was prejudiced as hell," Pollard said in a 1976 interview in the *Los Angeles Times*. "When I first went there, they said the last football uniform was gone... One day, the athletic director called me in and said, 'Are you the brother of the football player at Dartmouth?'"

Pollard said he was.

"Don't you want to play for us?"

"They told me there were no more uniforms," Pollard said. "He picked up the phone and called up and said, 'Give Pollard a uniform.'"

Pollard quickly ingratiated himself with his teammates, especially after they realized he was so good he could help them win games.

"I ran the ball an average of twice every four downs," he said. "When we started winning everything, I didn't have any more trouble at Brown."

While Pollard got along with his teammates, that was not the case with opposing players.

"The other teams raised hell," he said. "They called me all the names in the world and tried to massacre me. But when the other teams called me n—r, my teammates went after them. My brothers had taught me to roll over and keep my knees to my chest, cover up my face with my hands and if anybody hit me afterwards, if they piled on, I'd hit."

He eventually met a man who would help him. When he met with the school's president one day, Pollard noticed another man sitting in the office.

"The president called me back later and said, 'Do you know who that man is?'"

Pollard did not.

"He's Mr. Rockefeller. He's taken an interest in you and made arrangements for your room and tuition."

It was John D. Rockefeller, the New York businessman and philanthropist who graduated from Brown in 1897. And the richest man in the world.

Another of the NFL's Black players in the league's formative years was Paul Robeson, an end and tackle who was a two-time consensus All-American at Rutgers and played with Pollard's Akron Pros in 1921 and the Milwaukee Badgers the following year. Robeson, of course, went on to a celebrated career as a concert singer and stage and film actor. He was also active in the Civil Rights Movement and often criticized the U.S. government, for which he was blacklisted during the McCarthy era.

Duke Slater was a magnificent tackle for the Milwaukee Badgers, Rock Island Independents, and Chicago Cardinals, earning five first-team All-Pro awards and—at long last—induction into the Pro Football Hall of Fame in 2020.

But the vast majority of NFL teams had white players only, and by the 1933 season, Kemp and Lillard were the two remaining African-Americans in the league.

Kemp had been a standout offensive lineman at Duquesne University in Pittsburgh, and he was asked by Art Rooney to play for his semipro team, the J.P. Rooneys, in 1932. The following year, the team joined the NFL as the Pirates, and Kemp made the roster.

After four games, the Pirates were 2-2, but Rooney said he had to reduce the roster to twenty-two players, and Kemp, who had shared time at tackle, was among the cuts.

"We had no fault to find with Kemp's playing ability," Rooney said, but Kemp was a "sub" and not a "regular," according to the *Pittsburgh Courier*.

"Kemp, surprised that he was not valued any higher than to be considered among those to be 'let out,' declared that rather than be temporarily suspended, he would quit altogether," the newspaper said.

In their first game after Kemp's departure, the Pirates lost to the Packers, 47–0, and won just one game the rest of the season, finishing in last place in the league's Eastern Division.

Despite his untimely ouster, Kemp had made peace with the team.

"I met Ray Kemp, and he loved my grandfather," Jim Rooney said. "They had a good relationship."

Lillard had played for the Cardinals in 1932 and 1933 and was one of the league's best running backs. A former schoolboy star who grew up in Mason City, Iowa, and played at Oregon, where he was eventually stripped of his amateur status because he'd played semipro football, Lillard was also known to be hot-tempered and would get into fights during games. But he was given no indication it would lead to his removal from the team.

During an extensive interview with the *Globe-Gazette* published on November 24, 1933, Lillard sang the praises of the NFL game over college football, which was much more popular at the time.

"The crowd goes to a football game for thrills, and the pros are giving the customers as many sensational plays as the college gridders," Lillard told the newspaper. "In a college game, you see stars in two or three positions on the team, while in a professional contest, every man needs to be a star to retain his place on the team. That's why pro football is a more finished product than the amateur sport."

By the end of the season, though, he was gone. Cardinals coach Paul Schissler, who once said Lillard had been "terrific" for the Cardinals, said he was releasing Lillard for his own safety, as well as the team's.

"He was a fine fellow, not as rugged as most in the pro game, but very clever," Schissler told *Brooklyn Daily Eagle* writer Harold Parrott in a 1935 interview. "But he was a marked man, and I don't mean that just the Southern boys took it out on him, either. After a while, whole teams, Northern and Southern alike, would give Joe the works, and I'd have to take him out...It got so my Cardinals were a marked team because we had Lillard with us, and how the rest of the league took it out on us. We had to let him go, for our own sake and for his, too."

Lillard suggested to Parrott in a subsequent interview that Schissler's reaction was an exaggeration.

"The pro league and the way they are supposed to hand out the bumps is a joke," he said, referring to whether or not he was roughed up.

Pollard claimed there was little reason to suggest the inclusion of Black players led to danger for their well-being, an excuse some owners used when trying to defend the absence of African-Americans in the league.

"I played for 20 years with white teams and against 'em," Pollard told Parrott. "And I was never hurt so bad I had to quit a game. I took Jim Thorpe's $1,000 dare that I'd never go near Canton, Ohio, in 1920. Not only did the Akron team and myself go there, but we beat 'em, 10 to 0...

"I weighed 160 or so, and they never made me or the other colored boys—Paul Robeson, Inky Williams, Duke Slater and the rest who followed in the pro league—quit either. So, they needn't say that's the reason they're keeping us out of the league. Joe [Lillard] is as good as any back in that league right now, and he always took it while he played."

Pollard became convinced that there was a concerted effort to keep Black players out of the NFL. And while many have pointed to Marshall's leading role in the exclusionary practices, Pollard suggested that Bears owner George Halas and Giants owner Tim Mara were also behind the ban.

"[Halas], along with the Mara family, started the ball rolling that eventually led to the barring of Blacks," Pollard said in a 1971 interview.

Pollard and Halas both grew up in Chicago at the same time, with Pollard attending Lane Tech and Halas attending Crane Tech.

"George basically got beaten by my grandfather in football, baseball, and indoor track all through high school," said Fritz Pollard III. "That's where [Halas's] animosity came from."

When the two competed against one another in the fledgling NFL, there was more ill will. In the league's inaugural season in 1920, Halas's Decatur Staleys played to a scoreless tie against Pollard's Akron Pros in what Halas called the championship game, which drew twelve thousand fans to Cubs Park. Halas declared the 10-1-2 Staleys champions, but the league subsequently awarded the title to Akron, which finished 8-0-3 and won by virtue of its unbeaten record.

While Halas didn't spend much time on Pollard in his 1979 autobiography, *Halas by Halas*, Pollard discussed the game in a 1976 interview.

"We were on our way to California for exhibition games when George Halas sent word to me to ask if we could stop off in Chicago and play," Pollard said. "I didn't like the idea because George Halas wasn't the friendliest fellow in the world, and I didn't like the idea that he didn't allow any Blacks to play on his team. But I was going to Chicago, and Chicago was my home, and I couldn't turn it down."

Pollard suggested that Halas tried to keep him out of the league after that.

"Halas refused to play Akron the next year unless Akron dropped me," he said in 1976. "And he refused to play Milwaukee the next year when I went up there [as player-coach]. George Halas used me to get every goddamn thing he could. Then, after he used me and got power, he raised the prejudice barrier. If George Halas was still like he was then, he wouldn't have allowed a Black player in Chicago, because he was prejudiced as hell."

Halas was incensed after Pollard's remarks were relayed to him by *Los Angeles Times* sportswriter Ron Rapoport.

"He's a liar," Halas said. "At no time did the color of his skin matter. All I cared about was the color of blood. If you had red blood, I was for you."

When asked why his teams didn't play against Akron and then Milwaukee, Halas said, "We never refused to play anybody. You just tried to get the best attraction. We always wanted to play Jim Thorpe and the Cardinals and Green Bay after 1921. We may have already been scheduled."

Halas was asked by Rapoport why no Black players were in the league from 1934 to 1946, and the Bears' Hall of Fame owner said, "I don't know. Probably the game didn't have the appeal to Black players at the time. Probably they didn't realize the possibilities of the game at the time."

Halas added, "This is ridiculous. [Pollard] is trying to involve me in something so he can have something to talk about. There is nothing to it. He was a fine football player... But Jesus."

Halas's daughter, Virginia, who took over the team's ownership and management roles after George Halas died in 1983, said her father never discussed the league signing Black players.

"In our family of four, we didn't sit in the living room or at the kitchen table and talk about any of these things," she told longtime *Chicago Tribune* NFL writer Don Pierson.

Iowa's star running back Ozzie Simmons, who played from 1934 to 1936 and was one of the country's first Black All-Americans, had visions of playing in the NFL, although he was not naïve to the idea of facing racial discrimination. He recalled being subjected to late and vicious hits at Iowa, and in one 1934 game against Minnesota he was knocked out of the contest three times.

"There was quite a bit of piling on, and the referees didn't call it," he said in a 1989 interview. "They were kneeing me out in the open."

Tensions were so high in the run-up to the next year's game that Governor Clyde L. Herring suggested Hawkeyes fans might take matters into their own hands if Simmons was roughed up. In an attempt to defuse the situation, the governor of Minnesota, Floyd B. Olson, issued a friendly wager on the game. Whoever won would receive a prized pig from their state. Minnesota won the game without incident, and Herring arranged to have a pig from Rosedale Farms given to Olson. He named it "Floyd." Olson made a bronze replica of the pig, and the "Floyd of Rosedale" is now given to the winner of the annual Iowa-Minnesota game.

After his college career, Simmons played on a barnstorming basketball team and later played for a minor league football team in Paterson, New Jersey. Football remained his greatest passion, and he yearned to play in the NFL.

Halas wanted him in the league, according to Simmons.

"George Halas said, 'Ozzie, I'd like to use you, but we have one unwritten rule in the National League, and that is Blacks can't play,'" Simmons said in a 1989 interview.

Even so, Halas's grandson George McCaskey remains skeptical about whether there was an official ban on Black players:

> There are repeated references to a gentlemen's agreement, an understanding, a secret agreement. I'm a journalist and a lawyer by training, so I'm skeptical without proof.... I can't find any proof, and my difficulty, other than the result—everybody knows that there were no African-Americans on NFL rosters from 1934 to 1945, but what is the cause? The skeptic in me is looking for proof, and so far, I haven't found it. Any time there's an allegation of collusion or conspiracy,

> you're looking for a letter, a memo, minutes from a meeting, or something you would think the last few years would have come up. I haven't found that yet.

McCaskey acknowledges questions linger, however:

"The fact of the matter is that George Halas was such a dominant force in the National Football League that he could have done what he wanted," he said. "He could have signed an African-American player if he wanted, and quality African-American football players were available during that time period. That's what I'm trying to get to—why that didn't happen."

It is especially difficult for McCaskey to wrap his arms around it because of how he knew his grandfather. "The George Halas I knew was a progressive in race relations," he said.

> I have not heard of a single instance of any [Bears] player claiming discriminatory treatment or bigoted conduct by George Halas. His record, even going back to that time period, is one of a progressive, in my opinion.
>
> In 1938, he agreed to have the Bears play an exhibition game against a team billed as the "Negro All Stars," and it was for charity. Two of the charities were entities that, to this day, emphasize that their services are available to all, regardless of race, creed, gender, background. In 1941, he invested in a Broadway play that was based on Richard Wright's novel, *Native Son*. That, to me, is an indication that he knew there were issues that needed to be addressed in the public realm, and he was willing to do what he could to support that.

Halas's actions after the NFL was eventually integrated revealed a man who had accepted and embraced the need to promote diversity, according to McCaskey.

"The Bears were the first team to draft an African-American player, in 1949," he said, referring to George Taliaferro, a three-time All-American at Indiana who played halfback, quarterback, defensive back, and kicker. Taliaferro signed with the AAFC's Los Angeles Dons that season instead of joining the Bears. "They were the first team in the modern era to have an African-American play quarterback in 1953 with Willie Thrower."

Halas later signed off on an idea put forth by McCaskey's father, Ed, to have the first interracial roommates.

"In the 1960s, at the height of racial tensions in this country, he had Gale Sayers and Brian Piccolo be roommates," McCaskey continued. "That was a tremendous symbol, in my opinion, of the fact that we need to get along and we can get along. I'm trying to balance that record with what happened between 1933 and 1946."

* * *

While the complicity of other NFL owners has to be judged in the context of the times and on a case-by-case basis, for George Preston Marshall, keeping Black players off his rosters in Washington was an unequivocal decree.

When he moved the team from Boston to the nation's capital, he had the league's southernmost team and actively sought to appeal to white fans in the South. During the preseason, when teams played eight exhibition games, he'd barnstorm his team to several towns and cities south of Washington. He also built an extensive radio network to help build interest in the team.

"His strategy and his rationalization was that this was the only team in the South," longtime *Washington Post* NFL writer Len Shapiro said of Marshall. "He had his own radio network all the way down to Florida that would carry his games. He would not integrate his team because he felt it would hurt him with his fan base in the South, and even in Washington, which was segregated in the 1930s, '40s, and '50s."

Marshall himself barely hid his racism. He was raised in the small railroad town of Grafton, West Virginia, the child of a local newspaper publisher whose ancestors were Confederate officers. The family moved to Washington when he was a teenager, and he attended the Friends Select School before briefly enrolling at Randolph-Macon College, from which he dropped out in his first year.

As Marshall built his wealth in the laundry business and later invested in the Washington Palace Five, he was one of the city's biggest socialites who adored attracting a crowd and carousing at nightclubs. In 1920 he married Elizabeth Morton, who had danced in the Ziegfeld Follies, and they had two children before divorcing in 1935. He later married film actress Corinne Griffith. On the occasion of their engagement, he presented her with a gift: a Confederate flag that had been in the family since the Civil War.

Corinne wrote the lyrics to the team's now-famous fight song replayed after every Washington touchdown at home games. "Hail to the Redskins" was not without controversy, though. The song in its initial version included several lines that played to stereotypes of Native Americans:

"Scalp 'em, swamp 'um, We will take 'um big score, Read 'um, Weep 'um, Touchdown!—We want heap more."

There was also a time when the last line of the song—"Fight for old D.C."—was "Fight for old Dixie," a reference to the Confederate South. The song quickly became a tradition, and the scalping references were eventually removed entirely.

Oddly enough, the song actually worked against Marshall in his quest to maintain NFL exclusivity in the South after more than thirty years of dominance. When the NFL considered expanding to Texas, Marshall fought against the move, threatening what had become his monopoly in the South. Dallas businessman Clint Murchison Jr., who inherited his father's oil fortune, wanted to land the expansion franchise but faced fierce resistance from Marshall.

Murchison pulled off an ingenious move by purchasing the rights to "Hail to the Redskins" from the song's originator, Barnee Breeskin, and threatening to prevent the song from being played at home games in Washington. Marshall was infuriated by the move, but eventually an agreement was reached to bring the Dallas Cowboys into the league in 1960. Murchison returned the rights to the song.

Even in death, Marshall's feelings about race were clear: Marshall wrote in his last will and testament that he wanted his money to go toward the establishment of a foundation that dedicated all proceeds to the betterment of "health, education and welfare" of children in the Washington, DC, area. There was a caveat: No money from the foundation could ever go toward "any purpose which supports the principle of racial integration in any form."

When word of the clause got out, area clergy publicly denounced the clause as "onerous and racist." One of Marshall's granddaughters, Jordan Wright, told the *Washington Post,* "It was so absolutely ridiculous that he put it in there, but he did put it in. But with the family, when we saw that, it was all, 'Egads! Why did he put that in?' It was never acceptable to anybody in the family."

The clause was eventually thrown out in court, and the George Preston Marshall Foundation has since awarded millions of dollars to children's causes.

Marshall brought halftime entertainment to the league, including the NFL's first organized marching band, pushed for rules changes to open up the game, and was the driving force in dividing the league into two divisions with a playoff to determine a champion.

But it wasn't until after he'd grudgingly agreed to integrate his own team that he was selected for enshrinement in the Hall of Fame. And there is no mention of his decades-long refusal to have Black players on his roster in his Hall of Fame biography in Canton.

By the time he was inducted into the Hall of Fame in 1963, Marshall had fallen ill and could not attend the ceremony. His induction speech was made by longtime associate Milton King.

"His long and faithful service to the National Football League is well illustrated by his induction into the Hall of Fame," King said. "No man deserves it more."

Many would disagree, including Hall of Fame defensive end Deacon Jones, who finished his career in Washington after starring with the Rams and head coach George Allen, who signed him in 1974 to play in Washington. Jones knew full well of Marshall's refusal to have Black players on his teams, so before every home game, he'd walk past the monument built for the team owner and spit on it.

Marshall became the lightning rod for the NFL's ban on Black players, but the fact remains that his fellow owners didn't challenge him on it—or at least didn't push back forcefully enough—and thus tacitly endorsed the practice.

"There's a concerted effort to blame it on George Preston Marshall, that he forces the other teams to get rid of African-Americans," said Damion Thomas, curator of sports at the Smithsonian National Museum of African American History and Culture. "But I think he's used as the scapegoat in many ways. I can't attribute it just to George Preston Marshall. The NFL grows out of the working class, and some of the attempts to keep African-Americans out of those industries in the 1920s and 1930s show up in the sports arena. I don't think those two things are separated."

Marshall's unapologetic attitudes about race in particular negatively impacted people in the Washington area who might have become fans, but were instead alienated to the point of rooting against his team. Even to this day, the scars of that period are not forgotten.

"There are Dallas Cowboys fans everywhere, but there are a lot of Dallas Cowboys African-American fans, and the Dallas fans in Washington, DC, are 90 percent African-American, and it has a lot to do with that history," Thomas said. "Dallas had African-American players in the 1960s, and now a lot of people understand why their grandfathers and uncles were Cowboys fans. I have family members who are Dallas Cowboys fans."

Joe Horrigan, the longtime executive director of the Pro Football Hall of Fame who has studied the ban on Black players in the 1930s and '40s, believes there needs to be a reckoning of the league's past.

"The sins of the fathers go all the way back, and it's been here since slavery came to this country," Horrigan said. "We haven't talked fully about why things were the way they were in sports that we celebrate the end of. They never really ended. They *began* to end."

The inability and unwillingness of NFL owners to reconcile their ban—even if it wasn't decreed in writing or made official in any other way—only delayed the reckoning and later forced an eventual change. The fact that it wasn't talked about or acknowledged undoubtedly exacerbated the dilemma.

"There were three telephones in our house and they rang twenty-four hours a day, and I never heard a conversation, personally or privately [about keeping Black players out of the league]," said Upton Bell, whose father, Bert, owned the Eagles from 1933 to 1940 and was the NFL commissioner from 1946 to 1959. "Never once heard a racial slur. I never heard of any type of secret agreement to keep African-Americans out of football. You would think that with all the conversations he had as an owner, you would think that somewhere along the way, if there was some type of deal, I'd have heard about it. Either where he said maybe it's time to let Blacks into football, or we can't have these people play. I never heard that. That's the mystery that I think nobody has ever solved."

Bert Bell became a part owner of the Steelers along with Art Rooney before being elected commissioner, but even then, there were no direct discussions. At least none that Upton had become aware of.

"I know that he and Rooney, both before and after he became commissioner, I never heard them once ever discuss anything about it," said Upton Bell, a former Colts personnel director who helped the team to two NFL Championship Games and two Super Bowls. Bell became the Boston Patriots' general manager in 1971. "Never once heard them say, 'I don't think we can hire that guy or sign this guy.' You would pick up on something like that, but I never did."

While the owners were either unwilling or unable—or both—to voluntarily address the issue of keeping Black players out of the NFL, they came under increasing pressure, particularly from the African-American press, which had significant clout in several larger cities, including New York, Chicago, Pittsburgh, Baltimore, and Los Angeles.

Sam Lacy, columnist for the *Baltimore Afro-American*, once said of Marshall's team, "Only in the capital of the nation, in a stadium bedecked by flags of freedom, does the spirit of democracy get kicked in the pants."

Ted Carroll of the *New York Amsterdam Star-News* suggested the NFL needed to allow Black players back in the game to level the playing field, especially after the start of World War II meant that African-Americans were being summoned to serve in the military. He wrote:

> [The NFL's] action in admitting colored Americans for a time and then excluding them when things took a turn for the better is perfect anti-democratic propaganda.
>
> With enemy agencies everlastingly at work among the color population seeking to poison its loyalty to the country, their work is made easier by every extension of the color line. Japanese propagandists seize upon such policies as this

> and disseminate the information throughout the world to the detriment of the Allies.
>
> Were the attitude of the pro football league an isolated one, it might not loom so large. Unfortunately, it represents the path followed by so many organizations in our country, all of whom look to our armed forces, including thousands of colored boys to die if necessary for a way of life under which these organizations have fattened and prospered.

Another prominent African-American writer, William Claire "Halley" Harding, also criticized the NFL for prohibiting Black players. But Harding did more than just write about the problem.

He would help change the course of history by prying the door open.

Chapter 10

JACKIE, KENNY, AND WOODY

By the time he'd finished his two years at Pasadena Junior College, the legend of Jackie Robinson was already widely known up and down the West Coast.

Robinson had starred in four sports at Pasadena Junior College, had broken records his older brother, Mack, had set at the school. (And by the way, Mack had finished second to Jesse Owens in the 200 meters at the 1936 Olympic Games in Berlin.) Still, Jackie thrived. Whether it was football, basketball, baseball, or track, Robinson had dominated the competition in every sport. He was even a terrific tennis player, having won the junior boys singles title in the Pacific Coast Negro Tennis Tournament in 1936.

Robinson might have been the best young athlete in the entire state of California and certainly one of the best in the country. In a single day, he set a junior college broad jump record of 25 feet, 6½ inches and later helped his baseball team win the league title. Robinson played shortstop and hit .417 with 25 stolen bases as a freshman, and ran for more than 1,000 yards and 17 touchdowns in football the following year. He averaged 19 points a game in basketball, leading Pasadena to the California Junior College title, and was named Southern California

Junior College MVP after leading the school's baseball team to the league championship. This while also competing in track-and-field.

But now that it was time for his next step, UCLA made the most aggressive pitch to bring Robinson to big-time college athletics. It was not an easy situation for Robinson, because young Black athletes in his situation had far fewer options then. In fact, fewer than forty African-Americans played football at major universities throughout the country.

But UCLA already had two Black players on the squad—Washington and Strode, who had teamed up to help the Bruins to a much-improved 7-4-1 record in what turned out to be Bill Spaulding's final year as head coach. And now it was Spaulding, as the school's athletic director after Babe Horrell took over as head coach in 1939, who played a pivotal role in bringing Robinson to Westwood.

One of the team's scouts walked into his office to tell Spaulding about Robinson.

"He led the conference in touchdowns," the scout said. "Only, there's one problem, Bill."

"What do you mean, the [USC] Trojans have already got him?" Spaulding asked.

"No, no. He's a colored boy," the scout said. "I heard somebody squawking about giving colored boys too many athletic scholarships."

Spaulding looked at the scout and replied, "Colored boys are all right with me if they're the right color."

"The right color?"

"I like a good, clean, American boy with a B average," Spaulding said. "If that's the kind of boy you're talking about, his colors are blue and gold."

"UCLA colors, huh?" the scout said.

"That's right," Spaulding said, "and you can tell it to Robinson for me."

That was good enough for Robinson, who agreed to attend the

school, in large part because UCLA was one of the few schools that didn't entirely spurn African-American students and athletes, but also because he was encouraged by his older brother, Frank.

That Jackie had decided to attend UCLA was in many ways a tribute to his mother, Mallie, who had raised him and his siblings on her own. Her husband, Jerry, had abandoned the family six months after Jackie was born. Jackie hadn't realized how many hardships she'd endured until he was older.

Jack Roosevelt Robinson was born on January 31, 1919, to a family of sharecroppers in Cairo, Georgia. He was the youngest of five children, and his middle name was in honor of former President Theodore Roosevelt, who died less than a month before Robinson was born. After Jerry left the family in 1920, thirty-year-old Mallie took her five children to Pasadena, California.

"As I grew older, I often thought about the courage it took for my mother to break away from the South," Robinson wrote in his autobiography, *I Never Had It Made*. "Even though there appeared to be little future for us in the West, my mother knew that there she could be assured of the basic necessities."

The Robinsons were poor for much of Jackie's childhood, with Mallie making ends meet with a job washing and ironing clothes.

"Sometimes, there were only two meals a day," he said, "and some days, we wouldn't have eaten at all if it hadn't been for the leftovers my mother was able to bring home from her job."

Unlike Washington and Strode, who led relatively comfortable and conflict-free lives growing up in Los Angeles, Robinson experienced racism early.

"I must have been about eight years old the first time I ran into racial trouble," Robinson said. "I was sweeping our sidewalk when a little neighbor girl shouted at me, 'N—r, n—r, n—r.'" Robinson called the girl a "cracker," and the girl's father came outside. He and Robinson threw rocks at one another before the girl's mother made her husband go inside.

Were it not for the influence of two men—a mechanic named Carl Anderson who convinced Jackie he shouldn't join a neighborhood gang because "it would hurt my mother as well as myself" and a young minister named Rev. Karl Downs, the pastor at the family's church—that Jackie found his way.

"Often when I was deeply concerned about personal crises, I went to [Rev. Downs]," Robinson said. "One of the frustrations of my teens was watching Mother work so hard. I wanted to help more, but I knew how much my college education meant to her."

Sports became young Jackie's passion, and he quickly developed into a transcendent athlete, dominating the competition at every age. He suffered a broken ankle that briefly interrupted his first season at Pasadena, but, as he wrote, "I made up for lost time when I got back into action playing first-string quarterback."

Robinson's competitiveness was well known to both teammate and opponent alike, and his temper sometimes got the better of him. On January 25, 1938, he was arrested after arguing with police about the detention of a Black friend. There were other confrontations with police that didn't result in arrests, but Robinson had developed a reputation for not backing down when he felt he or people around him were subjected to racism.

Robinson received a two-year suspended sentence, and word of his arrest and other confrontations had preceded him when he went to UCLA. But there was something even more unsettling that happened before he started college. His older brother, Frank, was killed in a motorcycle accident. Of all his siblings, Jackie was closest to Frank, and his loss was incalculable.

"I was very shaken up by his death," Robinson said. "It was hard to believe he was gone, hard to believe I would no longer have his support."

Strode and Washington didn't entirely warm up to Robinson during their time at UCLA. While there was no outward hostility, there were some signs of strain.

"To be honest, Jackie was not well-liked when he was at UCLA," Strode said in recounting their time together with the Bruins. "Jackie was not friendly," he continued.

> When he came to UCLA, he was very withdrawn. Even on the football field, he would stand off by himself. People used to ask me, "Why is Jackie so sullen and always by himself?" Well, for one thing, Jackie's brother Frank was killed in a motorcycle accident just before Jackie got to UCLA. People hardly ever mention that.... They had a relationship similar to the one Rocky and Kenny shared.... I remember Jackie [once] said, "I wanted to win, not only for myself but also because I didn't want to see Frank disappointed."

Strode came to understand why it was harder for Robinson than for him and Washington:

> To someone like Kenny or me, Pasadena seemed like a million miles away.... Pasadena was where all the rich white people lived.... Those people controlled the community, and Pasadena was a segregated and prejudiced town. So it was much harder for someone like Jackie Robinson growing up than it was for someone like Kenny Washington, who grew up with nothing but poor Italians.

Strode said Bill Ackerman, UCLA's head of Associated Students who helped recruit Washington and assisted Strode's transition to the school, found it sometimes difficult to relate to Robinson. But

Ackerman also realized that at least some of Robinson's intensity was caused by his experiences with racism. He told Strode:

> Jackie always seemed to have a chip on his shoulder. I wasn't close to Jackie like I was to you guys. Maybe he was rather ahead of his time in his thinking with regard to the Black's situation. I think it hurt him emotionally to see how some of his friends were treated. The result was he kept pretty much within himself; to a certain extent, he was a loner.

Robinson was a very good teammate, however, and his addition to the UCLA backfield alongside Washington gave the Bruins a dimension that made them an even greater threat than the year before. It also helped Robinson that his childhood friend in Pasadena, Ray Bartlett, had also enrolled at the school and was an end on the Bruins' football team.

There was an unmistakable sense of excitement around the team and on campus, because the Bruins, long considered the second fiddle to perennial powerhouse USC in the southern California market, had the makings of their most competitive team.

The UCLA-USC rivalry itself began in 1929 and was so one-sided in the first two years—USC won the games by a combined 128–0—that UCLA declined to play again until 1936. And even with the improvement UCLA had shown with the additions of Washington and Strode, the Bruins were demolished in 1938, 42–7, just a year after Washington had nearly brought the Bruins back in an epic comeback attempt the year before in a 19–13 loss.

With a backfield that now included Washington and UCLA's prized recruit, Robinson, and with Horrell having replaced Spaulding to inject new life into the head coaching position, the optimism was justified.

"The Bruins of UCLA will hoist their hopes upon a triple staff of (1) new coaches, (2) new players, (3) and a new system when they dash out of the tunnel onto the Coliseum turf to tangle with the strong Texas Christian footballers one week from next Friday evening," *Los Angeles Times* writer Dick Hyland proclaimed in advance of their regular season opener against defending national champion TCU.

Horrell would stick with the single wing offense, using Washington as his left halfback and Robinson as the right half—also referred to as tailbacks and Robinson sometimes a wingback—but the coach also planned to introduce some other wrinkles, according to Hyland:

> Undoubtedly, Mr. Horrell is counting upon two factors to give needed aid to UCLA [linemen]. One, his spread formation will force opponents to spread also. Second, he is probably considering the speed of his backs.

The backs, of course, being Washington and Robinson.

Horrell's new approach would undergo a huge test right from the start, as the Bruins hosted the 1938 national champions. The 1938 Horned Frogs, coached by Dutch Meyer, went 11-0 and were voted by the Associated Press as national champions. They outscored their opponents by a combined 269–60, and quarterback Davey O'Brien was selected as the Heisman Trophy winner. (Another prestigious college honor—the Davey O'Brien Award—is now presented each year to the NCAA's top quarterback as judged by the Davey O'Brien Foundation.)

Fortunately for the Bruins, O'Brien had graduated after his championship season, but TCU, unbeaten in fourteen straight games going back to the 1937 season, was still considered a formidable opponent and Meyer an elite coach. He certainly had better credentials than Horrell, whose only prior coaching experience was as a UCLA assistant from 1926 to 1938.

Horrell didn't exactly cover himself in glory in his head coaching debut.

Hoping to fool Meyer and the Horned Frogs early on, Horrell started the game with . . . his backups.

That's right. Even with a team featuring Washington, Robinson, Strode, quarterback Ned Matthews, and fullback Leo Cantor, Horrell tried to psyche out the visitors by going with a lineup that included left halfback Chuck Fenenbock in place of Washington, right halfback Dale Gilmore instead of Robinson, and Ben Kvitky over Matthews.

Horrell eventually put his regulars in, but not before the early-game chicanery fell flat.

For the most part, TCU dominated the game, outgaining UCLA 259–179 in total yards and 107–25 in passing yards.

But it was Washington and Robinson who established some level of consistency for UCLA, with both accounting for the bulk of the team's rushing yards. Washington led the way with 11 carries for 65 yards, and Robinson was next with 6 carries for 56 yards. No other UCLA runner had more than 20 yards.

A 71-yard drive in the third quarter—keyed by Washington and Robinson—set UCLA up for its first and only score, as fullback Bill Overlin ran up the middle for a 9-yard touchdown.

TCU got to within four points, 6–2, on a safety, but UCLA prevailed in the defensive struggle.

Ralph Welch was among the sixty thousand people in the Coliseum stands to watch the game, and he was duly impressed by what he'd just seen. A scout on head coach Jimmy Phelan's University of Washington staff, Welch reported back to his boss in advance of the upcoming game against UCLA.

"Welch says that Jack Robinson is as good as he has been touted, being dazzlingly shifty," *Seattle Times* columnist George Varnell wrote. "The addition of Robinson to the UCLA backfield also adds effectiveness to Kenny Washington's play, giving the Bruins two of the fleetest backs in the conference. The Huskies defense must be airtight to stop them."

Washington, Robinson, and Strode combined to beat the Huskies, 14–7, in Seattle, with the Bruins recovering from an early 7–0 deficit. In his game story for the *Seattle Times,* Alex Schults reflected just how much of a novelty it was that UCLA had three African-American players on their roster.

And not in a good way.

"Just when the Washington Huskies thought they had their first 1939 Pacific Coast Conference football battle won yesterday in the stadium," he wrote, "the Midnight Express from UCLA got rolling, with Engineer Jack Robinson tooting the whistle, and it wasn't long until what looked like a 7–0 Washington victory became a 14–7 defeat...There will be fried chicken and watermelon on the dining car table."

It wasn't the only time racism reared its ugly head. In a game two years earlier at Washington State, Washington became enraged when he heard a coach use the N-word during the game. Strode said Bab Hollingberry used the invective as Washington ran near the Cougars' sideline. "You didn't call Kenny Washington a n—r without a reaction," Strode said, adding, "Kenny stopped the whole proceedings and went after the coach."

Strode said Washington once told him opposing players tried to take lime used to mark the field and rub it in his eyes. "Kenny would come back to the huddle and say, 'That son of a bitch tried to hurt me.'"

At 2-0, UCLA faced Stanford in Palo Alto, making it two straight road games against Pacific Coast Conference foes. Horrell once more tried to play mind games with the opposition, again putting his second-string offense into the game at the start in hopes of rattling the Indians (Stanford's team name at the time).

Again, it didn't work.

It was only when Horell went with his regular lineup that the Bruins got going. The first time Robinson touched the ball, he ran 52 yards on a reverse. The Bruins didn't score on the drive, but settled down and remained competitive in a 7–7 first half.

But Stanford appeared headed to victory in the fourth quarter, leading by 14–7, until Washington fired off a 15-yard completion to Robinson to the Stanford 9. Washington ran three times to the 2, and on fourth-and-goal, Cantor ran in to make it 14–13. Robinson kicked the extra point to pull even.

It ended in a 14–14 tie, but not before Robinson saved the day with a critical interception after Stanford drove deep into UCLA territory.

It would be Washington's turn to shine the following week in a 20–6 win over Montana to improve the Bruins' record to 3-0-1 and continue the momentum in what was turning out to be a special season. But this was not just another transcendent game for Washington, who had one of his best performances ever in running for 164 yards and 3 touchdowns before the first half had ended.

This was a performance that left Montana coach Doug Fessenden comparing Washington to one of the greatest football players who ever lived.

"That fellow Washington is even greater than Red Grange," Fessenden said after the game. "No wonder he ran wild against us."

Better than Red Grange?

Yes, he said it. And Fessenden knew exactly who he was comparing Washington to, because Fessenden himself had attended Illinois at the same time as Grange, who came to be known as "The Galloping Ghost." A three-time All-American who led the Illini to a national championship in 1923, Grange went on to play for the Bears in 1925 and captured the country's imagination during the fledgling years of the NFL.

It was a heady time for UCLA football, with the school beginning to get noticed around the country—albeit not yet to the point where they were nationally ranked.

That would come soon.

In the meantime, it was a fitting season to introduce what would soon be called the "Liberty Bell," a gift that had been bestowed upon

UCLA by the school's alumni association. The bell would be rung after every point scored by the Bruins, a reminder of the program's newfound respect.

The brass bell was eventually stolen by some USC students as a prank before both schools decided in 1942 that the bell would go each year to the winner of the USC-UCLA game—now commonly referred to as the Victory Bell game. The bell's mounting is painted with the school colors of the team that wins the game each year.

The Black press was particularly enthused about the play of Washington, Robinson, and Strode. Dubbed the "Three Dark Horsemen"—a play on the "Four Horsemen" of Notre Dame's legendary 1924 team under Knute Rockne—their collective performances in what was turning out to be a dream season were duly noted. Especially Washington.

"Of the 'Three Dark Horsemen'—Kenny Washington, Woodrow Strode and Jackie Robinson," read a dispatch of the Montana game from the Associated Negro Press in the *Baltimore Afro-American*, "it was General Washington who made three scores, Strode and Robinson doing their bit by interference and blocking. Washington was the hero of the day to his white schoolmates, the over 20,000 fans and the opposing team. Altogether, Washington carried the ball 164 yards in 11 tries to add new laurels to the leader of the 'Three Dark Horsemen' of UCLA."

Robinson was amazed by Washington's performance.

"The Montana game was probably the best I saw Kenny play in 1939," he said in an interview after Washington's death in 1971. "He completely dominated play. Over the years, people have downgraded Kenny's speed, but he could run 100 yards in 10 seconds flat—in full uniform. For that era, and for his size—6-1, 195 pounds—that was good running."

Because he was both pigeon toed and knock-kneed, Washington's unusual style made him even more dangerous. In addition to the nicknames "Kingfish" and "the General" (as in Gen. George Washington), teammates called him "Ken Bones," a reference to his slender legs.

"One of Kenny's great talents was the fact that he could run almost as fast sideways as he could straight ahead," Robinson said. "Tacklers found it nearly impossible to bring him down, because he could spin away from them so quickly, they couldn't stay with him."

Washington and Robinson would star again the following week against Oregon, as the Bruins scored a 16–6 win to improve to 4-0-1. It was a game that Robinson remembered as if it were yesterday while reminiscing about the plays more than three decades later. And it was a game marked as much by what Washington did with his arm as much as he did with his legs.

"Kenny was probably the greatest long passer ever," Robinson said. "He could throw sixty yards on the fly consistently. He was so strong that his short passing game suffered. He threw the ball so hard that receivers just couldn't catch it. But on the long throws, nobody could ever touch him. We were the first team to rely heavily on the long passing game that became so popular in later years."

It was especially formidable against Oregon.

The win over Oregon vaulted the Bruins into the conversation when it came to nationally ranked teams; UCLA made it to No. 19 and then climbed to eleventh overall with a dominant 20–7 win over the University of California, Berkeley at the Coliseum. Once again, Washington was brilliant, and this time he had to do it without Robinson, who missed the game with a knee injury.

Washington led the Bruins with 141 rushing yards on 22 carries and had a hand in all three UCLA touchdowns. He ran for a 35-yard score in the first quarter, threw a 35-yard touchdown pass to Don MacPherson in the second quarter, and fired a 22-yard touchdown strike to Strode in the third.

A surprisingly strong Santa Clara team gave the Bruins a much tougher game than they might have expected, but coming off consecutive wins over Purdue, Stanford, and Michigan State, the Broncos were thinking upset on November 18 at the Coliseum. It nearly happened.

Santa Clara got to the 2-yard line in the second quarter and the 9 in the third, but UCLA's defense held both times, forcing the Broncos into a missed field goal try on the second drive. But Washington struggled to take control offensively as he had in previous weeks, and the Bruins were held scoreless throughout.

The 0–0 tie wasn't frowned upon too badly when it came to the rankings; UCLA fell to thirteenth and then stayed there after another tie, 13–13, against Oregon State.

With hopes for a Rose Bowl berth still intact and the possibility of being unbeaten going into the regular-season finale against USC, the Bruins took care of Washington State, 24–7, thanks to more fine work from Washington and Strode, as well as Robinson, who had returned from his knee injury.

On to USC for the unbeaten Bruins, a chance to play in the Rose Bowl and a chance to win a national title to finish off what could be the greatest season in school history.

"We were a tough group of dead-end kids, and we came together that year to form UCLA's first great football team," Strode said. "And, to the best of my knowledge, UCLA was the first major university to have four Black kids playing key roles. Kenny and Jackie were the first one-two Black backfield men, I started every game [with the exception of the ones in which Horrell chose to go with the backups as a failed ploy], and Ray Bartlett saw considerable playing time as a reserve. We were unique in America."

What was even more unique was the fact that the most integrated football team in the country was in position to win a national championship.

It all depended on what happened against USC.

"The week before the big game we practiced in secret," Strode said. "Both schools had spies, and we caught two of theirs with binoculars and notebooks. We had guards patrolling the perimeter of the field, and they caught these guys hiding in the bushes. They tied them up and took them out to fraternity row. The kids out there shaved UCLA in their hair, painted them blue and gold and sent 'em home. That's how the war escalated."

Each school had a bonfire and a pep rally the night before the game, only this time some UCLA students snuck into the area where the USC bonfire was being held and lit the gigantic stacks of wood before it was scheduled to start. Strode was told USC had burned him, Washington, and Robinson in effigy.

"They made figures out of straw, hung us and burned us," Strode said. "That wasn't racial, that was fear. Just like whenever Pete Rose showed up at Dodger Stadium, the fans would boo the hell out of him. Well, they weren't booing him, they were booing his ability. That's how they show their admiration."

The tension was extraordinary.

A headline in the *Los Angeles Daily News* blared, "USC Boss Fears Westwooders," as the Trojans' legendary coach Howard Jones called UCLA "the most dangerous team in the country." Dozens of Hollywood celebrities showed up, including Douglas Fairbanks, Jane Wyman, and Joe E. Brown.

Strode picked Washington up the night before the game, and they met their teammates and coaches at the school for a bus ride to the Beverly Hills Hotel. After a mostly sleepless night, they headed over to the Coliseum for the biggest game of their lives.

The winner would go to the Rose Bowl and receive more than the $100,000 prize for playing in the prestigious game. A tie, and USC would go to the bowl game, by virtue of its 7-0-1 record heading into the game, versus UCLA's 6-0-3 record. As Strode wrote:

> The crowd started arriving around noon. We were still in the locker room at that point. I remember sitting with Kenny in the trainer's room waiting to get taped up. As I sat there I could feel the vibration of the crowd. Those thick concrete walls were pulsing, boy, and my heart was keeping time. Kenny turned to me. "You nervous?"
>
> "No way...how about you?"
>
> "Nope, I just want to get this thing started."
>
> The butterflies were swirling, and as we dropped our heads to hide the lie, I could see Kenny cross himself.

The game started as if the Trojans would make the Bruins their eighth straight victim, with USC threatening to score on three different occasions. Washington set up one of those opportunities with a fumbled snap, but Robinson rescued his team with a punishing hit that forced USC quarterback Grenville Lansdell to fumble at the UCLA 3. Strode recovered the ball in the end zone.

"The ball shot off the Trojan's chest like it had been blown from a gun barrel," Hyland wrote of the Robinson hit. "No man's arm could have withstood that blow from Robinson's body."

After seeing the loose ball, Strode wrote, "I woke up quick like I had stuck my finger in a socket. I saw a picture of myself in the papers; my eyes looked like a frightened deer's, and I was striding the goddamndest stride...I was thinking six points when Bob Hoffman brought me down on our own 13. To this day, I don't know where he came from, but he saved a sure touchdown."

Washington saved another scoring threat in the first half with his own defensive brilliance, as he intercepted a deep pass by Lansdell at the UCLA 10 and returned it 28 yards. The half ended in a scoreless tie.

As the teams went to the locker rooms, Washington noticed his Uncle Rocky waiting for him.

"You're playing scared, boy," Rocky told him. "You've got to open up, start throwing the ball downfield. Go with what got you here. You're in a great position to win this game, but you've got to take the fight to them. I believe in you, Kenny. Now go out there and show them what you can do!"

The words hit home, and Washington seemed like a different player in the second half. Much more authoritative, much more willing to throw the ball down the field. He nearly had two touchdown passes to Robinson, had a long pass to Strode that was ruled just out of bounds, and commanded the offense to the point where the unbeaten Trojans began to worry that their streak might come to an end.

Still, no points.

From either team.

With time winding down and the Bruins' hopes of a Rose Bowl berth beginning to fade, there would be another chance for Washington. With five minutes left in the fourth quarter, the Bruins took over at their own 20, and Washington went to work.

Robinson started the drive with a 13-yard run, and Washington followed it up with a 10-yard gain. Washington then went to work through the air, completing four straight passes to MacPherson for 18, Robinson for 12, Strode for 6, and Ned Matthews for 5.

The Bruins got to the 6, where it was first and goal.

Fullback Leo Cantor would get the ball, as UCLA hoped he could use his sturdy two-hundred-pound build to power into the end zone. And it looked as if that was exactly what would happen, as he found a hole up the middle and churned ahead. Suddenly, Hoffman, the alert linebacker, swooped in to make the tackle at the 2. The hit was so hard that it left Cantor slow to get up. After Washington was stopped for no gain, Matthews, calling the plays for UCLA, had Cantor try again up the middle. Only this time, he was brought down for a 2-yard loss.

Fourth and goal at the 4, and a huge decision to make.

"It was a perfect spot for a field goal," Washington said years later. "But both of our field goal kickers had injured legs."

Meanwhile, in the USC huddle, safety Doyle Nave was worried about Strode.

"I was trying to figure out what I'd do if they tried a pass to Woody Strode," Nave was quoted as saying in Steven Travers's book, *The USC Trojans: College Football's All-Time Greatest Dynasty*. "Woody stands about six-five, you know, and I'm under six feet."

It was a mismatch the Bruins elected not to test.

Washington took the snap, but USC didn't bite on the fake handoff. MacPherson, lined up to the right of the formation, ran an out route to the right, but USC defensive back Bobby Robertson correctly anticipated that the ball was coming MacPherson's way. As Washington delivered the pass, Robertson got to the ball in time to swat it away.

USC had narrowly escaped.

Washington's offense had one more shot in the final minute, getting to the USC 40, but his long pass was picked off by linebacker Chuck Morrill to end hopes of a miracle finish.

And with fifteen seconds left in the game and UCLA's unbeaten season assured—if not ending with the hoped-for berth in the Rose Bowl—Washington was summoned to the sidelines by his coach.

Years later, Washington called that walk to the sidelines, with cheers of appreciation surrounding him, "my greatest thrill."

Four years earlier, he had walked off that same field to the applause of Lincoln High School fans who had watched him win the city championship. Now he was leaving to an ovation few had ever received before or since.

"Kenny Washington was the greatest football player I have ever seen," Robinson said. "He had everything needed for greatness—size, speed, and tremendous strength. That 1939 season was something special, and it was all because of Kenny Washington."

Washington's three years represented arguably the greatest career of any UCLA player in history. He produced a school-record 1,915 rushing yards, adding almost 1,300 passing yards. He had 1,370 yards of total offense in 1939 alone. His average of 37.8 yards per interception return is still first in UCLA history.

And get this: He played 580 of a possible 600 minutes as a senior.

"Records are here to be broken," he said long after his career was over, "but when someone breaks my endurance record, let me hear about it."

It will never happen.

Washington was the first UCLA player to lead the nation in total offense, and he was the first consensus All-American in the school's history. The Bruins would eventually retire his No. 13. He would earn a well-deserved place in the College Football Hall of Fame.

He would not, however, get a chance at playing in the NFL. At least not at a time where he might have been the first player taken in a league that prized running backs.

He walked off to a hero's celebration on the final day of his college career on December 9, 1939.

But on that same day, when the NFL held its annual draft, Washington's name would not be called.

Nor would the name of any other African-American player.

Chapter 11

BLUEJACKETS

Marion Motley stood in line at the military recruiting center in downtown Cleveland and awaited his assignment. It was Christmas Day, 1944. World War II was in full force as one of the bloodiest battles in western civilization. Nearly half a million German soldiers pulled off a surprise attack on Allied soldiers. The Battle of the Bulge had begun.

In the Pacific theater, American-led Allied forces were beginning to make significant inroads against the Empire of Japan. It would still be two months before troops raised the American flag at Iwo Jima, one of the most impactful victories that foretold Japan's eventual surrender.

Motley wasn't sure how he would contribute to the war effort, only that he knew he must.

"The people in charge never asked 'em what branch they wanted," Motley said. "They'd just tell 'em, 'Army!... Navy!... Army!' But when I got up there, they said, 'What branch do you want?'"

The big man from Canton thought for a moment.

"I'd heard that in the Navy, you'd get to see the world, plus I'd heard the Navy was much cleaner than the Army and had the best food," he said. "So I said, 'Navy.'"

Motley was sent to the Naval Station Great Lakes, overlooking Lake

Michigan just north of Chicago. It was the Navy's largest training installation and home to its only boot camp. He spent the next several weeks preparing to go to war, and while there, he heard that Paul Brown was coaching the Great Lakes Bluejackets football team.

The two made contact, and Brown, who had enlisted in the Navy in 1944 after leading Ohio State to its first national championship, was eager to have Motley on his team.

Motley was happy to be playing *with* Brown this time; after all, the only three losses of his entire high school football career were to Brown's Massillon Tigers.

Brown's own journey had taken a fateful turn when he left Ohio State, and circumstances had changed.

Dramatically.

Brown left Ohio State after the 1943 season. Enlisting in the Navy felt like the right thing to do for Brown, whose patriotism ran deep and prompted him to do his part in the war effort.

But there was bitterness, too.

After his 3-6 Baby Bucks season—his only losing record to that point—the Army relaxed its rules and allowed ROTC members to resume playing. Brown had recommended that the Buckeyes hire his longtime assistant, Carroll Widdoes, to replace him until his military leave was over, and Brown had every reason to think he'd return to Ohio State.

But Widdoes had the luxury of using the players Brown had previously recruited to the school and now had their eligibility reinstated, and he responded with a 9-0 record. Ohio State outscored its opponents 287–79, and the Buckeyes were No. 2 in the Associated Press rankings. (The school has recognized only the AP ranking and does not claim any national title, despite subsequent organizations naming that team national champions.)

Even so, Brown had mixed feelings about the team's success.

Yes, Brown still had the opportunity to coach at Great Lakes, but it simply wasn't the same. That hit home after Brown had returned with his Bluejackets team to Ohio State for that October 21, 1943, game against his old team before 73,477 fans in Columbus. Even Brown's son, Mike, admitted to the coach he was pulling for Ohio State. And the fans, who had welcomed him home to warm applause before the game, were delighted at the fact that the Buckeyes had routed Great Lakes, 26–6.

After the game, Brown was angry, hurt and, most of all, frustrated by circumstances. Paul Hornung, a *Columbus Dispatch* sportswriter who had developed a close friendship with Brown over the years (and not the former Packers star of the same name), met with Brown in the losers' locker room.

Hornung was struck by how disheartened Brown had looked.

"Does this look like a losing locker room to you?" Brown recalled in his autobiography.

Hornung looked around the locker room and said no.

"The fact that I had coached at Ohio State meant nothing to our [Bluejackets] players, nor had losing the game," Brown told Hornung. "They just wanted to have a little fun, and the dressing room was a bedlam as they talked about all the things they were going to do later."

Part of Brown understood the fact that his team wasn't as invested in the outcome as the coach.

"Who knows, perhaps they were right—things like football games tended to dim in importance to men who, two or three months from then, might be lying dead on some beach in the South Pacific," he thought to himself. "[But] it was something I never could reconcile myself to while coaching service football."

Brown had a lot to live up to at Great Lakes. After all, he had taken over for Tony Hinkle, who led the Bluejackets to a 10-2 record the year before Brown arrived, earning Great Lakes the No. 6 ranking in the final Associated Press poll. That was heady stuff for the service team, one of several around the country that had fully scheduled seasons and played not only one another, but prominent college teams as well.

But Brown's loss to Ohio State while coaching the Bluejackets might have served as a wakeup call, even if he didn't feel his team had shown the kind of dedication and commitment he expected.

Things did get better after that game, and while his former Buckeyes team was conquering every challenge it faced during its unbeaten season under Widdoes—something Brown was keenly aware of, even if he wasn't on campus—the Great Lakes team showed steady improvement.

After the Ohio State loss, Brown brought his team to Wisconsin, where the Buckeyes had suffered that agonizing defeat in 1942—their only loss of the season—after many of Brown's players had become sickened by drinking tainted water on the trip to Madison. This time, Brown's team crushed the Badgers, 40–12. It was the first of five straight victories, setting up a season-ending showdown at Notre Dame.

But the Great Lakes team was outclassed from the start, as No. 9 Notre Dame rolled to a 28–7 win to drop Brown's record to 9-2-1. A highly respectable season, no doubt. But the loss to Notre Dame was a major disappointment, one he hoped wouldn't be repeated if the teams faced one another again.

By the time Brown was preparing for his second—and final—season at Great Lakes, the tide had turned in the war, and the Allied forces were inflicting heavy losses on the enemy in Europe and the Pacific. By now, the Western Allies had freed France from German occupation, the Soviet Union had repelled German forces, and Japan was losing territory it had captured in Asia. The Allies also had punished the Japanese Navy and wrested control of several important Western Pacific islands and other territories.

On May 8, 1945, not long after Hitler had committed suicide, Germany surrendered unconditionally. Japan would soon follow, although not before the United States dropped atomic bombs on Hiroshima and Nagasaki. Japan surrendered officially on September 2, 1945.

The mood at the Great Lakes military installation was particularly ebullient, considering all the sacrifices, and Brown shared the sense of relief that the war had finally ended.

His coaching responsibilities continued, however, and preparations for the 1945 season were well underway in the spring and summer months. He'd already made contact with Motley, his old high school foe, and looked forward to using the bruising fullback in a big way. What he particularly liked about Motley's situation was that few people had really heard of him, since he'd returned from Nevada and spent a year out of football while working in the steel mill in Canton and raising his young family before enlisting in the Navy.

Brown was privately ecstatic about the team he was about to field, because it included some of the country's best players who were in the service. One of those players was Buddy Young, a five-foot-four, 175-pound running back who made up for his lack of size with a speed and quickness rarely seen on a football field. He'd been a star at the University of Illinois before joining the Navy and heading to Great Lakes, and Brown looked forward to having both him and Motley in the same backfield.

And then Brown got the news.

After having organized what he considered one of the finest football teams in the land—college or pro—Brown was told that most of his top players would be leaving to play for the Fleet City base in Shoemaker, California, near Oakland.

"We thought we were ready to dominate the football scene," Brown said. "Just then, however, a Great Lakes officer who had been director of the service school was transferred to Fleet City and was told by his commanding officer that he wanted a great football team for his base.

As the season came closer, our players were transferred, one by one to Fleet City, by some means which I never did understand."

Brown was told that operations were being fortified on the West Coast because the war in Europe was winding down and the Japanese had not yet surrendered. It was important for morale purposes, Brown was told, that the soldiers stationed at the base had a great football team to rally around.

Brown, meanwhile, was crestfallen, privately likening his situation to the one he faced at Ohio State in 1943, when Army regulations had left him with the shell of a team just a year after he'd won the school's first national title.

As it turned out, there was hope this time. That hope largely rested with Motley, although he, too, nearly was swept up in the transfer of so many of Brown's great players.

Motley had actually received orders in August to transfer to Fleet City along with about 1,500 other troops. He was about to board a train at the Waukegan depot.

"I was right there at the train when I phoned Paul and told him what was happening," Motley said.

"Don't move," Brown told him. "You stay right there at that phone."

Brown quickly called the commanding officer in charge of the troop transfer and delayed the train's departure.

"[Brown] told him, 'If you want me to coach this football team, you better stop that player and any other player that comes through there,'" Motley said.

After a few minutes, Brown called Motley.

"You get your gear off that train and bring it back to the barracks," the coach told him.

Motley wasn't cleared just yet. He'd previously put his seabag in a boxcar for bulk shipment to the West Coast, and it required a search committee to go through the pile of equipment before the one labeled "Seaman Apprentice Motley" would be located.

"I'll never forget that day," Motley told veteran football writer John Steadman of the *Baltimore Sun*. "It would be hard to believe that, had I been an admiral instead of a 'swabbie' that any more fuss could have been made over me."

The fuss was made because Brown had been furious at the possibility that he'd lose Motley in addition to the other players he'd expected to be on his team. Relieved that he'd have his big running back on his team, Brown was also heartened by the fact that three players from the Notre Dame team that had routed Great Lakes the year before had enlisted and were stationed at the naval base.

Quarterback George Terlep, end Bucky O'Connor, and linebacker Marty Wendell would play for Brown's squad. Terlep and O'Connor would make a good enough impression that Brown eventually signed them to play for the Browns.

And there was another player Brown had been looking forward to coaching, someone who had come highly recommended by Harry Stuhldreher, an original member of Notre Dame's celebrated "Four Horsemen" backfield and the former Wisconsin coach. The player Stuhldreher recommended: Bud Grant.

Yes, that Bud Grant.

Before he became a Hall of Fame coach for the Minnesota Vikings, Grant was a terrific player at Wisconsin and then with the Eagles. But a big turning point in his career came as a result of playing for Brown's team at Great Lakes.

The original plan for Grant was to play fullback for the Bluejackets.

Motley changed those plans, however.

"I didn't know Marion Motley until I got there, and we had these blocking drills, and every time I was blocking this great big Black guy," Grant said. "I'm thinking to myself, how am I going to get around Marion Motley? Every time my turn came up, he was blocking me or I was blocking him or we had these tackling drills."

Grant told Brown he'd prefer to play end.

"Bud knew what he was doing, because no one could have competed with Motley," Brown said. "In fact, no one competed very successfully with Bud once he broke into our starting lineup. He was a natural athlete with tremendous leaping ability, and once he got his hands on the ball, he never dropped it."

Grant was such a fleet and sure-handed receiver that Brown once called the same play—a "go" route—three straight times in a game. The first was a touchdown called back on an offsides penalty. The second was a touchdown called back on an illegal motion penalty. The third was another touchdown; this time, it stood.

Motley wasn't only the leading playmaker on the team, but he was a terrific leader as well, especially for someone like the young Grant.

"I'd never seen a Black person until I went in the Navy," Grant said. "I didn't have any Black friends in northern Wisconsin. But with Marion, he was very easy-going. He was a guy who was always in good humor. He took everything in stride. Just a great guy."

And a great player.

The season got off to a slow start, however, in part because Brown didn't have the complement of star players he'd anticipated after the unexpected transfer of standouts like Buddy Young to Fleet City. Brown himself knew this would be his final season with the team, even before the outcome of the war was assured and Great Lakes and other service teams would be disbanded. He'd already been contacted to become the coach and part owner of a team in a start-up league called the All-America Football Conference. The discussions had begun in secret in February 1945, although Brown never let on that he would be taking the job until months later.

The season started with a humbling 35–0 loss to a college all-star team at Ross Field, and the Bluejackets were 0-3-1 after four games. But as had been the case in Brown's previous stops, his teams showed dramatic improvement as the season wore on. With Motley carrying the load in the running game and Terlep showing the form that helped Notre Dame beat Brown's Great Lakes team the year before, the Bluejackets won five straight games heading into the season finale—the last game in the history of the team, in fact—against Notre Dame.

It was a game Brown had been thinking of for months, because he'd never gotten over the previous year's loss at South Bend. This time, the game would be held at Ross Field, and Brown spent weeks preparing for the matchup.

"We practiced against Notre Dame formations for about a month, even though we were playing other teams," Grant said. "[Brown] was very serious about preparing for that game."

Notre Dame had a terrific team under first-year coach Hugh Devore, going 7-1-1 in its first nine games before the finale against Great Lakes.

Their only loss was a 48–0 drubbing at Yankee Stadium from an Army team that notched nine wins and a national championship in what has been called one of the greatest college football seasons in history. The Cadets would beat Navy on the same day as the Great Lakes–Notre Dame game, so Brown knew a win over the Fighting Irish would carry even greater weight.

Motley was under no obligation to play in the game, nor was halfback Grover Klemmer, a California sprint star who held the world record in the 440-yard run. Both players were eligible for discharge about two weeks before the game, and Brown needed to clear it with them before penciling his two runners into the lineup. He pulled them aside before a practice.

"I've been notified that you men have finished your tour and may leave," Brown told them. "Or I can arrange to delay your discharge until after we play Notre Dame. Which will it be?"

Both of them stared intently at Brown. Then Klemmer smiled.

"Coach, we've gone this far, and I don't think the extra ten bucks the Navy had to pay us is going to bust the government," he said.

Motley agreed.

Finally, Brown knew he had a team at Great Lakes that was as singularly focused as he was. He knew he had a chance against Notre Dame.

The Fighting Irish were three touchdown favorites heading into the game, something Brown relished as yet another reason to motivate his team. Motley set the tone early, smashing through the interior of the line and using his powerful build to literally run over Notre Dame defenders.

"Notre Dame simply could not handle Motley that day and even had trouble knocking him down as he ran several trap plays that became his specialty over the years," Brown said. "We had particularly told Marion in practice, 'If you come clear on this trap play, don't get fancy. If there is someone in front of you, just run in one end of him and out the other.' "

After the teams traded touchdowns on their first possessions, Motley's 37-yard kickoff return set up another Great Lakes touchdown drive, and Motley's 44-yard touchdown in the fourth quarter helped break the game open in a resounding 39–7 win.

"Afterward, our dressing room was positively flooded with emotion," Brown said. He called that win one of the most significant in his entire career—and that includes pro football championship seasons. The fact that Notre Dame was the opponent meant that the game had attracted national attention—all of it good for the team led by the great coach and his spectacular running back.

"Great Lakes Routs Notre Dame 39-7 For Smashing Upset," read the banner headline in the *Pittsburgh Press* on December 2, 1945.

"Great Lakes football team fired a farewell shot to the wartime prowess of the Navy today as they walloped Notre Dame, 39–7, in a dramatic season-ending upset before 25,000 rabid Navy officers and sailors," the lede to the United Press game story read. "The Blue Jackets, three-touchdown underdogs at game time, struck hard to make up for Navy's defeat by Army at Philadelphia and give Navy men scattered around the world something to cheer about."

It was a game Brown never forgot.

"My father had a handful of games that were, in his mind, games that were the most important ones he ever coached, that meant the most to him," Mike Brown said. "For some reason, this game was one of those, and one of the reasons was that Marion was free to go back to civilian life and my father pleaded with him to stay on for a couple of weeks to participate in the game against Notre Dame, and he did that."

And along the way in that final season, Brown had not only commanded the respect of his players, but he also awakened the imagination of two of his key players about the possibility of following Brown's career path: coaching.

For Motley and Grant, it would become a lifetime passion. But only one man would get to achieve his dreams of leading his own teams.

"I learned more from Paul Brown in one year at Great Lakes than at any time in my playing or coaching career," Grant said. "How to handle people, how to handle situations, how to evaluate players. If you just listened to Paul Brown, he wasn't a rant-and-rave guy. He just said things straight. That was new and different to me. It was one of the greatest experiences I've had in my life."

Grant would go on to a Hall of Fame career with the Vikings, winning the Canadian Football League's Grey Cup four times before leading the Vikings to four Super Bowl appearances in an 18-year NFL run. In 1994, he'd go to Motley's hometown of Canton and be inducted into the Hall of Fame.

Motley would never get that chance to coach.

* * *

While Motley's future after leaving the military remained up in the air, Brown's next move would take him on a journey he once never thought possible.

A journey that would eventually include Motley in a very prominent role.

Brown realized it might be awkward to return to Ohio State and replace Coach Widdoes just after they'd completed a perfect season.

Pro football would eventually be all the better for it.

* * *

Arch Ward may no longer be a household name in the sports world, but there was a time when he was one of the industry's most influential power brokers. He created baseball's All-Star game in the 1930s. He originated a football all-star game that eventually morphed into the Pro Bowl. And he brought Paul Brown into professional football, setting off a string of events that would eventually lead to the sport's reintegration and lead football into the modern era.

Ward was the bookish, bespectacled sports editor of the *Chicago Tribune* in the 1930s, having climbed the ladder in the newspaper and public relations business from the sports editor of the *Telegraph Herald* in Dubuque, Iowa, to Notre Dame's first publicity director in 1920, and eventually to the *Tribune* in 1925. He'd started as a copy editor but within five years was appointed sports editor.

Ward was a terrific sportswriter in his own right, but he had a knack for promotion. In Dubuque, he'd promote wrestling matches, combining his position at the newspaper with a gregarious personality and relentless work ethic. At Notre Dame, his job was to promote the school's program and build the legacy of Rockne, the All-American end who began his legendary coaching career the same year Ward got the school.

Ward's promotional gambits proved wildly successful, especially after coming through on a request by Chicago mayor Edward Kelly to come up with a way to create a sports event that would help celebrate the city's 1933 Century of Progress exposition—also called the Chicago World's Fair. Ward came up with the idea of a baseball all-star game that would feature the likes of Babe Ruth, Lefty Grove, and dozens of other luminaries in the nation's most popular sport.

It was a big ask, especially during the Depression, when baseball owners were struggling along with the rest of the country. But Ward sold the idea, writing almost daily about the possibilities and even soliciting fans' opinions about which players should be selected for the American and National League teams.

An overflow crowd of 47,595 packed Comiskey Park for the game, which was supposed to be just a onetime affair. But the event was so popular that it became an annual tradition that continues today.

Ward was again asked in 1934 to help boost attendance at the World's Fair, which extended through October 31 of that year. This time, he turned to football, and collaborated with Bears owner George Halas and others in the league on an idea that helped increase interest in the sports unlike anything before it.

Halas, of course, had been one of the league's founders in 1920 and was a dominant presence in the league over the following sixty-three years. Born in Chicago to immigrant parents Barbara and Frank Halas, who came to America from Austria-Hungary in the late nineteenth century, George grew up playing football, baseball, and basketball and helped the University of Illinois win the Big Ten Conference championship in 1918.

Halas represented the Decatur Staleys when pro football's first organizational meeting took place in Canton, Ohio, in 1920, eventually taking full control of the team that would soon move to Chicago and become the Bears. Halas would go on to coach the Bears to six NFL championships and a then-record 321 career victories over a forty-year coaching career.

At the time Ward was thinking of using football as the vehicle for the World's Fair promotional tool, Halas and his ten-team league were struggling. And it wasn't simply the Depression causing the financial hardships. The sport itself had not caught on the way baseball and college football had commanded fans' attention.

Pro football was still considered an inferior product compared to college, and the fact that the players were paid to play worked against the league. College football was considered more pure, in fans' minds, because the players competed for the love of the game and weren't motivated by money.

Consider this: When the Bears won their second straight championship in 1933, beating the Giants, 23–21, at Wrigley Field, just twenty-five thousand fans showed up. In their regular season finale at home against the Packers, the crowd was around seven thousand.

Just as the baseball All-Star Game buoyed the sport, Ward contended that an exhibition football game pitting a group of college all-star seniors facing the defending NFL champions could be a big draw. To entice the league further, Ward announced that proceeds from the game would benefit several charities.

The game was a huge hit, as 79,432 fans showed up to watch the College All-Stars, coached by Purdue's Noble Kizer, battle the defending champion Bears to a 0–0 tie.

Pro football would never quite be the same, thanks in large part to the vision of Ward, who was recently named the eighty-fourth biggest game changer in NFL history during the league's centennial celebration. So impressed were the owners by Ward that they offered him a chance to become the league's commissioner. Not once, but twice.

And both times, Ward turned them down.

But Ward remained interested in pro football, and by 1944 had hatched the idea of creating a competing league—the All-America Football Conference. With his formidable powers of persuasion, Ward convinced several wealthy businessmen around the country, some of whom had previously tried to own NFL teams, to form the new league. His plans were scuttled for a year because World War II was not yet over, but by 1945, he had lined up prospective teams in New York, Cleveland, Chicago, Buffalo, Los Angeles, San Francisco, Brooklyn, and Miami.

The league selected James Crowley, one of Notre Dame's famous "Four Horsemen," as commissioner. His NFL counterpart was Elmer Layden, who also played alongside Crowley on the legendary 1924 team.

Layden scoffed at the notion the league could compete with the NFL, suggesting Ward's league should "first get a ball, then make a schedule and then play a game." That line stuck in the craw of Ward and the owners of his startup league, and it served as motivational fodder throughout the league's history.

Washington owner George Preston Marshall piled on. "The worst team in our league could beat the best team in theirs," he said.

But before the AAFC could get off the ground, it needed something money couldn't buy. It needed legitimacy. Especially in the form of a big-name coach who would convince fellow coaches and players that the league meant business.

Ward had privately met with Brown at Great Lakes in 1944, trying to convince the coach that he'd have a unique opportunity to coach a pro team that would compete with the NFL. In Ward's grand scheme, he wanted to create a league that mirrored Major League Baseball, with two distinct leagues that would hold a playoff to crown an overall champion.

Brown was somewhat skeptical, but he at least gave the idea some thought.

Ward had secured the financing of Cleveland businessman Arthur B. "Mickey" McBride, whom he'd gotten to know in the newspaper industry, upon which McBride built a fortune in the Cleveland market. McBride increased his wealth even further when he purchased Cleveland's largest taxi company and was also a successful real estate developer in Cleveland, Chicago, and Florida.

In other words, money was no object for McBride in building a new team from scratch.

But his first choice as coach was the only coach he knew: Notre Dame's Frank Leahy. After some convincing, Leahy gave McBride a verbal assurance he'd work for him, but the school's president convinced Leahy to remain.

McBride asked sportswriter John Dietrich of the *Cleveland Plain Dealer* if he had any suggestions for a new coach, and Dietrich said Brown would be a great choice.

With Brown now having second thoughts about returning to Ohio State, Ward's offer was enticing.

By early 1945, Ward began to press Brown for an answer. After all, the Chicago-based newspaperman/entrepreneur had the teams lined up, but still no coaches yet. He needed to hit a home run here, and he knew Brown would be the answer.

On February 9, Brown agreed to a meeting with Ward, McBride, and Dan Sherby, another investor in the Cleveland franchise. As the meeting went on, the pressure increased for Brown to make a decision.

He asked if he might leave the room for a moment.

Brown called his wife, Katy.

"What are your feelings about this?" he asked her after describing the terms of a potential new deal.

"You do whatever you want to do," she told him.

Brown took that as a tacit acknowledgment that this was a good opportunity. He walked back into the room and signed a five-year contract that would pay him $25,000 a year and include a 5 percent ownership stake in the team.

"Most important to me," Brown said, "I had complete control of the team's operation, with total freedom to sign players and coaches. I told Sherby and McBride that I wanted to build a dynasty from the start and that I wanted our team to have the very best of everything, regardless of what it cost."

Brown hammered home his point this way:

"I'm sure you men are interested in making this go financially, but I'm not interested in your pocketbook. If we win the game and nobody is in the stadium, that won't bother me because I'll be satisfied with winning. If we lose the game in front of eighty-two thousand people, that's bad."

The men shook hands.

The Cleveland Browns were born.

Chapter 12

WHEN HOPE TURNED TO HEARTBREAK

A little more than eight months after walking off the field at the Los Angeles Coliseum to an ovation so thunderous that teammate Woody Strode suggested "it was like the Pope of Rome had come out," Kenny Washington boarded a train to Chicago for what he thought would be one more—and one final—chance to play a football game at the highest level of the sport.

With Arch Ward's College All-Star Game having turned into one of the most hotly anticipated games in the country—college or professional—Washington had been selected to play for the All-Star team that would face the previous year's NFL champions at Soldier Field. A then-record crowd of 84,567 would see the Packers take on the college stars on August 29, 1940, at the venerable stadium.

The Packers were in the midst of the first iteration of their glory days, having won the 1939 title with a 27–0 rout of the Giants in the championship game after a 9-2 first-place finish in the league's Western Conference. Curly Lambeau was coach of the Packers, winning Green Bay's fifth NFL championship and the first shutout in the title game.

Future Hall of Fame receiver Don Hutson was the star of the team, producing 846 receiving yards and 6 touchdowns—totals that were considered astronomical in a league that still relied mostly on the ground game. Arnie Herber and Cecil Isbell combined to throw 14 touchdown passes, and Clark Hinkle had a combined 9 rushing and receiving touchdowns.

In the days leading up to the All-Star game, Lambeau singled out Washington for his brilliance during UCLA's unbeaten season in 1939. In an article Lambeau penned for the *Chicago Tribune* a few weeks before the game, he wrote, "Washington and [Banks] McFadden (of Clemson) will likely be the collegians' stars, carrying on where Bill Osmanski of Holy Cross left off [as the game's MVP] in 1939. These two men are the pick of the finest set of backs ever assembled for the All-Star Game. Washington, UCLA's rugged halfback, is the epitome of football perfection. He was the toast of the Pacific coast, where great football players abound."

That's quite a compliment, since there were five first-round picks, as well as 1939 Heisman Trophy winner Nile Kinnick of Iowa, on the roster for the All-Stars. And one of those first-round picks was Hal van Every of Minnesota, who was selected by Lambeau himself.

Washington, of course, was overlooked in the previous month's draft, as was every other African-American player, due to the continuing exclusion of Blacks in the NFL. And despite being selected as an All-American by six different organizations, he received no first-team honors. Zero. He was named second-team on five ballots and third-team on the sixth. By not being named a first-team All-American, Washington was ruled out of the prestigious East-West Shrine Game that featured the nation's best college players. He would have been the first Black player to participate in the game had he been selected.

And make no mistake: He should have been a first-team All-American. After all, in a *Liberty* magazine poll among college players, Washington was the only one of the 664 nominees to be voted to the list by every player he faced.

The snub caused an uproar among many influential voices in California, including the state's lieutenant governor, Ellis E. Patterson, who wrote in a letter to the *Los Angeles Sentinel* that Washington's omission "was not the sentiment of the majority of the people. Such prejudice is un-American. If we believe in Democracy, there must be equal justice to all people irrespective of color and creed."

Participating in the College All-Star Game was all the more significant for Washington, and drawing praise from a future Hall of Fame coach like Lambeau was further validation for what he'd done at UCLA. And after a scrimmage in the days leading up to the game, Washington "stole the show," according to the *Chicago Tribune*.

Washington and his fellow college stars had their work cut out against the defending champions, but it was a surprisingly competitive game, with the Packers prevailing, 45–28, in the highest scoring game of the entire series, which ended in 1976. Washington scored a touchdown for the All-Stars and played well defensively, especially considering the fact that a Hall of Fame talent like Hutson, who is still considered one of the finest receivers in NFL history, was in the Green Bay lineup.

Chicago Defender columnist Fay Young was impressed with the performance:

> Kenny Washington . . . lived up to all expectations as far as an offensive back is concerned in the College All Stars vs. the Green Bay Packers, world professional football champions.

But the writer opined that Washington might have done even better if he'd had more of a chance:

> Washington scored a touchdown, driving over the line for the needed six inches, at the start of the second period. The coaches did not send him into the game in the first period, something which puzzled the fans. There were two things which cannot be forgotten about this game and Washington's

> play. His bullet-like passes and his runs were what over 10,000 of his own race wended their way to Soldier Field to see... [But] there is a general belief that Washington was not given the chance to start soon enough.

Fay went on to write that "the Packers respected Washington enough not to pass to his side of the defense. That was plain as the nose on anybody's face."

But Fay also criticized Washington for one defensive play on which he fell for a fake and allowed a touchdown. "It was the kind of play one would expect to see in a high school contest," Fay wrote. "I remarked to Coach Cleve Abbott, who was my guest, that many backfield aces in our Negro colleges could have given a far better account of themselves in the game than Washington showed, especially on defense."

It was a curious departure in a column that started with high praise for Washington and questioned the decision not to play him more early in the game. But Fay also was onto something else when it came to the idea that African-American players could ultimately help NFL owners with the bottom line, if only they'd allow Black players in the professional ranks.

"Dollars and cents erase color," he wrote. "An additional 10,000 on several Sundays during the short football playing season would make anybody think, especially when tickets are $1.10, $1.65 and $2.20."

But Fay suggested that Washington simply wasn't the right player at the right time to convince the owners that he could increase interest in the NFL.

"To get what we want, we have got to put somebody in there who can stand the gaff both on the offense and the defense. As it is, we will have to wait another year to put Jackie Robinson in there in the starting lineup and then watch things hum."

George Halas himself was far less critical of Washington. In fact, as Halas watched the game at his home stadium—surely miffed that it was the hated Packers representing the NFL—he thought Washington might be the one to change the owners' minds about allowing Black players into the pro game.

"Halas asked my grandfather if he could stick around Chicago," Washington's grandson, Kraig, said of what happened after the game. "He was very impressed with what [Washington] had done, and he wanted to see if he could sign him to the Bears."

Halas explained to Washington that he had to discuss his situation with the other owners before he could make any final decisions.

A day went by. Then two, then three.

As Washington himself later recalled it, the wait seemed interminable.

"George Halas kept me around for a month trying to figure out how to get me in the league," Washington said. "I left before he suggested I go to Poland first."

What Halas had to do was run the idea past his business partners. But in the end, there wasn't unanimous agreement that he should sign Washington.

"George Preston Marshall nixed it," Kraig Washington said, relating the story of what he'd been told by his father, Kenny Washington Jr. "And that was that."

Halas's grandson, current Bears chairman George McCaskey, isn't quite sure how things went down. And he's still searching for answers.

"To me, it seems like Kenny Washington was a talent that George Halas missed out on, and I'm trying to find out why," McCaskey said. "Now, Kenny Washington was on the College All-Star Team because he was one of the best, if not *the* best, college football players in the country. I haven't heard or seen anything about this meeting that supposedly took place [between Halas and Washington], and the skeptic in me says I don't see one person [Marshall] casting a dissenting vote which kills the idea. It turned out that he did not sign with the Bears, but it may have been for many other reasons."

That included the fact the Bears were at the beginning of their most dominating epoch. Starting in 1940, the "Monsters of the Midway" won championships in three of the next four seasons, which included a 73–0 win over Marshall's Washington team in the 1940 NFL Championship Game—the most dominating performance in playoff history. Sid Luckman was the quarterback. George McAfee, Bill Osmanski, Gary Famiglietti, Ray Nolting, and Joe Maniaci were outstanding running backs.

"The Bears had a potent offense, and it may have been that [Halas] didn't think [Washington] would get sufficient playing time, that there wasn't room on the roster for him," McCaskey said. He also acknowledged that Halas might not have been ready to bring all that would come with signing an African-American player to the roster at that time.

Excuses aside, Washington was heartbroken once he learned that Halas wouldn't sign him.

He confided as much in his great friend, Strode, who told his son, Kalai, during their long talks late in Strode's life. Kalai kept a journal of their conversations, noting that Washington was highly disappointed that he didn't have a chance to play professionally at that time.

Washington was not alone in his disappointment. Anyone who had watched him grow up in Lincoln Heights and seen him play at UCLA knew he was an elite talent, and if Washington didn't make his frustration public, others took up his cause.

NBC broadcaster Sam Balter delivered a blistering rebuke of the NFL's ban on Black players, delivering an open letter on the air and taking the league to task for ignoring the great halfback.

> [Washington was] not only the best football player on the Pacific Coast this season, but the best of the last ten years

> and perhaps the best in all that sport's glorious football history—a player who has reduced to absurdity all the All-American teams selected this year because they did not include him. And all know why. You have scouts—you know this better than I—you know their unanimous reports: He would be the greatest sensation in pro league history with any one of your ball clubs. You got that report. He was No. 1 on all your lists.

Still, there was silence among NFL owners, enough of whom were unwilling to go against the wishes of Marshall, who had never hidden his feelings about keeping Black players away from his team and out of the league.

The complicity was unmistakable. And it wasn't just Marshall.

"There's a concerted effort to blame everything on George Preston Marshall and that he forces the other teams to get rid of African-Americans," sports historian Damion Thomas said. "But you can't attribute it all just to him. I think the NFL needs to own its collective decision to not have African-American players for that period."

"Among the NFL's decision makers during those twelve years were some of the most storied individuals in the history of the game," author Andy Piascik writes in the book *Gridiron Gauntlet.* "Their commitment to apartheid was seemingly stronger than their commitment to winning championships."

* * *

Woody Strode had a stellar career at UCLA, although nothing close to Washington's. Still, the two had a loyal following in southern California, and fans would not soon forget the epic 1939 season that nearly resulted in a Rose Bowl appearance and a potential national championship.

With no opportunities in the NFL, Washington and Strode remained together on the football field, at first in a two-game exhibition series in Los Angeles, staged by promoter Larry Sunbrock, whom Strode described as "one of the slickest, slipperiest promoters you ever laid your eyes on." Sunbrock's idea was to stage two games featuring college all-stars against two minor-league teams in the area—the Hollywood Bears and the Los Angeles Bulldogs.

Sunbrock promised Washington $1,000 for each game, knowing that he would be the game's biggest draw. In fact, he'd called his team the Kenny Washington All-Stars. Sunbrock wanted to pay Washington with war bonds, but Uncle Rocky demanded cash, worried that the bonds were in Sunbrock's name. The promoter eventually relented. But when word got out that Washington would make that much—an exorbitant sum in those days—the Bulldogs threatened not to play. Sunbrock had to pony up some more cash to the home team to stage the game.

Strode was the second-biggest draw and got $750 per game, as Sunbrock took advantage of the former UCLA player's name recognition. But the games also connected Washington and Strode with Bears coach Paul Schissler.

He was the same coach who led the Chicago Cardinals during the 1933 season, when Joe Lillard was the last African-American in the NFL before what became the league's twelve-year ban on Black players. Schissler was the one who suggested that Lillard not play for his own safety and that of his teammates because of his hot temper, and the coach invited criticism that he, in fact, was racist. But he insisted then he meant well, and he had no problems having African-American players on his Bears team. In fact, he welcomed them, especially Washington and Strode, who were not only well regarded by their own teammates but also drew thousands of fans to the games because of how popular they'd been at UCLA.

"Paul Schissler was paying me $100 a game, plus a percentage of the gate," Strode said. "When we filled up Gilmore Stadium, I'd come home with $300. Kenny was making about $200 a game, plus his percentage. He took home $500 some weeks. We were making more money than the guys in the NFL."

The Bears would draw crowds as big as eighteen thousand, in part because Washington and Strode were featured, but also because there was no professional football being played on the West Coast. It would still be years before the Rams moved from Cleveland to Los Angeles, the American Football League days were decades away, and the 49ers weren't yet born.

There were plenty of fine players in the area, and the quality of football was actually quite good. Using Gilmore Stadium as its home field, the Bears finished 5–2 in Washington's first season with Schissler and Strode, as the team won six straight before dropping its last three games. Washington had just two rushing touchdowns that year, but he led the team with four touchdown passes. A former Giants fullback named Kink Richards, who played in New York from 1933 to 1939, led the team with 5 rushing touchdowns and added a touchdown reception.

Washington captivated fans who watched the former UCLA star in action. His dazzling open field runs and strong arm were familiar sights to anyone familiar with his college career, and he was almost always the best player on the field for the Bears. There was the story where he stood in one end zone at Gilmore Stadium and heaved the ball clear to the other side. "It was really ninety-three yards," Washington confided later. Still, ninety-three yards!

He and Strode connected on passes longer than sixty yards, and another speedy receiver—Ezzrett "Sugarfoot" Anderson—was also a favorite target.

"People would come on Sundays after church, all dressed up," said Brad Pye Jr., sports editor of the *Los Angeles Sentinel*, of the Pacific Coast league games. "Thirty to forty percent in attendance were Black.

Kenny was like a god. He did everything, and Sugarfoot Anderson could catch anything Kenny put up."

The Bears tore through the competition in 1942, going 8-0 to win the league title, with Washington leading the way in rushing and receiving, and also compiling a team-high 7 touchdowns. In the season's final game, Washington and Strode teamed to beat the rival Los Angeles Bulldogs, 17–10, in a game that also featured another of their Bruins' backfield mates.

Jackie Robinson had been playing semipro football with another former UCLA teammate, Ray Bartlett. Robinson was the Honolulu Bears' best player that year, but as the season wore on, attendance began to dwindle, and Robinson decided to head back to Los Angeles. His ship departed from Oahu on December 5, 1941.

Two days later, Bartlett woke up in the middle of the night to the sound of a plane flying low.

"When I looked up, I saw a red dot on the plane," Bartlett said. "I didn't know it was a Japanese fighter until later. I turned on the radio and they were announcing that the entire island was under attack."

Bartlett could never forget what he saw in the aftermath of the bombing of Pearl Harbor.

"I still remember the terrible sight of the bodies bobbing in the water," he recalled. "I saw the USS *Arizona* burning in flames for days after the bombing."

Robinson found out during a poker game on his ship returning to the mainland.

"We saw members of the crew painting all the ship windows black," Robinson said. "The captain summoned everyone on deck. He told us that Pearl Harbor had been bombed and that our country had declared war on Japan. When we arrived home, I knew realistically that I wouldn't be there long. Being drafted was an immediate possibility, and like all men in those days, I was willing to do my part."

Robinson, who would join the Army in May 1942, made it back

in time to play in the Bulldogs' final game against Washington and Strode's Bears. Robinson helped the Bulldogs to a 10–7 lead, but it was Washington who orchestrated a comeback in a 17–10 win.

When he wasn't playing football, Washington worked as a uniformed officer with the Los Angeles Police Department—a job he got with help from his Uncle Rocky, who'd been a highly respected LAPD officer for years. He also spent his first season after college as a UCLA assistant coach, and would soon finish his undergraduate degree.

And Washington had started a family, marrying June Bradley from Long Beach and moving into a two-bedroom house on West Thirty-Fifth Street. There was an announcement in *Liberty* magazine, as well as a picture of the couple.

"The caption read, 'Kenny Washington marries June Bradley (a girl of color),'" Strode said. "June was half-German, very pretty, and very light-skinned. They wanted everybody to be sure of what she was. I remember Kenny saying to me, 'Sometimes I'm with June and I feel funny because they think I've got a white girl.'"

It was an awkward position for Washington, especially with interracial marriages simply not being widely accepted at the time.

"The optics were a concern for him," Kraig Washington said of his grandfather.

Strode said Washington had a difficult adjustment to his new job as a police officer.

"I remember one night I was going home and I saw him having a confrontation with a drunk on Central Avenue," Strode recalled. "I got out of my car and thought I'd have to help him fight this guy. The ignorant Blacks had no respect for Kenny. To them, if you achieve success in the white man's society, you were an Uncle Tom."

Strode, meanwhile, found a job as an investigator in the Los Angeles district attorney's office, delivering subpoenas in the Black community. Strode eventually grew emotionally weary of the job.

"Part of my job was escorting prisoners to San Quentin and Folsom," he said. "That wrapped me up. I knew right then I'd never make it as a cop. Those prisons looked like dog pounds, the human beings like dogs. I'd take the prisoners up there on the train. They'd be handcuffed, and I'd have my .45 in my waistband."

Strode eventually left that line of work, but not before running into the woman he'd met in Hawaii when the Bruins played two games there at the end of the 1938 season. He was in a bar with acquaintances and noticed a Hawaiian woman with friends sitting across the room. She kept looking over at him, and Strode became uncomfortable because she was with another man.

Strode got up to leave and the woman grabbed his arm.

"Woodrow, don't you remember me?" she said.

"No!" Strode replied.

"Well, you were in Hawaii two years ago. Remember the little girl that kissed you goodbye and was crying?"

It was Princess Luana.

The two would soon be married.

While the Pacific Coast league gave Washington and Strode the chance to continue playing and make some decent money, the sport was not kind to Washington's knees. Already hobbled at various points during his college career, Washington's knees were further battered in the semipro league, and he was forced to miss a season after undergoing a surgical procedure.

There would be more problems in the years ahead, but in the time he was healthy enough to play, Washington flashed the form that made him such an important part of college football history. Schissler knew it, too, which was why the coach included Washington's name in every promotional tool there was.

After the 1941 season, with the United States now on a war footing, Schissler was called upon to serve as an officer at March Field. It was there he would coach the football team—called the Flyers—similar to Paul Brown's stint as coach of the Great Lakes Bluejackets. Schissler wanted Strode and Washington on his team, but Washington's knees kept him out of the service, meaning he could continue playing for the Bears.

Strode, meanwhile, enlisted as a private in the Army and played for Schissler. As it was with all the other service teams across the country, the idea was to help build morale for the enlisted soldiers and give them a chance to enjoy sports as a diversion.

Strode was reunited with former UCLA fullback Leo Cantor, who had nearly scored a touchdown against USC that would have sent the Bruins to the Rose Bowl.

It was through Cantor and his own experience in the service that Strode felt firsthand the pain of racism and anti-Semitism. Cantor was a Russian Jew, but he kept his religion a secret from his fellow enlistees, who routinely expressed disdain for Jews.

"Woody, I can't put up with this shit," Cantor confided to Strode one day. "It's driving me crazy. I go to bed, but I can't sleep."

Strode was twenty-seven. Cantor was twenty-two.

"That's when we were introduced to serious prejudice in this country," Strode said.

When he first enlisted, Strode was told he had to stay with Black soldiers in separate quarters from whites.

"What a slap in the face that was," he said. "For twenty-seven years, I thought I was equal. Now we had the goddamndest war going and I found out how bad things really are... Things I had been doing all my life I could not do now."

Strode considered attending Officer Candidate School, but Schissler said he might not be able to play. So he remained a private. "As a private, I had more prestige than the Black officers," Strode said. "That was from athletics. If you're white and rooting for your own team and one of the guys on the team is Black, well then, he's one of yours and he's all right."

Schissler vouched for Strode as far as living arrangements were concerned; Strode would stay with the rest of his teammates in a gymnasium.

One of Strode's most enjoyable games came against the USC team he'd never beaten while at UCLA. Playing alongside grown men, many of whom had starred in college football before, Strode and the Flyers visited the Coliseum on November 15, 1943, to face the Trojans.

The Flyers rolled up a 35–0 lead at halftime, and Schissler had to beg his team to stop pouring it on.

"If you guys keep this up," he told the players, "I'm through forever as a coach."

Schissler went with substitutes the rest of the game, and neither team scored another point.

And it wasn't as if USC had a bad team that year. In fact, they went 8-2. Their only losses: to the Flyers and the San Diego Naval Air Station Bluejackets.

Strode played well in his third and final season with the Flyers in 1944, catching 9 touchdown passes.

With the war raging and the need for soldiers continuing to grow, orders came down that even the athletes had to serve overseas. Strode was initially going to fight in the European theater, but Schissler went to Strode to ask if he had a preference. Strode, having familiarity with Hawaii and the South Pacific, asked to be deployed to the Pacific. He was stationed at Tinian Airfield in the Mariana Islands and was assigned the duty of guarding B-29 bombers.

Eight months after he arrived, the United States dropped atomic bombs on Hiroshima and Nagasaki.

After the war ended, Strode was sent home on an aircraft carrier and arrived in San Francisco, where Luana was waiting for him.

"The whole team is on its way up here," she told her husband.

The Hollywood Bears were coming to play the San Francisco Clippers.

"I've got Kenny with me. I'm bringing your uniform," Schissler told Strode over the phone. "Are you in shape?"

Strode played forty minutes, doing his part in helping the Bears to an 8-2-1 record and another Pacific Coast Football League title.

Washington was again the star of the team, leading the Bears with 68 points and finishing with 542 rushing yards and 765 passing yards.

While Washington enjoyed playing during the war years, he'd hoped to contribute to the military effort, but was rejected by the Army because of his bad knees. The worst injury came late in the 1941 season with the Bears. "Kenny went to make a cut," Strode said. "He planted his foot and when he went to push off, the knee just gave out. I could hear that thing go clear across the field; it sounded like a guitar string popping."

Washington's biggest contribution during the war years was his participation in USO Tours, as he delivered speeches to troops and played in some exhibition football games. He may not have fought, but "the government did use Kenny Washington," Strode said. "They sent famous Black athletes like Kenny overseas to talk to the segregated Black units...The idea behind these USO tours was to keep the Black soldiers quiet by promising them things would get better after the war."

Things would get better after the war, at least incrementally. With an economic boom that would bring the United States out of the Great Depression era once and for all, there would be room for opportunity ahead. But it would not be a straight line toward success, and many struggles were yet to be waged.

Racism would certainly not be eliminated, and that issue was not about to go away. In many ways, things would get worse.

Chapter 13

KENNY WASHINGTON BREAKS THROUGH THE LINE

Dan Reeves knew he had a problem, and as far as the Cleveland Rams owner was concerned, there was only one way out after the 1945 season. He had to move his team.

Immediately.

No matter that the Rams had just won the NFL championship, following up a 9-1 season with a 15–14 win over George Preston Marshall's Washington team on December 16, 1945, in subzero conditions at Cleveland Municipal Stadium. No matter Reeves's coach, Adam Walsh, was selected as the NFL's coach of the year. No matter his rookie quarterback, the former UCLA star Bob Waterfield, was the league's MVP. No matter the Rams had the makings of an NFL dynasty with that kind of coach-quarterback synergy.

Reeves was hemorrhaging money.

And with Paul Brown about to begin operations with the team that bore his name in Year 1 of the All-America Football Conference, Reeves knew there wasn't a moment to wait.

Never before—or since—has an NFL team won a championship in one city one year and played in another the next. But that was the level of desperation Reeves felt. He knew there was no future for his team in Cleveland, not with such tepid support from local fans. Only once in that championship season did the Rams draw more than twenty thousand fans at League Park at the northeast corner of East Sixty-Sixth Street and Lexington Avenue. The stadium was home to the Cleveland Indians at the time, and the Rams were interlopers and renters.

In the title game at Municipal Stadium, only 32,178 fans showed up, although the weather didn't help. Game time temperature was eight degrees below zero, with a fierce wind off Lake Erie. The Browns beat a Washington team that featured renowned quarterback "Slingin'" Sammy Baugh, whose first-quarter pass from his own end zone hit the goalpost and caromed into the end zone for an early Rams safety.

With the early safety playing such a pivotal role in the final outcome, Marshall was so infuriated that he convinced the league the following year to change the rule to make a pass that hits the goalpost an incompletion. That rule remained until 1974, when the NFL moved the goalpost ten yards behind the goal line.

The Rams won 15–14. Reeves was jubilant about the victory, but it didn't change the fact that he was struggling to turn a profit. He believed there was much more of an opportunity to make money in the untapped southern California market. And now with Brown, whose deep roots in Ohio presented a very real threat to the Rams' viability in Cleveland, about to coach his first pro team, Reeves knew he had to get out.

Reeves made his intentions known shortly after the title game, and he would never turn back. In many ways, it was a radical move at the time, since there were no pro baseball or football teams on the West Coast. It wasn't until 1957 that Major League Baseball's Dodgers and Giants moved from New York to California. The AAFC had awarded teams to Los Angeles and San Francisco, but they'd yet to play there.

Reeves was thus ahead of his time in many ways, and the NFL's owners were hopeful he could capitalize on the new market.

All he needed now was a stadium, and the Los Angeles Memorial Coliseum was the logical solution.

William Claire "Halley" Harding had other ideas.

On January 15, 1946, Harding delivered a speech that changed the course of sports history.

It would be the fitting culmination of his life's work, a transcendent, if largely forgotten, moment that set in motion a chain of events to transform football. And, by extension, American society.

Harding was sports editor of the prominent Black-owned newspaper, the *Los Angeles Tribune*, and he was never shy about promoting the interests of African-American athletes in his hard-hitting weekly columns. Born in 1904 in Wichita, Kansas, Harding played college football at Wilberforce University in Ohio—he was a quarterback and punter—and briefly played basketball for the Harlem Rens (short for Renaissance, the name of the New York dance hall that hosted their games). The Rens were the predecessors to the famed Harlem Globetrotters basketball team that continues to provide entertainment the world over. Harding went on to play Negro league baseball for the Indianapolis ABC's and Kansas City Monarchs, where he was a teammate of legendary pitcher Satchel Paige. He also played semipro football.

But it was Harding's career as a sportswriter that provided the forum for his lasting influence, and his cherubic face and easy smile belied an intense passion for trying to make right in a world he couldn't accept. He was particularly miffed at the absence of Black baseball players in the minor and major leagues, especially during World War II.

"I really wonder if the powers that be in baseball know that a speeding bullet does NOT veer when it gets to a colored person; nor does a bomb from a plane fail to explode simply because the target turns out to be colored soldiers," he wrote. "It is high time that the same people who unhesitatingly ask them to sacrifice their lives in time of war fix it so that in time of peace, this liberty they are supposed to have bled and died for becomes reality.

"Last season's baseball contributed many dollars to worthy causes, and rightly so," he wrote, "but baseball also provided America's enemies with their greatest single piece of propaganda, by barring the colored American."

He and other prominent Black journalists in southern California argued with Pacific Coast League owners in hopes of allowing Black players to participate, to no avail. But Harding was never afraid to challenge, always willing to speak truth to power.

The incongruity of conscripting African-Americans into the military while at the same time shutting them out from opportunities, especially in sports, was simply unacceptable to Harding, and he was never afraid to point it out.

While baseball was his primary target, especially since it dominated the pro sports scene in America, Harding also took up his fight with football. And when Reeves attempted to bring his Rams to California, Harding saw an opportunity to advance his mission.

NFL owners were initially against the move; in fact, on January 12, 1946, Reeves's request to relocate to Los Angeles was denied. The league was concerned that the Los Angeles market wouldn't support a team, but Reeves was convinced he had no alternative. He threatened to sever his ties with the league, but a settlement was brokered and the move was allowed to go through.

Three days after the owners decided not to stand in the way of Reeves's relocation, the Los Angeles Memorial Coliseum Commission held its regular meeting to consider the owner's request to use the venue for the Rams' home games. The expectation was that the commission would simply rubber-stamp the request and allow the Rams to play there.

Harding had other ideas.

Since the Coliseum was a publicly owned property, Harding devised a shrewd argument that the Rams should be prevented from playing there. During a public comment session at the meeting, Harding took the floor. The room grew quiet as his voice took over:

> Thank you, Mr. Commissioner, fellow commissioners, sportswriters, concerned citizens and fans of football. I came here to speak for many in this room and in the African-American community. We all know that baseball is a national sport and that football is its neglected stepchild everywhere except here in Los Angeles. We have two fine semipro football teams here, the Hollywood Bears and the Los Angeles Bulldogs.

As he continued, Harding built his factual argument and stirred the passions of those in the room, appealing to their senses of fairness and equality. Charles "Chile" Walsh, the general manager, had expected little pushback from the team's request, and he was startled as Harding continued:

> We have players of all races and creeds on those teams. It is our way here in the west to give every person a chance to succeed and excel. You can even see this at the college level. Three quarters of UCLA's 1939 backfield were Negroes. We have always had integrated teams out here in the west. But unfortunately, that is not the case everywhere in our great nation. Today, you will not see a Negro on any NFL football field. Maybe as a janitor or a waterboy.

Harding brought up the NFL's unofficial but strictly held ban on African-American players:

> The NFL is segregated and has barred Negro players since 1933. It wasn't always that way. We had many, many Negro ballplayers until that fateful year. Charles Follis... Fritz Pollard, Rube Marshall, the great Paul Robeson... Duke Slater... Joe Lillard and Ray Kemp, who was the last Negro

> player in the NFL before the door was closed. There hasn't been another now for thirteen years.

Harding reminisced about the unforgettable USC-UCLA battle that ended in a 0–0 tie, at the conclusion of which Washington walked off to a breathtaking ovation in which fans of both teams saluted his Bruins career.

> We all remember that great UCLA-USC game back in 1939. Kenny Washington, Jackie Robinson, and Woody Strode held the Trojans to a 0–0 tie. We were all so proud when Kenny went to play in the All-Star game of 1940 in Chicago. He scored a touchdown against the Green Bay Packers, and many of the players who were on that field with Kenny were invited to play on NFL teams. But nobody invited Kenny.

And then Harding finished with a rhetorical flourish that drew attention to the irreconcilable notion that African-Americans could be conscripted into military service yet couldn't participate in professional sports:

> It's a shame, a shame. America fought Adolf Hitler because he was a racial supremacist, yet our Army is still segregated. We fought a Civil War against those who believed that Negroes should be enslaved and excluded from society, yet exclusion still exists.
>
> Even our Declaration of Independence tells us that all men are created equal, yet opportunity is still not equal. We cannot allow a segregated NFL team to use a stadium paid for by our taxes. We cannot play segregated football here in Los Angeles. It's just not our way. I oppose any team that will not give our citizens an opportunity to try out, an opportunity to be included, and an opportunity to play.

"Thank you," he concluded. "Thank you very much."

This reconstruction of Harding's speech, compiled years later by Strode's son, Kalai, after extensive research on the subject, hit on the major themes used by the outspoken sportswriter to drive home the point: The time had come to allow Black players—starting with Washington—a chance to play in the NFL.

Post–World War II was a particularly transformative time in American history—a period that changed the dynamic of race relations and led to a bigger voice for African-Americans.

"There was a second migration [of Black Americans] that accompanied World War II, in that they started to move west, to California in particular," said Damion Thomas, curator of sports at the Smithsonian National Museum of African American History and Culture.

> The second migration and the number of African-Americans moving to the North and West was a really big deal. You began to see the emergence of much stronger Black communities, dense Black communities out west. That's a major part of what was going on here.
>
> A lot of people talk about World War II and people beginning to rethink their policies on race. It's an important point, how Americans fought in the war against Hitler and Germany and the evils there. Victory abroad and at home, linking the struggle against Nazism to the struggle against racial segregation in the United States. It's this moment where people are really trying to work toward a new future.

Harding's speech was met with applause from many who had attended the meeting. And Chile Walsh, the Rams general manager who had expected a smooth process in which the Commission would grant the team's request to play in the Coliseum, was stunned by the turn of events.

Commission president Leonard Roach responded positively to Harding's speech and delivered his own message about standing against racism. Commissioner John Anson Ford also commended Harding for his speech.

And Walsh, now realizing that he needed to address the concerns raised by Harding, spoke on behalf of the Rams and promised that the team would be open to giving an African-American player a chance to make the team.

"Any qualified Negro football player is invited by me at this moment to try out for the Los Angeles Rams," Walsh said. He mentioned the idea of signing Buddy Young, the fleet Illinois running back once coveted by Paul Brown for his Great Lakes service team, trying out. But Young still had college eligibility remaining, so he was not immediately available.

Harding demanded right then and there that Roach make a formal commitment to integrating the team as part of any lease agreement with the Rams. Roach did so, and then suggested that Walsh and Harding meet separately to further discuss the subject.

Officially, there was no mention of the move to integrate the Rams; the minutes for the Coliseum Commission meeting did not include any details of the discussion, according to Commission records.

Several days later, Walsh and Harding met, along with other influential Black sportswriters joining Harding's push for integration, and the subject eventually turned to Washington's hoped-for tryout. Walsh initially balked at the idea, citing Washington's contractual relationship with the Hollywood Bears. Unbeknownst to the GM, Harding had already worked out an agreement with Bears owner/coach Paul Schissler that he would allow Washington's contract to be bought out.

It was yet another deft move on Harding's part, one that went a long way toward bending the arc of pro sports history toward justice and helping others. And this came after his own athletic dreams had been snuffed out in an era when Blacks were not wanted in pro sports.

"Harding's athletic career was an example of the cruel racism against which he crusaded so ardently," wrote Charles Livingston in a tribute to Harding after his death in 1967.

> Halley himself would have made it big as a basketball, baseball and football star, had it not been for "Old Man Jim Crow."... So with his own athletic career as an example of the restriction suffered by outstanding Negro athletes, Harding turned to crusading for their rights, and took up the pen as a weapon... Thus, it was as a crusading writer that Harding made his most effective mark in sports.

There would be no bigger impact than the one he had just made.

On March 21, 1946—just over three months after Harding's impassioned speech in front of the Coliseum Commission—Chile Walsh purchased Washington's contract from the Bears and signed the twenty-seven-year-old halfback to "a five-figure salary," according to Harding.

But neither the Rams nor the NFL trumpeted the move. In fact, there was a notable disclaimer in the Rams' press release announcing Washington's signing.

"The National (Football) League has never had a rule against the use of Negro players and no precedent is being set in the signing of Washington," the statement read.

Yet history had been made, and there was no going back: For the first time since African-American players were effectively barred from the NFL in 1934, pro football's color barrier had been broken.

It was an undeniably transformative moment, as re-integration finally took hold and the NFL would eventually become a league that today is comprised of 70 percent African-American players. But the reaction around the country was decidedly muted. The news of Washington's signing was a three-paragraph story on page five of the sports section—with no picture—

in the *Hilo Tribune Herald* in Hawaii. The story was buried on a page that featured a banner headline about a high school basketball tournament.

In the *Racine (WI) Journal Times*, a four-paragraph story—no picture—was printed beneath a story out of Jacksonville, Florida, about Jackie Robinson, who was then a minor-league baseball player in Montreal. The story reported that Robinson and fellow African-American player John Wright would be prohibited from playing in an exhibition game in Jacksonville against a team from Jersey City. A city official said "the Montreal club could bring Second Baseman Robinson or any other Negro player it wished to Jacksonville but that no Negro player would be permitted to play."

The *Cincinnati Enquirer* had just a one-paragraph story; there was a two-paragraph item in the *Pasadena Star-News*.

North Hollywood's *Valley Times* sports editor Claude Newman included a picture of Washington and Chile Davis at his signing, with Davis winking for the camera and Newman writing in the cutline below the picture, "When Walsh winks like that, he isn't kidding, and he is pleased! He knows it's a good deal to sign the greatest football player the Coast has ever seen, meaning Washington."

It would be more than another year before Robinson signed with the Dodgers on April 10, 1947, breaking baseball's color barrier. And while the NFL can claim it achieved integration before Major League Baseball, Washington's was far less of a purposeful signing than Robinson's. After all, Dodgers general manager Branch Rickey made it known that he was taking the definitive step of having Robinson play, regardless of how anyone else felt about it.

Yet even Rickey may have needed reassurance about his choice, and Washington's signing may have helped him along.

"It's always been my feeling that Washington's signing finally tipped Rickey over to do what he did with Robinson," former Rams head coach Bob Snyder once said. "Washington's signing took the pressure off."

There's no question the Rams were pressured to sign Washington, as they gave in after Harding campaigned to prevent them from playing at the Coliseum if they didn't sign a Black player.

And Reeves's fellow owners—who six years earlier had decided against signing Washington when he was in his prime coming out of UCLA and might have been the first overall draft pick had Blacks been allowed into the NFL—had no choice but to go along with it.

"Reeves had the league over a barrel," Washington said after his career was over. "The Coliseum people warned the Rams if they practiced discrimination, they couldn't use the stadium. When those NFL people began thinking about all those seats and the money they could make filling them up, they decided my kind wasn't so bad after all."

Kenny's uncle, Rocky, who had taken him in as a young child and had watched over him his entire life, was again front and center for his nephew. He made sure Kenny was paid fairly, but also demanded—and received—a "no-cut" clause in the contract that made sure the Rams wouldn't simply use Washington's signing as a publicity stunt and not include him in their plans that fall.

"Rocky wanted to make sure that they weren't signing Kenny to use as window dressing," Strode said.

It was a wise move.

"The Rams were smart in signing Kenny, because with him on the roster, they were assured of drawing X number of people," Strode said. "The Rams almost folded when they first started playing out here, and without Kenny, they probably would have."

It wouldn't be long before Strode joined his teammate and best friend.

The Rams were concerned that Washington might feel overwhelmed as the only African-American player on the team—and in the entire NFL. So they solicited his input about whether he'd feel more comfortable having someone join him. There was only one person Washington considered.

"He could have gotten along with the white boys on the team, Bob Waterfield and Jim Hardy and all those boys from UCLA and USC," Strode said. "But the thinking then was that he had to have a running mate, another Black person to live with on the road. They asked him to select somebody. Kenny told them he wanted me."

There was a problem, though.

"They spoke of my marriage to a Hawaiian," Strode said. "They tried to use my marriage to keep me off the team."

Years later, Strode told his son, Kalai, how his signing with the Rams went down:

Walsh met with Washington while he and Waterfield were working out, with the quarterback showing his new teammate how the team's T-formation—much different from the single wing that Washington thrived on at UCLA—worked. Walsh went over to Washington and showed him a list of potential roommates.

"I don't see Woody's name," Washington told Walsh.

"He's not on the list," Walsh said.

Washington demanded to know why he wasn't. And after Waterfield told Walsh to reveal the whole story, the general manager cited Strode's age, and the fact that he was married to a Hawaiian woman.

Washington ripped up the list.

"If I can't have Woody," he said, "you can't have me."

Walsh tried to make the point that Washington was throwing away his opportunity to play in the NFL, but Washington told him he wanted no part of an organization that wouldn't sign Strode.

As Washington walked off the field, Walsh turned to Waterfield. "Damn it, what the hell do we do?" he said.

"You put Woody on the team," Waterfield replied.

On May 7, 1946, the Rams bought out Strode's contract with the Bears and signed him to a one-year deal.

Washington and Strode were together once more.

Chapter 14

TRYOUTS FOR THE BROWNS

Bill Willis never got a response to the letter he'd written to Paul Brown. Which was unsettling for Willis, because the two had corresponded regularly.

Brown and Willis had formed a tight bond during their time together at Ohio State, where Brown had seen so much potential in Willis and helped turn him into one of the country's best players—a terrific blocker on offense and a playmaking lineman on defense. And he did so despite the fact no African-Americans had previously played for the Buckeyes.

But when Willis sent a note of congratulations to Brown after word got out in 1945 that he'd become the head coach and part owner of the Cleveland franchise in the All-America Football Conference, he didn't hear back.

For Willis, it was yet another reminder that there was no room in pro football for African-Americans.

Or so he thought.

Willis wasn't just writing to congratulate Brown on his new football journey. He was privately hoping for a chance to be a part of it.

After graduating from Ohio State following an illustrious career in which he was a two-time All-American, Willis still yearned to play. With the NFL still not allowing African-Americans on their rosters, and with Brown already having given Willis an opportunity at Ohio State when few white coaches were willing to recruit Black players, Willis figured there might be a chance.

But as Brown began assembling a team that wouldn't take the field until 1946, Willis was not a part of the plans. At least not in the initial phase. Despondent that he couldn't find a place to use his unique talents that had made him one of the country's finest college players, Willis tried coaching for a year.

He got a job as head coach and athletic director at Kentucky State College—a historically Black school—for the 1945 season, and lost only twice in ten games. But this really wasn't what he wanted to do with his life just yet.

"We were a small school and played similar Black schools in the area," he said. "My heart was not really in coaching."

He followed up on his letter to Brown with a phone call, again urging him to consider giving him a chance to play, but Brown was vague.

"Paul told me he would get back to me in the near future," Willis said.

But there was a chance for Willis to play—in Canada. The Montreal franchise invited him to play, and Willis was ready to go.

What he didn't know at the time was that Brown was actually thinking of a way to bring him to Cleveland. The coach just had to figure out a way to make it happen without drawing negative attention to it.

"Though the constitutions of the All-America Conference and the National Football League did not forbid Black players from competing, none ever had in the [twelve] years since football's modern era had begun," Brown said. "I knew the fierce attention we would receive would create some unfair pressure. I wanted to avoid that dangerous ground."

There was no question in Brown's mind that Willis had what it took to play at the next level. In fact, he felt he could dominate. Now it was a matter of finding a way to quietly bring him to the team so Willis could concentrate strictly on football and not bear the extra burden that being African-American might have created.

"I didn't care about a man's color or his ancestry," Brown said. "I just wanted to win football games with the best people possible."

Brown hatched a plan and enlisted the help of *Columbus Dispatch* sportswriter Paul Hornung, who served as an intermediary between the coach and Willis.

In early August, Brown had Hornung reach out to Willis.

"I was on my way to Canada when Paul Hornung called," Willis said.

"Why don't you go to Bowling Green University where the Browns are training and try out for the team?" Hornung said.

"I'm going to Montreal tomorrow to try out for Montreal in the Canadian League," Willis replied.

Hornung pressed the matter. "I really think you should stop in Bowling Green," he told Willis.

"This was done under the pretense that [Willis] would just go up to watch practice," said Mike Brown. "Maybe talk with my dad, who could advise him on a coaching job."

Willis showed up shortly before noon the next day and briefly met with Brown. It would be more than just talk.

"When [Willis] got there, it was for [Paul Brown] to talk him into playing pro football for the Browns," Mike Brown said.

"Bill, get your uniform from the equipment manager and I will meet you at the other end of the field with the center, two guards, and Otto Graham," the coach told him.

Once he got onto the field, Willis lined up opposite center Mo Scarry.

It took one play for Brown to realize what he had in Willis.

Not that the coach didn't believe Willis was an outstanding talent. He'd already seen that firsthand. But it was nearly three years since they'd last been together on a football field, so Brown wasn't quite sure what to expect.

Graham stood under center and called for the snap from Scarry.

"The first time he hit me, I fell over backwards into Otto and Otto fell down, too," Scarry recalled. "Otto said, 'What the hell happened?' Then we put [Frank] Gatski at center. Same thing. Then we tried a guy named Mel Maceau. Same thing. Everybody got knocked down."

On one snap, Scarry stepped on Graham's foot as he tried to block Willis. Graham yelped.

Brown called all the players to the middle of the field.

"Now men, someone stepped on Otto's foot, and we can't very well have a good practice if that keeps happening," Brown told them. "So, would you please take care not to step on his toes?"

The players laughed, but what happened in that moment led to a strategic change that continues in today's game.

Brown realized that Graham would need to line up his feet differently to account for Willis's quickness. Like all quarterbacks of his era, Graham would line up with both feet even with the line of scrimmage when he got under center. But Brown, looking to find a way for Graham to be in a better position to backpedal, had him line up with one foot angled slightly toward the backfield so he could begin his drop just a split second sooner. That split second could make all the difference in dealing with a player that had Willis's quickness.

Just watch any quarterback in an NFL game line up under center, and you'll see his feet lined up in a similar fashion. You can credit Willis for the change.

Brown was so enthralled by Willis's speed off the ball that he had to see for himself how he did it. Brown once got down on his knees before the snap so he could make sure Willis wasn't offsides.

Nope. He was onsides.

How quick was Willis after the snap? Photographers had to adjust their camera's shutter speed so their pictures weren't blurry. The team's press guide eventually had a line telling photographers that Willis had to be shot at 1/600th of a second so the pictures would be clear.

Willis earned the nickname "the Cat" for his speed and quickness.

But there was more to Willis's burst than just his physical gifts.

"I had developed a technique of watching the center and charging as soon as I saw his hands tighten on the ball," Willis said. "My reaction time was so fast that I was in the backfield before the quarterback could receive the ball and pivot to start the play."

Scarry made an adjustment, too.

"We used to just line up over the ball and snap it," he said. "With Willis, you had to put the ball as far as you could out in front of you, to get as far away from him as you could. He changed the whole way we snapped the ball."

Within hours of his first practice, Willis had signed a contract. His starting salary: $4,000.

* * *

A few days after helping Paul Brown's Great Lakes team produce a resounding win over Notre Dame in the final game for both men at the naval base, it was time for Marion Motley to return home to Canton, Ohio.

At twenty-five years old and his career behind him, there was no reasonable hope of ever playing organized football again. Married with two children, he needed a means of supporting his family, and the only realistic alternative was to go where he had already been: the steel mill.

Like Willis, Motley had asked Brown about the possibility of playing for his new team in the AAFC. And like Willis, Motley didn't get an answer.

He figured that was it.

But as had been the case with Willis, Brown hadn't ruled out Motley. And while there is some debate about whether the coach was more interested in Motley as a running back and a linebacker or as a roommate for the newly signed Willis, Brown did reach out to him shortly after Willis signed his contract.

Once again, he relied on a familiar face to help convince Motley to join the Browns.

"I called Oscar Barkey, a friend from Canton, and asked him to drive Marion to our training camp and have him ask for a tryout," Brown said. "I felt that was the best way to handle the situation, again in the light of the potential publicity, because there was nothing unusual in a player's coming to his former coach and asking him for a chance to play."

Despite his powerful build and formidable skills, Motley was a mostly forgotten player once his enlistment was over. But not with Brown.

"No other professional football team was interested in him at the time because he had not played enough in college or in the service to attract any attention," Brown said. "That was their loss."

But Motley himself was unsure whether he'd be able to make the team, even with his connection to Brown.

"When Bill Willis was there with the Browns, they didn't have any other Black players on the team, so Paul Brown really brought my grandfather to be Bill's roommate," said Tony Motley, Marion's grandson. "It wasn't that Marion couldn't play, and he never fathomed what it was going to turn out to be. But the initial reason was to be his roommate, because at that time, no white and Black players had ever been roommates on the road. He needed another Black player."

Longtime NFL writer and author Dan Daly suggested that Brown had contacted Motley and Willis after two other players had decided they no longer wanted to play with the Browns.

"He'd signed two Pro Bowl quality NFL players to play fullback—Ted

Fritsch—and linebacker—Vince Banonis," Daly said of Brown. "They got cold feet and wanted to go back to the NFL, so Brown let them go back. They didn't want to play for him? OK, go back. So, suddenly, he has two gigantic holes. He's like, how do I fill these holes? Well, Bill Willis was available. Marion Motley was available."

Mike Brown believes his father was interested in Willis and Motley regardless of the circumstances. And once he saw how quickly Willis had blended in with the team, he felt it was a natural fit to reach out to Motley.

"My father had great confidence and belief in Marion Motley," Mike Brown said. "There was one time at Great Lakes where they ran a sprint. They used to do a forty-yard test even then, and my father had two players run together, and they ran Marion against one of the other players who was an NCAA hurdles champion. It was just nip and tuck, a very close race. Marion was very fast, and people overlook that when they think about him."

Motley made the most of his chance with the Browns. And made some of his teammates pay for it in the process.

"Gene Fekete was the fullback, and I worked at linebacker," Motley said of his initial time with the Browns. "One day we had this scrimmage, and I was making a few tackles and shaking a few people up and someone asked Willis, 'What's the matter with Motley today? He trying to kill somebody?' 'No,' Bill said. 'He's just trying to make this football team.'"

He did just that.

Chapter 15

GREAT EXPECTATIONS AND DASHED HOPES

It was a glorious day in southern California, the sky so blue it almost didn't seem real, the sunshine warm and comforting, the pungent mix of sea air and earthy fragrances combined with eucalyptus and pine...it's almost as if Upton Bell can still feel and smell it three quarters of a century later.

It's what hit him as he and his father, then–NFL commissioner Bert Bell, got off the train after arriving from Chicago.

They'd made the pilgrimage from the 1946 College All-Star Game and into southern California to see the birth of pro football in Los Angeles. And the beginnings of integration in the sport that had not included African-American players for more than a decade.

Upton was just nine years old and adored spending the time with his father, the former Eagles owner and Steelers co-owner who was now presiding as the NFL's chief administrator. Bert Bell had taken over as commissioner the same month the Rams moved from Cleveland to Los Angeles and set off the chain of events that eventually saw them sign Washington and then Strode to break the league's color barrier. He was anxious to check in on the Rams and see for himself how the league's westward expansion was proceeding.

His son never forgot the experience, especially the first time he laid eyes on Washington and Strode.

"I remember going to practice, standing there and seeing Kenny Washington run out in his cleats and then Strode come out soon after," Bell said. "It struck me, not only the difference in color, but they seemed to stand out from the rest of the players. And there were so many great players with that team, we're talking some future Hall of Fame players."

That included quarterback Bob Waterfield, the MVP in the Rams' championship run in Cleveland the year before. Waterfield followed Washington and Strode at UCLA, helping the Bruins to another Pacific Coast Conference title as an all-league quarterback. He'd also made news off the field, marrying actress Jane Russell in 1943.

"I can remember listening to Jane Russell talking about her husband," Bell said. "It was surreal. It was the Hollywood scene."

What he remembers most, though, was beholding the sight of Washington and Strode—larger-than-life images for a boy who had grown up in the NFL yet who had never seen a Black man play in a game. "They were just so impressive," Bell said.

To help build interest in the team, the Rams hosted the team they'd beaten in the previous year's NFL Championship Game in Cleveland. In the *Los Angeles Times*' second annual charity all-star game, it would be the Rams against George Preston Marshall's Washington team.

While the game didn't sell out, more than sixty thousand fans did show up to the Coliseum, nearly double the crowd the Rams had drawn in Cleveland for the championship game. And the fact that a large chunk of the Rams' roster included players from USC and UCLA—including Washington, Strode, Waterfield, Jim Hardy, and Pat West—surely added to the interest.

"Big things are ahead for Kenny Washington in the future plans of the Los Angeles Rams," the lede to a pre-game story in the *Los Angeles*

Times read. "But just how much duty he will see in the game against the Redskins Sept. 6 depends on the condition of his left knee."

Actually, it was both knees.

Less than a month after Washington's signing, the Rams released the news that the running back would require surgery on both knees—the fourth and fifth of his career.

"A torn cartilage will be removed from the left knee and a growth from the right knee," read an Associated Press story on April 11, 1946.

A little more than a month later came an encouraging prognosis, as Washington "is now walking without a limp and expects to start bicycle-riding exercises this week. Dr. Daniel H. Levinthal, who performed the surgery, reports that Washington should be ready for topnotch football next fall if his present rate of improvement continues."

Still, it was a lot to ask of a twenty-eight-year-old man who'd physically been through so much. *Times* columnist Dick Hyland once called Washington the greatest football player he'd ever seen—better even than Red Grange and Tom Harmon, the former Michigan star who was now with the Rams. But Hyland suspected Washington couldn't summon the level of play that once made him so good.

"Coming into the National League with a reputation, Kenny Washington is going to find himself on a hot seat every time a ball is snapped into play," Hyland wrote. "Washington has become a beaten-up ball-player who is neither so strong nor so quick in his reactions as he was before the war."

Hyland predicted that Washington would be used only as a spot player for Walsh.

"Kenny Washington will work his head off to prove this prediction wrong," Hyland wrote. "And I hope he does."

Walsh himself was coy about how he'd use his newly signed player.

"We'll use him where we can get the most good out of his many outstanding abilities," Walsh said. "We will use Kenny where his assets as a passer and runner will give us the strongest possible four-man combination on the field at one time."

Strode remained skeptical.

"In other words," he said, "Adam Walsh didn't know how he was going to use Kenny."

Walsh delivered only a hint of his plans in the exhibition game against Washington. Much to the dismay of many in the crowd who had come to see him and Strode play, they barely got in the game. Which left some to wonder whether signing the two was a publicity stunt after all.

Los Angeles Daily News columnist Gordon Macker called the Rams on it in his column the Monday after the Friday night game.

"Plenty of Central Ave. carriage trade was lured through the turnstiles with the idea of seeing Kenny Washington and Woody Strode," Macker wrote, referring to the increase in African-American fans' interest. "The 'Kingfish' got in for one play in the first half; saw a couple minutes of action just before the final [gun] exploded. Strode, they left in Kokomo."

Macker suggested the signings were simply to placate the team's critics, including Harding, who had pressed the Rams to integrate the team.

"If Washington and Strode aren't good enough, then take 'em off the payroll," Macker said. "Just to sign 'em to win the affection [not to mention the business] of Halley Harding's customers and then only use 'em on billboards and splinters is strictly four ball.

"This skam [*sic*] of advertising names to hustle the chumps and then letting the names only be numbers in the program (25c please) seems to be an accepted practice with the promoters. Well, this town won't go for it."

There may have been some truth to Macker's words, because the Rams drew less than half the crowd for the Washington game as they did for the regular season opener against the Eagles. Only 30,500 showed up for a listless debut, as the Rams lost, 25–14, Waterfield led a 21–17 upset of the Packers the following week, and Harmon's 83-yard touchdown run highlighted a 28–28 tie against the Bears in Chicago in Week 3.

That road trip proved to be an important one in several respects, and not just because of the exhilarating game between the two teams. When the team arrived in Chicago, Washington walked up to Strode after getting off the team charter with a frustrated look on his face.

"What's wrong?" Strode asked.

"You know we can't stay at that stinking hotel?" Washington said.

The team was staying at the opulent Stevens Hotel on South Michigan Avenue across from Grant Park. But the Rams were told Washington and Strode couldn't get rooms there.

Strode was stunned; he had previously stayed at the hotel when he was with the UCLA track team for a competition in Chicago. Washington said he was told the Rams would give him and Strode $100 apiece to find another place to stay.

They found a room at the Persian Hotel.

"Back then, it was the most plush Negro hotel in the city," Strode said. "They booked the greatest jazz bands into that place. Count Basie was playing in the club downstairs, and all the white people had come to hear him play."

Strode and Washington sat at the bar listening to the music and having some drinks. Later in the evening, Waterfield showed up at the bar.

"You crazy sons of bitches, what are you doing here this late at night?" he said.

Waterfield told them he had convinced the Rams to let Strode and Washington stay with the rest of the team.

"Forget that, boy," Strode told Waterfield. "I'm going to be segregated, spend this hundred dollars, stay right here, and listen to the Count play his music."

Waterfield smiled and joined them for a drink.

It was a moment that drew the three closer. And it was also a testament to the ability of teammates to get along, despite their differing backgrounds. In fact, Strode and Washington rarely had any problems interacting with their teammates.

That was not always the case on the field, however.

Bob Snyder, a Rams assistant coach who helped Waterfield make his spectacular transition into the pros by winning a title as a rookie in Cleveland, said Washington was often a target of opposing players. In one game against the Packers, Snyder, who went on to become the Rams' head coach in 1947, saw a Packers player smash his elbow into Washington's jaw. Snyder heard the player call Washington "a Black bastard."

Washington started to go at the player but then thought better of it.

"Listen, that was a pretty good shot," Washington told the player, according to Snyder. "I want to tell you something else, you white trash. If you want to wait till the game is over, meet me under the stadium and I'll knock your goddamn block off."

"Well, our other players heard about that," Snyder said, "and I think if we had an election, he would have been elected captain."

Strode recalled another instance where an opposing player went at Washington.

"In one of the early games, Kenny had made a block and the play was going away from him," Strode recalled. "He was flat on his back when their left end came across and took a run like he was going to kick off. Kenny happened to see him coming and raised his head. This guy just missed or he would have kicked Kenny's head clear up to the press box."

After the game, the players discussed the incident, and Hardy, one of the Ram quarterbacks, asked his teammate about it.

"It's hell being a Negro, Jim," Washington told him.

But there were also moments of inspiration for Washington and Strode, things they discovered now that they were out of the southern California bubble in which they'd been largely insulated from the rest of the country. They came to realize that they themselves were a source of hope for others.

"Traveling with the Rams made a big impact," Strode recalled. "We discovered how popular we were across the country. The Black kids outside California used to tell Kenny and me how much they enjoyed listening to our games on the radio while we were still playing at UCLA. Until that time, we didn't realize what a unique thing they had done. We discovered that very few Blacks received the opportunity Kenny and I had received. We had it better in Los Angeles than any other area of the country, but we still suffered from prejudice."

Washington and Strode understood they had a unique opportunity to blaze a trail for others, which served as a source of motivation as the season went on. Yet from a football perspective, they couldn't help but feel out of place. It was particularly challenging for Walsh to find the right spot for Washington. He used him at halfback, at fullback, and yes, even at quarterback. In fact, Washington probably had the strongest arm of anyone on the team, including Waterfield, who was coming off a championship season as a rookie and was virtually assured of keeping the job.

A *San Pedro (CA) News-Pilot* story about the start of training camp at Compton College was headlined, "Rams to Try Washington in Signal Calling Role":

> Coach Adam Walsh's most newsworthy decision on the eve of taking his world champion Los Angeles Rams to training camp was made today when he announced that the first position at which Kenny Washington will be given a trial will be quarterback.

> The versatile 190-pound Negro All-American from UCLA has always played tailback in the single wing, where he could make equal use of his running and passing powers and... he has been equally devastating at either chore. In the T-formation [used by Walsh], Washington would be called upon chiefly as a ball carrier if he played either left or right halfback or if he were to be used at fullback. The quarterback's job is to handle the ball on virtually every play from center and to do nearly all of the passing but very little running.

Walsh soon decided that Washington would be better suited at one of the running back positions, with Waterfield continuing as quarterback. Washington's switch to fullback fairly early in the season seemed to be a good fit. In fact, Washington had his best showing of the season in a Week 4 matchup against the Detroit Lions. Waterfield was the star of the 35–14 win with two touchdown passes, but Washington had a season-high 6 carries for 49 yards and a touchdown. Included in his day's work was a 20-yard run to set up a touchdown.

But Washington remained mostly an afterthought in Walsh's offense as the season wore on. The Rams were blown out the following week by the Cardinals in Chicago, and went to 3-3-1 after losing to Halas's Bears at the Coliseum.

Still, the team was competitive enough to draw nearly forty thousand fans to a November 17 game at home against the Cardinals, and Waterfield's 28-yard touchdown throw to Steve Pritko was the deciding score in a 17–14 win to make the Rams 4-3-1. All hope of a Western Conference title ended the following week, however, as the Rams lost, 40–21, to the previously winless Boston Yankees.

Impressive wins over the Giants at the Polo Grounds and the Packers at the Coliseum, where forty-seven thousand fans showed up, left the Rams at 6-4-1 to finish behind the 8-2-1 Bears. Chicago then beat the Giants, 24–14, to win the NFL title.

If Washington was left to play only a small part in his first NFL season, it was worse—much worse—for Strode.

He played even less than Washington, and finished with just 4 catches for 37 yards—the lowest production of anyone on the team. For the most part, Strode didn't complain about his lack of playing time, although he acknowledged later in life that he would have spoken out more in hopes of seeing increased action.

And he sensed that the team's management, particularly Reeves, was uncomfortable because he was married to a Hawaiian woman. Remember, Hawaii hadn't achieved statehood until 1959, so Luana was considered a foreigner, and an interracial marriage was not accepted by a large segment of American society. Even Washington, married to a light-skinned woman, was self-conscious about people's reactions to seeing him with his wife.

"I had the ability to play in the NFL but the Rams weren't concerned with that," Strode said. "They spoke badly of my marriage to a Hawaiian, and I think if they had their choice they would have selected somebody else. They weren't really glad to have me, so I spent considerable time sitting on the bench, collecting my $350 a week."

Eventually Strode's lack of playing time got to him. When they faced Chicago at the Coliseum—a game that drew the largest crowd of the season—he ran into Bears defensive lineman Fred Davis, with whom he played when the two were with the March Field Flyers service team during the war. At halftime, Strode jawed with Davis on the way to the locker room.

"Woody, what the hell are you doing on the bench?" Davis asked.

Strode stumbled through an answer, but he was embarrassed he hadn't gotten into the game.

In the third quarter, Walsh needed someone on defense to try and contain the Bears' rushing attack, and Strode volunteered.

"I was getting through their line, and each time I broke through, I punished their left halfback, Dante Magnani," Strode said. "Five times, I dropped my shoulder and laid him out. The sixth time, he couldn't take it anymore and flinched. I went right around him and caught Sid Luckman looking out the window. I sacked him for a ten-yard loss, undressed him right there in front of 70,000 people."

That was one of the few highlights for Strode; otherwise, it was a frustrating season because he felt there was no meaningful role for him on the team. And he'd continued to have a sinking feeling that his marriage to Luana was frowned upon by management.

But there was also joy for the Strode family; eight days after the team's final game, Woody and Luana welcomed their first child. Woodrow Wilson Kalaeloa Strode was born on December 16, 1946. His parents called him Kalai.

Woody Strode kept in shape during the off-season, now even more motivated to provide for his growing family. But at age thirty-two, and with the gnawing sense that he simply wasn't wanted on the Rams, he was concerned about his future.

Those fears were justified.

In an exhibition game against Washington, Strode got in for only one play.

The next day, line coach George Trafton delivered the news: Strode was being released.

"Woody, it's not because of your ability that you're getting fired," Strode recalled Trafton telling him. "They're trying to say you're too old and that they're trying to rebuild. I tried to tell them Negroes don't age like white people."

Strode wept.

He saw Washington not long after and asked if he had any idea why he was released.

"It's not your ability. It's your lifestyle," Washington told his friend, according to Strode's memoir. "Dan Reeves does not approve of your marriage to Luana."

A few days later, after Strode had returned to his Hollywood apartment, Strode got a knock on the door. Some of Washington's friends had paid a visit. They'd heard that Reeves and Snyder—who took over as coach after Walsh left to return to a previous college job at Bowdoin in Maine—had released Strode for reasons other than his play. They asked if Strode would like them to deliver their own message to the owner and coach.

"I've lived here thirty-two years, and I've never had a racial incident," Strode told them. "I don't want to start one now." He thought to himself, "How do you fight someone with 100 million dollars? I'm talking about Dan Reeves."

Strode carried a grudge against Reeves until the owner died in 1971.

He looked back on his time with the Rams as one of his most trying periods.

"Integrating the NFL was the low point in my life," he told *Sports Illustrated* in an unpublished interview before he died. "There was nothing nice about it. History doesn't know who we are. Kenny was one of the greatest backs in the history of the game, and kids today have no idea who he is," he said, displaying a mix of sadness and anger.

"If I have to integrate heaven," he added, "I don't want to go."

Chapter 16

GREATNESS TAKES ROOT IN CLEVELAND

For Bill Willis and Marion Motley, life was now about opportunity.

Paul Brown had given them the chance no one else in the country dared consider, and now there was hope of playing the game they loved and making a living at it.

Brown knew what he was getting into by having the only two Black players in the fledgling All-America Football Conference. There would be pushback—even inside his own locker room—but Brown believed Willis and Motley deserved the chance.

"My father believed thoroughly that everyone had the same opportunity to a job," said Mike Brown, son of the Hall of Fame coach. "The fact that they did it better than others is why he hired them. They were great players. My father knew Marion from his days at Canton McKinley, and of course he knew Bill from Ohio State.

"Bill was a remarkable individual," Brown said. "People trusted him. People liked him. He had a way about him that was special."

Mike Brown was just a boy when Motley and Willis joined the Browns, but he gravitated toward the two players early on.

"Those days, I was a young kid and we had training camp at Bowling Green," Brown recalled. "I would stay in the dormitory with the players, and I would go up to the second floor where Marion and Bill Willis had their room. A corner room. I'd go up there and they would let me come in and play [the card game] 'Hearts' with them. Marion would huff and puff when we played. They would laugh, I would laugh. It was a good time. They were my heroes."

Neither Motley nor Willis could have known during those first weeks that they'd become part of one of the greatest teams in pro football history. At that point, they just wanted to do whatever it took to make the team.

Paul Brown had no doubt they would.

Brown constructed the team brilliantly, taking advantage of an unusual set of circumstances. Unlike the NFL teams the AAFC clubs were competing with, Brown could negotiate directly with players and offer the contracts to lure them away from the NFL.

When it came time to select the quarterback for his new team in Cleveland, Brown went after Otto Graham. He'd been drafted by the Detroit Lions and had enlisted in the Navy during World War II, but once Brown had agreed to run the Cleveland franchise in the AAFC, he made signing Graham his top priority.

"Paul Brown remembered me from my days at Northwestern when I was running to the left and I threw a long pass right-handed," Graham said. "It was a God-given ability, but he remembered it, and when he put the Browns together, he remembered me."

Brown offered Graham a contract worth $7,500 a year, although Graham would only earn the money once the league began play. Brown sweetened the deal with a $250 monthly stipend until the war ended, and Graham agreed to the deal.

Brown had his man.

He took advantage of the uncertainty about player availability due to the war and aggressively pursued other standouts like Graham.

"Every player in the service was fair game in those days because the war had disrupted professional sports so severely," Brown said. "Many players had gone into the military after their contracts had expired, and since there wasn't any competition at that time, the NFL teams had figured they would return to their former teams. Contractually, however, most of them were free agents, and we went after the ones I knew could help us."

Brown even plucked several players from the Rams team that moved to Los Angeles in 1946. Since some of the players preferred to remain in Cleveland, Brown signed the likes of tackle Chet Adams, defensive back Tom Colella, running back Gaylon Smith, defensive back Don Greenwood, and center Mo Scarry.

By any measure, but especially for a start-up league, Brown's team was extraordinarily talented and very deep, and he went into his first season prepared to back up the vow he'd made to AAFC founder Arch Ward and team owner Arthur McBride: He wanted to build a football dynasty.

His offense was led by Graham and featured Motley at fullback, speedy end Dante Lavelli, right halfback Don Greenwood, and left halfback Edgar Jones. The defense included Willis at middle guard and Motley at a linebacker spot, with superb backfield coach Blanton Collier minding the details on pass coverage. Another key contributor in that first season: Lou "the Toe" Groza, an offensive and defensive tackle who also proved to be an excellent kicker. It was his first of twenty-one seasons with Cleveland.

The Browns couldn't have been more prepared for their inaugural game on September 6 at Cleveland Municipal Stadium. With the Rams having left the city for Los Angeles in January, and with Paul Brown's widespread popularity in Cleveland, a crowd of 60,135 fans showed up. That was nearly double the crowd that had turned out for the Rams' championship game against Washington the year before.

Also driving attendance for the newly created Browns team: the presence of Willis and Motley on the team, which drew a sizable crowd of African-American fans and provided an important reminder to anyone who believed that using Black players was not economically advantageous.

The Browns' opponents that first game—the Miami Seahawks—were not of the same mindset. Miami is now one of the country's most diverse cities, but in 1946 it was part of the deep South and a deeply segregated city. In fact, it was illegal for Black players to participate in a game in the Orange Bowl, the Seahawks' home stadium—something the Browns would deal with later in the season.

Seahawks owner Harvey Hester, like the NFL's Marshall, wanted his team to represent the South. He reminded Brown of that minutes before his team faced the coach in Cleveland.

"Boy, I feel sorry for you in this league," Hester told him. "You don't have enough Southern boys on your team."

Hester would soon discover it was his own team that was lacking.

The Browns demolished Miami, 44–0.

Graham, who didn't start the game because he was still new to Brown's offense, threw his first touchdown as a pro, Groza kicked three field goals, and Cleveland had two defensive touchdowns, including a 76-yard interception return by Ray Terrell.

Week 2 would bring another victory—a 20–6 win over the Chicago Rockets in front of a crowd of 51,962 at Soldier Field. Yes, a bigger crowd than the NFL's Bears would draw at Wrigley Field, their home stadium at the time.

Motley had his first of many signature games, scoring the first touchdown of his pro career on a 20-yard rush in the first quarter and finishing with a game-high 122 yards on 12 carries. Willis again excelled on defense, as the Rockets didn't score until the fourth quarter.

But something else happened in that game to draw the Browns closer together and help set them on a path toward greatness.

Willis and Motley were subjected to several cheap shots by the Rockets during and after plays, to the point where many of their white teammates retaliated against the Chicago players. And while the Rockets might have thought they were sending a message to Willis and Motley, the incidents served to motivate the team's white players to rally around their Black teammates.

It was therefore no surprise to Brown two years later that Willis befriended fellow guard Weldon Humble, who was acquired in a trade with Baltimore.

"Weldon was Texan all the way," Brown said. "He always wore cowboy boots and a big ten-gallon hat. Weldon and Bill Willis sat together on every flight and shared a tremendous camaraderie since both were guards and respected each other's ability. It was a tremendous display of what people today call brotherhood, since Willis was Black and Weldon was white, but it was typical of the feelings all our players had for one another. The friendship between Willis and Humble seemed perfectly natural to me."

Willis and Motley would endure many more moments of bigotry. Motley recalled having his hands stepped on repeatedly after he was brought down.

"It was rough for us on the field," Motley recalled after his career was over. "The officials called back touchdowns of mine. Players stepped on my hands so much that I still have scars on the backs of them."

Yet there was little he could do, knowing that complaining would fall largely on deaf ears. Or worse.

"The other teams' players were very adamant against us playing," Motley said. "I remember Bill and I used to sit in our room and talk about making sure we didn't get into fights, that we didn't call anybody names, that we kept our mouths shut."

They felt that drawing attention to the physical and verbal abuse "would have set Black players back another 20 years." The concern: Fighting back would only reinforce stereotypes among white fans that the time wasn't right for African-Americans to play.

Willis once recalled a player from the Los Angeles Dons would slip razor blades in his hand pads and jam them into Willis's body if he got the chance. Willis refused to react.

"I knew I was a much better player than they were," he said. "Along about the middle of the third quarter when they realized that what they were doing wasn't having an effect and that they couldn't beat me, you'd be surprised how quiet they would get."

Brown was adamant that his players support Motley and Willis. There was little he could do about how opponents treated them, and the fact that teammates defended them on the field was the sort of organic reaction cultivated by Brown's overarching philosophy of putting the team before everything.

But what happened in the days leading up to Cleveland's rematch against the Seahawks in Miami rose to a different—and far more dangerous—level than anything Brown had seen. The team received written death threats against Motley and Willis in the event they played in the December 3 game.

"I still remember reading the death threat," Motley said in a 1999 interview. "It came to the Browns and was addressed to me. It said if the two of us played, they would kill us."

"They received credible death threats that if they were going to show up at the field, they'd be shot," said Joe Horrigan, one of pro football's great historians and a longtime executive at the Pro Football Hall of Fame. "They lived in a world where they faced those kinds of threats."

Brown had a decision to make: Does he refuse to be intimidated by the threat and take his players to a state in which it is illegal for Black athletes to compete against whites? Or does he not put Motley and Willis at risk of physical harm—or worse—and keep them home?

"Unfortunately, not every situation was under our control," Brown said.

The coach confirmed with police that the threats were genuine. He decided not to bring his players.

Brown didn't tell Motley and Willis why they weren't playing until after the season; he simply gave them their week's pay, and the players didn't question the move.

As they did in the regular season opener, the Browns again routed the Seahawks, 34–0. Their two wins over Miami that year were by a combined 78–0.

The Browns extended their record to 11-2 after trouncing the Seahawks, while Miami was on the way to a league-worst 3-11 season. The Seahawks would cease operations after just one year.

The win over the Seahawks clinched the Western Division championship for the Browns and earned them a spot in the championship game against the New York Yankees, who won the Eastern Division with a 10-3-1 record.

It was a spectacular debut season for the Browns, as the coach's conviction on Graham as his most important offensive player was realized and his faith in having Willis and Motley was justified. In fact, Willis and Motley might have even surpassed the expectations that Brown had, especially after they'd arrived so late in the team-building process.

Motley frequently referred to the notion that he was brought in after Willis to be his roommate—sometimes kidding, sometimes not—but the bruising fullback became one of the team's most reliable performers. Even after missing the game in Miami, he led the team with 601 rushing yards and an astonishing 8.2 yards per carry average.

One of his best games came in a 31–14 win over the Los Angeles Dons at Cleveland Stadium before what was then a record crowd for a professional football game—71,134. Motley had touchdown runs of 47 and 68 yards, as the Browns exploded in the second half after trailing 7–3 at intermission.

The victory over the Dons extended the Browns' record to 7-0.

Willis was a mainstay on defense, playing a middle guard position specifically designed to capitalize on his quickness and later moving off the line to act as a quasi linebacker. In fact, Willis was the forerunner to the middle linebacker, as his versatility allowed Brown and Collier to move him around to maximize his speed.

And while Motley and Willis were repeatedly stepped on, received countless cheap shots, and were verbally taunted during the season, they purposely chose not to retaliate, lest they give anyone an excuse to believe that Black players shouldn't participate. Motley sometimes burned with anger at the way he was treated.

"Sometimes I wanted to just kill some of those guys, and the officials would just stand right there," he said. "They'd see those guys stepping on us and heard them saying things and just turn their backs. That kind of crap went on for two or three years until they found out what kind of players we were."

Willis recalled a game against the Brooklyn Dodgers early in his time with Cleveland when racial tensions ran high.

"In the beginning, I played offense and defense, and up there at the line I'd hear the opponents getting ready for Marion, especially the Brooklyn Dodgers, who had quite a few bigoted players," Willis recalled. "You would hear them yell, 'Get that big Black blankety-blank!' or 'Look over this way! That Black so-and-so is coming around here this time.' They also had some choice words for me. When they stopped Motley, they would hold him up, keep him on his feet, so they could take shots at him.

"The first time we played the Dodgers, just about the whole lot of them piled on Marion," Willis said. "I started pulling guys off, saying, 'Ok, boys, the play's over. Let's go!' Well, they had a five-by-five type, a guy about 260 pounds, and he wheeled around and said, 'Keep your black hands off me!' I stepped back a pace in case he tried to reach me with a punch, but I was angry and I kept my hands on his shoulder pads. Before anything more could happen, some of our players—Lou Rymkus, Lou Groza, and some of the others—raced over and broke it up. Then Rymkus told me there was no point in my getting into fights and risking being thrown out of the game. He said, 'If anyone gives you a bad time, you just tell us. We'll take care of him.'"

Opponents eventually learned that concentrating on stopping both players was more important than trying to intimidate them.

"They found out that while they were calling us n—rs and alligator bait, I was running for touchdowns and Willis was knocking the shit out of them," Motley said. "So they stopped calling us names and started trying to catch up with us."

Motley admits, though, that there were times he felt enraged over the way he was treated. But he had an acceptable means of getting back at opponents.

"I had an advantage because I played defense," Motley said, referring to his role as a linebacker. "When a guy would say something to me, it made me want to kill him on the next play. Kill him. It made me want to hit him with everything I could."

It was particularly galling that officials let the dirty play continue.

"They never called what they should have been calling," Motley said. "And they were just waiting for Bill and me to do something."

But there did come a time when officials began to call penalties on players who took liberties with Motley and Willis. In fact, the first time it happened, Motley was stunned.

"Guys used to take their cleats and dig them into his hands," Horrigan said of Motley. "Marion once told me he remembered the first time an official threw the penalty flag for unsportsmanlike conduct. It was a game in Buffalo, and this little official—Tommy Hughitt, an All-American quarterback at Michigan who was maybe five eight—called the penalty. That meant something to Marion."

James recalled an incident when the team was at a hotel on the road and the players went to get a bite to eat in the bar. "They asked the Black players to leave. They weren't allowed to order," James said. "But Paul Brown put an end to that. Those guys ate with us."

It was that kind of camaraderie that Brown fostered, while at the same time building team chemistry on the field. That the Browns had come together so quickly that first season was therefore not a surprise to the coach.

But Brown wasn't immune to disciplinary issues coming up from time to time. By the end of the AAFC's inaugural season, the Browns had earned a spot in the championship game against the New York Yankees, who were owned by Dan Topping, president and co-owner of the legendary Yankees baseball team. The 12-2 Browns earned home field advantage by virtue of a better record than the 10-3-1 Yankees, with the championship game set for December 22.

A week before the game, three of Brown's players were arrested during a drunken confrontation with police, after which Brown released team captain Jim Daniell, who had been booked on public intoxication. Teammates Mac Speedie and Lou Rymkus had been given lesser charges, but it was Daniell who was released by Brown because of his failure to live up to his leadership role.

There was plenty of buildup for the game, and Yankees coach Ray Flaherty, a two-time NFL champion, added fuel to the matchup by suggesting that these teams were better than anything the NFL had to offer. "I think either the Browns or the Yanks can lick the pants off the Bears or the Giants in the National League," he said. "And don't forget, I coached some championship teams in that league."

A crowd of 41,181 showed up for the title game—less than the Browns' more well-attended regular season games but still more than most NFL Championship Games. Motley gave the Browns their first lead of the game on a touchdown run in the second quarter, and a Graham touchdown pass to Lavelli made it 14–9 with less than five minutes to play.

Cleveland held on, with Graham, who played defensive back as well as quarterback, coming up with a late interception to seal the win for Brown's first championship. It would be the first of many for the coach and for Motley and Willis, both of whom were selected to All-Pro as rookies.

* * *

Motley kept the handwritten letter in his scrapbook, and even as the years went by—the paper yellowing, the words fading, the edges fraying—he often looked at it. His heart swelled with pride every time he read the words.

It was from Branch Rickey, the owner of the AAFC's Brooklyn Dodgers and general manager of the Major League Baseball team. Rickey had taken more than a casual interest in seeing how Motley and Willis performed as the only two Black players in the AAFC. He was months away from making a decision that would have even greater ramifications in pro sports.

Rickey had great familiarity with the world of football, having played for the Shelby Blues of the Ohio League, a forerunner to the NFL. One of his teammates on the Shelby club was Charles Follis, widely regarded as the first African-American professional football player.

Rickey was also a teammate of African-American catcher Charles Thomas on the Ohio Wesleyan baseball team he coached in the early 1900s. Rickey was impressed by the way Thomas remained composed while experiencing racism.

Rickey would be similarly impacted by how Motley and Willis conducted themselves in that first season in the AAFC. The two Black players didn't realize Rickey was even aware of them, no less understand that the football Dodgers owner and baseball team's GM was studying them.

Motley didn't understand until later how he had affected Rickey's decision. The letter finally made sense.

"In the letter I saved," Motley said, "Branch Rickey says, 'If Marion Motley and Bill Willis can break the color barrier in a contact sport, then Jackie Robinson sure can do it in a non-contact sport.'"

On April 10, 1947—eight months after Willis and Motley joined the Browns and less than a year after Kenny Washington and Woody Strode signed with the Rams—Rickey signed Robinson to a major league contract with the Dodgers.

Five days later, Robinson became the first African-American to play in the major leagues since Moses Fleetwood Walker in 1884.

Chapter 17

SEPARATE WAYS

There were no outward indications that Kenny Washington and Woody Strode would never be teammates again.

In fact, as they prepared for their second season together with the Rams, Washington and Strode showed up to practice eager to continue their careers together, just as they had when they first started at UCLA eleven years earlier.

But behind the scenes, there had been changes that might have foretold their partnership was about to end.

The biggest change was that Adam Walsh was no longer the coach. Even his brother, Rams general manager Chile Walsh, couldn't convince Adam to stay on for a third season. Adam had done a magnificent job in leading the Rams to their first-ever NFL championship in 1945, the team's final year in Cleveland.

But the coach was quietly miserable in his role.

Walsh had been the All-American center and captain of the 1924 Notre Dame team that featured the Four Horsemen under legendary coach Knute Rockne. Walsh was a legend himself, having played one game with broken bones in both hands, yet never missing a snap as part of the team's unbeaten season.

Walsh set out on a coaching career, starting at Santa Clara University and then at Yale for five years and another at Harvard coaching the offensive and defensive lines. But it was at Bowdoin College where he found a home, coaching at the small school in Maine and winning at least a share of the state championship in seven of his first eight seasons.

Bowdoin suspended its program in 1943 because of World War II, and Walsh coached at Notre Dame in 1944. He joined his brother with the Rams as head coach in 1945 and did spectacular work in a 9-1 regular season that was capped with his 15–14 win over Washington for the championship.

But Walsh was privately unhappy when the team was uprooted and headed to Los Angeles, and while he did a solid job in finishing second in the NFL's Western Division in 1946, he missed coaching at Bowdoin.

"He really liked living and coaching in Brunswick, Maine," Horrigan said. "While successful and certainly having options in both the pros and major colleges, he preferred the small school Bowdoin. He used a clause in his Rams contract to be released and he went back to Bowdoin."

Walsh coached ten more seasons at Bowdoin and added four state championships before retiring in 1958. An immensely popular figure in Maine, Walsh won two terms in the state's House of Representatives and served as the U.S. Marshal for Maine under Presidents John F. Kennedy and Lyndon Johnson.

When Walsh stepped down from the Rams, Reeves named Bob Snyder, who'd done a fine job with Waterfield during the championship season in 1945, as head coach. Snyder was the league's youngest coach, and there was no way to know what his future would hold. But his was an itinerant career in which he coached with thirteen different teams over twenty-eight years—mostly for one season and never for more than three with the same team.

Snyder had only one question for Reeves before taking the job: Was Waterfield under contract with the team?

"As long as Waterfield is around," Snyder said, "he'll make any coach look good. Right now, he's greater than ever."

Washington's roster spot was also secure, and Strode seemed safe as well, especially the way he looked in camp.

"Woody Strode beat all ends in the 50-yard dash," *Valley Times* columnist Pete Kokon gushed about the fleet receiver after an August practice at Loyola College, where the team had moved for its second camp. Later in his column, Kokon described Snyder as a coach who demanded accountability, particularly when it came to being on time for practice. "Look, you have just three minutes to get on that field," he quoted the coach telling one of his players. "And if you're any later, bring $25."

Strode himself knew the value of practice, especially after his first season, when he was used only sparingly on offense. He treated practice like the game, because that was when he knew he'd have a chance.

But after barely playing against Washington in the first exhibition game, Strode knew his time was over with the Rams and the man he'd shared so many football experiences with. As he would discover in the coming weeks, however, his football life wasn't quite over.

Washington, meanwhile, was shaken by Strode's release, but he accepted that he'd have to carry on without his best friend. He was also beginning to get comfortable in the Rams' offense after an unremarkable rookie season the year before.

It was a spectacular debut for the Rams in Snyder's first regular season game, as they routed the Steelers, 48–7, at Forbes Field. For Washington, it was further evidence that he was finding a niche in the offense, as he scored 2 touchdowns—the first on a pitch from Waterfield that went for 9 yards and then a 6-yard touchdown off a Waterfield handoff.

The Rams improved to 3-1 after a 27–7 win over the Chicago Cardinals before its highest attendance—69,631, the most to ever see an NFL game to that point—at the Coliseum. Washington was again showing the kind of form that made him one of the game's greatest players during his time at UCLA. Washington needed only a few minutes in the first quarter to provide a highlight run.

"With the ball on the Cardinals' 31, Kenny Washington circled left end," Sid Ziff of the North Hollywood *Valley Times* wrote. "He was trapped momentarily, shook loose, swivel-hipped through a half dozen arms, and then picking up fine blocking in the last 10 yards, scored easily standing up."

It was a familiar sight to southern California fans who'd seen this before. At twenty-nine years old, and after five knee surgeries, Washington still had it.

The Rams were listless the following week in a 14–7 loss to the Eagles at Philadelphia's Shibe Park, and at 3-2, they headed to Chicago for a rematch against the Cardinals. And if his 31-yard touchdown run at the Coliseum was good, what he did against the Cardinals on the afternoon of November 2, 1947, at Comiskey Park was sublime.

It was a pleasant day in Chicago, with game-time temperatures of around fifty degrees under partly cloudy skies and winds gusting to nineteen miles per hour. In other words, about as good a football day as there could be at this time of year. There were heady times for the Cardinals, a mostly hard-luck franchise who'd usually played second fiddle to George Halas's Bears but were now in the midst of the team's greatest days.

Coach Jimmy Conzelman's team featured what came to be known as the "Million Dollar Backfield" of Charley Trippi, Elmer Angsman, Paul Christman, and Pat Harder. The Cardinals were coming off a much-improved 6-5 season that followed a last-place finish in 1945. Their loss to the Rams at the Coliseum earlier in the season would be their only defeat in their first eight games, so the rematch was particularly important. Especially as they attempted to contain Washington, who'd had his best game against the Cardinals in Los Angeles.

As in the first meeting against the Rams, Washington's brilliance came in the first quarter. With the Rams backed up at their own 8-yard line, they looked to Washington to get some breathing room.

Instead, they got history.

Just over ten minutes into the game, with the Rams at their own 8-yard line, Waterfield handed off to Washington, who ran to his left between a hole created by left tackle Dick Huffman and guard Hal Dean. Cardinals defender Red Cochran had a clear shot at Washington, but Washington slipped out of the tackle. Marshall Goldberg then got in position to tackle Washington, but he couldn't bring him down either. Washington was now in the open field, with one more Cardinals defender to beat.

Washington slowed up just a bit to take on safety Walt "Bull" Rankin, but just as Rankin approached him near midfield, Washington delivered a stiff-arm that knocked Rankin to the ground.

Washington was gone.

It was a 92-yard touchdown run for the twenty-nine-year-old Washington, a defining moment for one of the most talented athletes to ever traverse a football field.

And it had come in a fitting location. Seven years earlier in this city, his hopes were raised when George Halas asked him to stay behind after the College All-Star Game to see if the Bears owner could convince his NFL colleagues to let a Black man join the league. Those hopes were dashed when Halas opted not to go against George Preston Marshall, the most outspoken opponent of reintegrating the league, and a forlorn Washington returned home.

If only for a few moments, Washington had enjoyed his own piece of retribution, proving that his talent was enough to make sure he belonged in this league. Even if the color of his skin had once prevented it.

Washington earned his slice of history, and his record continues to stand alone: No Rams running back has run for a longer touchdown since.

* * *

Washington's feelings of exultation would not last long. And while he couldn't have known it at the time, this would be his final transcendent moment as an athlete.

His touchdown run gave the Rams a 7–0 lead, and he would complete an 18-yard pass to Waterfield on a trick play later in the game. He had an interception on a similar play after that, as the Cardinals eventually rallied for a 17–10 win.

Washington finished with a career-high 145 rushing yards on 11 carries, including his record-setting run.

But the physical problem that had haunted him through most of his life surfaced yet again. And this time, the damage from yet another injury to his left knee would signal the eventual end to his career. The duality of Washington's career was perhaps illustrated no better than on page twelve of the *Los Angeles Times*'s November 7, 1947, edition—published just five days after Washington's spectacular run.

A sub-headline for one blurb in the Rams Notebook column read: "Still the Kingfish," and the column described his magical play. Two columns to the left, the headline "Kingfish Out" introduced a different article:

> The real hard-luck gent in the Ram backfield is named Kenneth Stanley Washington. Troubled with bad knees ever since he joined the Rams a year ago, he was busily making himself the sensation of the league this fall until he was taken out of the Chicago Card game last Sunday with a bad leg injury. The Kingfish had been proving in big time football all the things that had been said about him in college, with sensational runs and fine defensive play.

Kenny Washington was a legendary player at Lincoln High School in Los Angeles. His team won the city championship in 1935, and his coach, Jim Tunney Sr., recommended that he attend UCLA. *(Courtesy Kenny Norwood)*

Woody Strode played football and ran track at Jefferson High School, where he was coached by Harry Edelson, a blocking back on USC's "Thundering Herd" teams in the late 1920s. Strode went on to play at UCLA, where he developed a lasting friendship with Washington. *(Courtesy ASUCLA Photography)*

Bill Willis was skeptical about attending Ohio State after the school passed over his older brother, Claude. But because Paul Brown was one of the few college coaches willing to have African-American players on his team, Willis agreed to play there and developed into an All-American defensive lineman. *(Courtesy Willis Family)*

Marion Motley starred at the University of Nevada after transferring from South Carolina State. He was involved in a fatal car crash and faced the possibility of jail time, but school administrators, faculty, and fellow students raised money for a successful legal defense. *(Courtesy University of Nevada)*

In 1939 Kenny Washington became the first All-American player in UCLA history and was arguably the most talented college player in the country. But because of the NFL's ban on Black players, he went undrafted and played with the Hollywood Bears of the Pacific Coast Football League. *(Courtesy Kenny Norwood)*

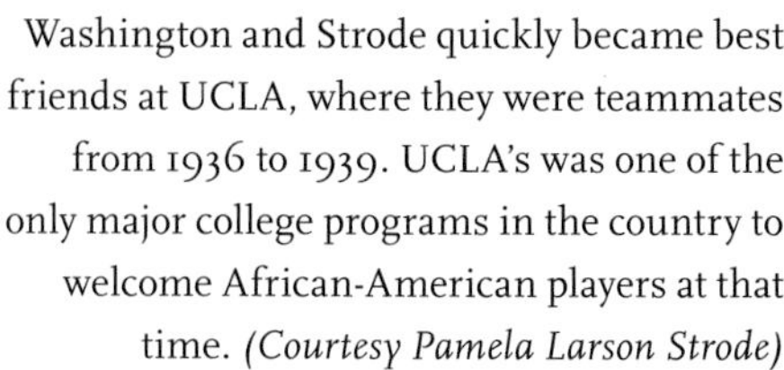

Washington and Strode quickly became best friends at UCLA, where they were teammates from 1936 to 1939. UCLA's was one of the only major college programs in the country to welcome African-American players at that time. *(Courtesy Pamela Larson Strode)*

Washington and Strode were teammates with Jackie Robinson *(center)* on the 1939 UCLA football team, and all three went on to play professional ball. Robinson, of course, gained fame by becoming the first African-American in the modern era to play Major League Baseball, while Washington and Strode have been far less celebrated as the first two Black players to reintegrate the NFL. *(Courtesy ASUCLA Photography)*

UCLA preserved its unbeaten season in a 0-0 tie against rival USC in the final regular season game in 1939. Robinson forces USC's All-American quarterback, Grenville Lansdell, to fumble as Strode *(left)* and Washington *(right)* look on. Strode recovered the ball in the end zone to help preserve the tie in a game that was attended by more than 103,000 fans. It was the final college game for Washington and Strode. *(Courtesy USC Athletics)*

There were no African-American players in the NFL between 1934 and 1945, and George Preston Marshall, who owned the Washington franchise, was the league's most outspoken advocate of the ban. His team was the last to integrate, in 1962, and it did so only after intense pressure applied by the Kennedy administration. *(Pro Football Hall of Fame)*

When Washington played in the College All-Star Game in 1940, Bears owner George Halas asked him to stay in Chicago while he attempted to convince fellow owners to let Washington into the NFL. But Washington went home to Los Angeles when he wasn't offered a contract. *(Pro Football Hall of Fame)*

On March 13, 1946—more than a year before Jackie Robinson broke the MLB color line—Kenny Washington signed a contract with Los Angeles Rams general manager Chile Walsh, thus officially ending a dozen-year ban on Black players in the NFL.

Woody Strode joined the Rams shortly after Washington did. Washington had insisted that the team sign his former UCLA teammate and best friend. *(Courtesy Los Angeles Rams)*

Bill Willis *(No. 30)* was technically considered a defensive lineman, but he was so fast that he was often asked to drop back into pass coverage. He is considered a forerunner to the modern middle linebacker. *(Courtesy Cleveland Browns)*

Hall of Fame coach Paul Brown signed Motley and Willis to play for the Cleveland Browns team of the All-America Football Conference in 1946. Brown believed in giving players a chance based on their talent, not their race. *(Courtesy Cleveland Browns)*

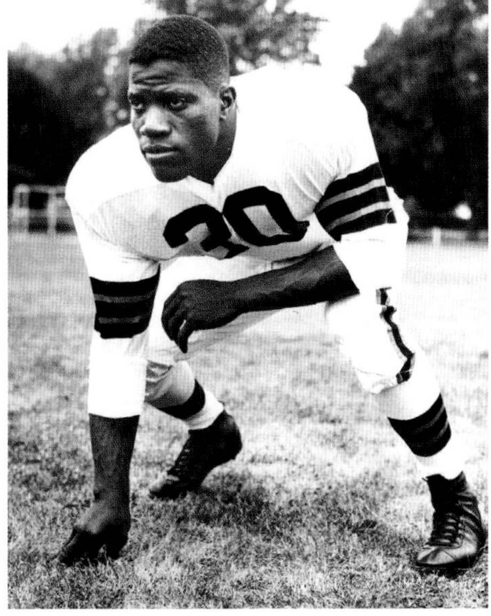
Paul Brown had coached Willis at Ohio State and then brought him over to the Cleveland Browns. Willis was so quick coming out of his three-point stance that the Browns' public relations department told photographers to adjust their shutter speeds so pictures wouldn't be blurry. *(Courtesy Willis Family)*

Marion Motley became the AAFC's best fullback after joining the Browns in 1946. At 6-foot-1 and 232 pounds, Motley was one of pro football's greatest blockers and runners, and he helped his team win a league championship when the Browns were absorbed into the NFL in 1950. *(Courtesy Cleveland Browns)*

Motley was one of the toughest players to bring down because of his size and power. Through the early part of his career, defenders often used cheap shots against him and issued racial taunts. *(Courtesy Cleveland Browns)*

Washington was a teammate of celebrated Rams quarterback Bob Waterfield (*No. 7*), who considered Washington a quarterback as well as a running back. Washington was in fact the first African-American to play quarterback in the NFL when he briefly filled in for an injured Waterfield in 1946. *(Courtesy Los Angeles Rams)*

Keyshawn Johnson stretches before a USC game in 1995, a year before becoming the first overall pick by the Jets in the NFL draft–exactly fifty years after Washington, Strode, Motley, and Willis had broken the color barrier in pro football. *(Courtesy USC Athletics)*

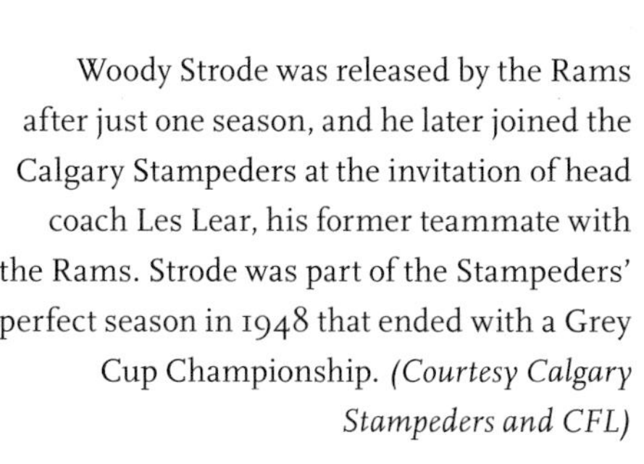

Woody Strode was released by the Rams after just one season, and he later joined the Calgary Stampeders at the invitation of head coach Les Lear, his former teammate with the Rams. Strode was part of the Stampeders' perfect season in 1948 that ended with a Grey Cup Championship. *(Courtesy Calgary Stampeders and CFL)*

Following his pro football career, Strode became a professional wrestler and later an actor. He was nominated for a Golden Globe Award as best supporting actor when he appeared in *Spartacus* in an iconic fight scene with actor Kirk Douglas.

After retiring in 1954, Willis took a position as the city of Cleveland's assistant recreation commissioner and later became chairman of the Ohio Youth Commission, working with three governors during his tenure. Pictured here with NFL commissioner Roger Goodell and wearing his Hall of Fame gold jacket, Willis regularly interacted with current and former NFL players and executives until his death in 2007. *(Courtesy Willis Family)*

On August 3, 1968, Motley became the second African-American player to be inducted into the Pro Football Hall of Fame. In nine pro seasons, he averaged an astonishing 5.7 yards-per-carry. *(Pro Football Hall of Fame)*

Willis asked Paul Brown to be his presenter at his induction into the Pro Football Hall of Fame, in 1977. *(Courtesy Willis Family)*

Washington had even been mentioned as a leading contender for "Comeback Player of the Year" honors.

"Kenny Washington, UCLA immortal and Los Angeles Rams halfback, is highly deserving of a mythical badge of glory award for his tremendous comeback in the ranks of play for pay football this season," *Pittsburgh Courier* columnist Herman Hill wrote. "There were plenty who claimed he was through and should retire to [the] old rocking chair."

Hill wrote that Washington "reached his zenith at Chicago when he raced [92] yards to pay dirt against the Cards a fortnight ago... Proof that Kenny Washington has come back is best shown by the fact that he is the leading ground-gainer in the Western Division of the league with better than an eight-yard average per try!"

Snyder announced that Washington would miss three games because of the injury. And while he didn't undergo an additional surgery, this would foretell more problems ahead.

* * *

Strode was distraught when he was told he wouldn't make the Rams' roster in 1947, and was incensed over what he believed was the team's disapproval of his marriage to a Hawaiian woman. He also now had no means to support a family, including Kalai, who was barely nine months old when Strode was released.

"After I got cut from the Rams, I completely shut down," he said. "I kept myself busy cleaning and cooking, washing diapers and taking care of the baby. [Kalai] and Luana were my only joy at that time."

While Strode's release signaled an end to his NFL career, it turned out to be the start of a journey. In the short term, however, Strode was devastated.

"He was so torn up to not be able to play football with Kenny anymore," said Pamela Larson Strode, Woody's daughter-in-law and Kalai's widow. "Kenny was like his brother, and he was happy for him that he was still with the Rams. Their friendship was never affected when Woody was cut. They were both devastated to be apart, but they remained like brothers."

Strode once confided to his son how despondent he was. He told him he had once considered suicide, but he didn't take his own life only because he was a new father.

It wasn't until he was asked about trying out for the New York Yankees of the AAFC that he began to emerge from his self-described funk. He had his doubts about what was behind the request to play in New York, however. This was a year after Willis and Motley had joined the AAFC's Browns, and their successful debut season served as encouragement to other league owners to integrate their teams.

Bitter over the way things panned out with the Rams, Strode at first declined.

"At first I said, 'No, they don't want me to play football,' and I was through integrating anything," he wrote in his memoir. "But finally, not knowing what else to do, I decided to give it a try."

He took a train to New York and met with Dan Topping, who at that time was the Yankees general manager, and Topping seemed surprised that Strode appeared so young and fit.

"Son, from the way they talk about you, we thought you were fifty years old!" Topping told Strode.

The Yankees did integrate that year, but it was former Illinois star Buddy Young who became the team's first African-American player.

Strode didn't make the team, and again rejection hit him hard.

He took the train back from New York and stopped off to visit some cousins in Chicago.

"I got drunk for one week and licked my wounds," he said. "I was a warrior, I didn't know anything but football; now they weren't allowing me to play. I didn't know how I was going to support my wife and baby."

While Strode was drowning his sorrows, his next opportunity had presented itself.

When he returned home, Luana told him that Les Lear, a former Rams teammate, had been calling him from Calgary, where he was now a player-coach with the CFL's Stampeders. Lear had grown up in Manitoba, won two Grey Cup titles with the Winnipeg Blue Bombers, and then was a guard for the Rams from 1944 to 1946, winning an NFL title when the team was in Cleveland in 1945.

He was named coach of the Stampeders before the 1948 season, and with the ability to sign four American players, Strode was one of his first targets.

"Woody, I got a job for you," Lear told him. "Bring your shoes and your shoulder pads. I'll get you all the money I can."

Lear sent his former teammate a contract for $5,000, and threw in $100 a week for expense money. His hotel accommodations would be paid for.

Strode was going to Canada.

"When I stepped off the plane in Calgary," he said, "it was like stepping back into the Old West. It was cowboy country...Their land was wide open. The plains between Calgary in the Alberta province and Regina in the Saskatchewan [province] were just an extension of our great plains here in the United States."

It was an invigorating environment for Strode—and not simply because of how cold it got during the fall and winter months. He felt welcome by the people of Canada, a rare experience for him. The only others who had made Strode feel that way were Hawaiians, who had embraced him when he played college ball in Hawaii, returned for visits while in the military, and later married Luana.

Lear proved to be a capable coach from the start, and Strode became one of his best players.

"My Calgary teammates were just kids and ignorant about the game," said Strode, who was then thirty-four, "so Les gave us only seven plays. Around end, off tackle, over guard, center; he simplified it."

Success came quickly; the Stampeders went 12-0 in the regular season, outlasted Regina in the Western Conference playoffs, and qualified for the Grey Cup final against Ottawa.

The teams traveled to Toronto for the title game, and Strode was in his glory, with a chance to win a championship for the first time in his life. He'd become an immensely popular player, both in the locker room and among Calgary fans, some of whom he came to know because of their Indian heritage.

"The Canadian Indians used to bring wild game to my hotel room," he said. "I'm part Indian, but you never walk up to them and announce it. They'll see it in you. They came to all the football games, and it took them a month to ask me what kind of Indian blood I had. I told them, 'American Blackfoot.' The guy who asked me had an interpreter talking for him; he replied, 'We are Canadian Blackfeet.' Well, that made us like brothers."

Strode was also popular with the press, often providing entertaining quips to the writers. That included the buildup to the Grey Cup title game, when he was asked about his impressions of Ottawa.

"After all this business, I'm not worried about playing against the Ottawa Rough Riders," he said. "I'm more worried about trying not to freeze to death."

Staying warm was a challenge in those days.

"We trained hard and we drank hard," Strode said of his CFL experience. "We used to drink rum and scotch before practice just to stay warm. In fact, we used to have rum in our coffee at halftime. As we used to say, it was solely for medicinal purposes."

On this day, Strode would save the drinking for later.

Amid subfreezing temperatures at Toronto's Varsity Stadium, with the Grey Cup championship on the line, he produced the most consequential play of his football career.

With the Stampeders trailing 7–6 in the fourth quarter, Strode was on defense when Ottawa had possession near midfield. Rough Riders quarterback Bob Paffrath attempted a lateral to running back Pete Karpuk, but the ball popped loose. The players stopped for a moment when it appeared that a penalty for offsides would be called, but Strode alertly picked up the ball and raced toward the end zone.

"I looked at that ball on the ground and then I looked right into the mouth of the referee as I reached for it," Strode said in the locker room afterward. "He didn't blow his whistle, so I just picked it up and ran. I went for it because I suddenly realized it was a lateral that went wrong."

Strode returned the fumble deep inside Calgary territory before lateraling to teammate Chick Chickowsky, who was tackled at the 10. Two plays later, Pete Thodos scored the game-winning touchdown.

"I was the hero," Strode said. "I left the field on my teammates' shoulders, a bottle of rye whiskey in my hand. No Black athlete in the world had ever done that."

The celebration at the iconic Royal York Hotel lasted into the wee hours, with Strode lapping up every moment. Hundreds of fans from Calgary who had made the trip east poured into the streets of Toronto. Strode spotted an acquaintance in front of the hotel and got an idea:

> I met an Indian friend... and he let me borrow his horse, a pure white multi-breed. I saddled up and walked that horse right up to the front entrance. The doorman watched me coming, frozen in his boots. My friend held the door for me as I moved inside...
>
> I walked that horse right through the crowd. I was wearing a white linen cowboy-type suit, reddish lizard-skin boots,

> and a navy blue silk scarf around my neck. I held the reins and my rye whiskey in my left hand, my white ten-gallon hat in my right. I walked to the center of the lobby and pulled back on the reins. I kicked that horse hard and he reared up and spun around. I leaned way back in the saddle, looked up towards the ceiling and let out a war cry. The place erupted in applause and shouting. And when the police showed up, I sliced through them like cutting a cake as I charged out of there.

It was the culmination of the greatest season in CFL history; Strode's Stampeders remain the league's only unbeaten team.

* * *

Strode received the telegram while he was still in Calgary. It was from Kenny Washington, asking Strode if he could make it back to Los Angeles as soon as possible.

Washington was retiring from the NFL after three seasons.

They'd both done their part as trailblazers, breaking the NFL's color barrier. But after five knee operations and a devastating hit to his left knee in the same game he scored his record-setting 92-yard touchdown, Washington knew it was time to walk away—while he still could.

"Hell, even a half-step slower is fatal," Washington told Strode. "Not only that, I notice I get up a lot slower."

By now, Washington had gained weight and didn't have the speed that once made him one of the NFL's best runners—even with his bad knees. By the 1948 season, he'd gotten up to around 220 pounds—although he told reporters late that year that he was "a sylph-like 200." His ideal playing weight was 190, so there was simply no way he could justify continuing to play.

At age thirty, he knew in his heart it was over.

Washington played in just ten games in his final season, rushing for 301 yards on 57 carries while scoring two touchdowns. His knees—particularly his left knee—continued to cause problems. He acknowledged publicly in November that his final game would be December 12 against the Steelers at the Coliseum.

When word got out about Washington's plans, area sportswriters—including Halley Harding, who had led the charge for the Rams to sign Washington—pushed for a special celebration in honor of his last game. Momentum built quickly, and within days, longtime Los Angeles mayor Fletcher Bowron proclaimed December 12, 1948, "Kenny Washington Day." Many of Washington's ex-coaches and teammates would show, and he'd receive gifts at halftime commemorating his brief but meaningful time with the Rams.

It was also a chance to reflect on what might have been for Washington.

What might his career have been like had he been allowed to play in the NFL at the peak of his physical powers, when he was considered arguably the greatest college football player in the land after the 1939 season?

Many believed that he could have produced a Hall of Fame legacy.

"Kenny would have been the greatest player of all time," former Rams coach Bob Snyder said, "and that includes Thorpe, Nagurski, Nevers and the rest, if he had played in the National League as soon as he got out of college in 1939."

His former backfield mate, Jackie Robinson, called Washington "the greatest football player I have ever seen" and suggested that he'd have been even greater if he wasn't asked to do so much on the football field, particularly in college.

"If he had been able to concentrate on playing exclusively either on offense or defense," Robinson said, "he probably would be better remembered today. But in 1939, two-platoon football was unheard of. Everybody played both ways."

For the third—and final—time at the end of a season, Washington would walk off the field at the Coliseum to the cheers of the home team. This would be a far more muted moment, however. A crowd of only 27,967 showed up for Washington's final game, indicative of how the Rams, who would finish the season 6-5-1, were again struggling to draw fans.

But those who did show up to offer a final salute to Washington showered him with applause throughout the game, especially during a halftime ceremony arranged by the Southern California Football Writers Association and the group's president, Rube Samuelsen.

Washington received an eclectic mix of parting gifts from people who touched him through all phases of his life.

Bill Schroeder, managing director of the Helms Athletic Foundation, gave Washington a huge trophy that was then presented to Lincoln High principal Thomas Riley. It would become a "perpetual trophy" given each year to Lincoln's most valuable football player.

Rams team captain Fred Naumetz gave Washington an expensive watch on behalf of the players.

He got a 1949 Ford sedan.

A combination radio–television set.

A $500 U.S. savings bond for his young son, Kenny Jr.

Mayor Bowron gave him a framed "Kenny Washington Day" proclamation.

And eight members of El Centro's touch football championship team surprised Washington with a large crate of the town's celebrated lettuce.

Washington delivered a brief speech.

"The cheers you fans have given me," he said, "went to my heart, not to my head."

So many who meant so much to Washington were there. Strode was by his friend's side once again. Schissler, the Hollywood Bears coach who adored having Washington on his team and was all too willing to let him out of his contract so he could join the Rams, showed up.

Jim Tunney, his high school coach, was there. Bill Spaulding, his first coach at UCLA, and Babe Horrell, who led the team's unbeaten season in 1939, now stood by their prized halfback.

Washington was invigorated by the sendoff and had one of his most impactful games of the season. He ran for 54 yards on 10 attempts, recovered 2 fumbles, intercepted a pass, and also attempted a pass. His retirement was the lead story in the following day's *Los Angeles Times*, with a series of four large photographs showing him on a rushing attempt, on an interception return, on a fumble recovery, and making a tackle in the 31–14 win.

Washington's pass fell incomplete, and he joked about it afterward.

"I should never have tried that pass," he said in the locker room. "I ran with the ball first, and I was afraid I would pass it too far. As a result, I wound up pushing it. It was a terrible toss and naturally was short."

Even so, it was a reminder that Washington, who once threw a pass 62 yards in the air at UCLA, could do just about anything and everything in a football game. And while he is remembered as a running back and safety, there is no question that a player with Kenny Washington's arm talent and versatility in today's NFL would at least be considered as a potential quarterback.

When it was over, when Washington had completed one final game at the place that held so much history for him, he walked off the field once more to the cheers of the Coliseum crowd.

Kenny Washington's football career, filled with such potential, such promise, and such expectation—but also heartbreak, injury, and disappointment—was over.

Chapter 18

A DYNASTY IS BORN

By any measure, the Browns' first season in the AAFC was a success. The team had won the Western Division with a 12-2 record. They scored the most points of any team—423. They allowed the fewest—137. They led the league with 67 defensive takeaways; to this day, no professional team has ever had that many.

And they won the championship, beating the New York Yankees, 14–9, at Cleveland Stadium.

The Browns had captured the imagination of Cleveland fans like no other professional team before. Crowds of more than sixty thousand showed up to some games, and team owner Arthur McBride's decision to hire Paul Brown was a stroke of genius.

But Brown was not content winning just one championship. As he'd done at Massillon in building one of the greatest high school football programs in the country, he wanted to produce a consistent winner. As he'd told McBride when the two shook hands on a contract that gave him part ownership of the team, Brown wanted to build a dynasty.

"This was the first layer of the Cleveland Browns then," Brown said of his inaugural team. "A solid base of championship caliber."

It was therefore no surprise to anyone who knew Brown that he made a number of changes in 1947 and then again in 1948. Among the players he added: halfbacks Ara Parseghian (who went on to become the fabled Notre Dame head coach) and Dub Jones, linebacker/guard Alex Agase and another familiar face for Brown going back to their days at Massillon: Horace Gillom.

Brown had first met Gillom before he went out for the team at Washington High, and gave him a few pointers on how to punt the football. Gillom turned out to be one of Brown's finest players at Massillon; in fact, the coach once called Gillom "the greatest high school player I ever coached."

He became the Browns' third African-American player.

Like Motley, Gillom was another of the Ohio players recruited to play for former McKinley Canton coach Jim Aiken at Nevada. Gillom played at Nevada after he'd enlisted in World War II, where he fought in the Battle of the Bulge and earned three bronze stars. A terrific all-around player, Gillom was used as an offensive and defensive end and punter for the Wolf Pack, and he was part of a 1946 team that led the nation in passing offense.

Aiken and Brown were two of the handful of white coaches of their era who didn't have an issue with having Black players on their teams, even if it meant having to confront those who did. Aiken had a showdown with a coach in Idaho who initially refused to play if Motley suited up. And when Gillom played for him, there was another confrontation that left a lasting impression.

Prior to a game against Mississippi State, athletic director C. R. Noble wrote to the University of Nevada and suggested that Gillom and his African-American teammate, running back Billy Bass, would not be welcome when the schools were to play in Mississippi.

"It is not custom in the South for members of the Negro race to compete in athletics with or against members of the white race nor members of the white race to compete against the Negro race in athletic contests," Noble wrote. "I am sure that you understand this traditional custom which Mississippi State College cannot under any circumstances violate."

Aiken met with his players, and they decided they wouldn't play unless Gillom and Bass were allowed to participate. The game was called off, even though Nevada had to pay a $3,000 cancellation fee.

The following season, Gillom joined the Browns and began what would become a ten-year career as one of the best punters in NFL history.

Brown's relentless pursuit of providing his teams with an edge was a perfect match with Gillom. Thanks in part to his coach's instructions, Gillom combined technique with his booming right leg and turned into a prolific punter who could change field position and thus have a profound impact on games.

Unlike traditional punters of his day, all of whom would stand ten yards behind the line of scrimmage, Gillom moved back to fifteen yards behind center. It afforded him an extra split second to get his kicks off, and he more than made up for the yardage lost by standing farther back.

Gillom also added depth at offensive and defensive end, giving Brown one more advantage as he went about the task of attempting a second straight championship.

The 1947 season started off in mostly auspicious form, as the Browns beat Buffalo, 30–14, at Cleveland Stadium. The Browns dominated the first half, building a 27–0 lead at intermission and prompting Brown to use his backups for much of the second half. Afterward, he took the occasion to tweak his own team.

"We got a good head of steam and took a commanding lead in the first half and let down and looked back in the last two periods," he said. "I started the kids in the second half, and Buffalo almost tore them apart."

But the quarterback they beat, Buffalo's George Ratterman, said something in the Buffalo locker room that indicated just how good the Browns were.

"Their line rushed me all night long, and I didn't have much chance to get the ball away accurately," Ratterman said. "I think the Browns are much better than the Bears, especially their [defensive] line."

And the anchor of that line? Bill Willis.

Even so, Brown returned to practice with an edge the following week.

Brown's intensity carried over into a Week 2 game against the Brooklyn Dodgers at Ebbets Field, as Cleveland destroyed the Dodgers, 55–7. The Browns scored three touchdowns in the first quarter, with Motley running for 111 yards and scoring two touchdowns. That included a 50-yard scoring run in the second half.

The game also led to the unexpected invention of one of football's most widely used plays.

It happened purely by accident.

As Graham dropped back to pass, he collided with Motley and started to fall down. Motley grabbed the ball and then raced up the middle for a decent gain. It might have been a botched play, but Graham and Brown noticed during a film session that the delay in getting the ball to Motley momentarily froze the defense, especially the linemen rushing the quarterback. The resultant hole that opened up allowed Motley to advance the ball forward.

"That later became the old '32 trap play' with the Browns," Mike Brown said. "Marion went across Otto's path, they bumped, and Marion grabbed the ball and there was a big hole and he ran through it. Next day, they looked at it and said, 'Gee, why don't we use that as a play?' "

The draw play was born.

"We didn't think much of it at the time, but looking at the game films, Otto said, 'I think that could become a play,' " Paul Brown said. "We developed blocking assignments and the techniques which went with it. At first, we called it a pick, but since that word was also part of the passing terminology, I changed the name to draw, because we wanted our offensive linemen to visualize it as drawing in the pass rushers."

Brown's conviction about Gillom paid off in a big way in a 28–0 win over the Baltimore Colts in Week 3 to give Cleveland a perfect 3-0 getaway. With Motley scoring one of three first-quarter touchdowns, Gillom smothered the Colts with poor field position the entire game. He averaged 55.7 yards on his punts and boomed kicks of 80 and 85 yards. And this was no fluke; Gillom went on to average 43.8 yards per punt for his career, by far the AAFC's best punter, and only Sammy Baugh had a higher average by the time Gillom's career had ended.

Gillom also played a role in a nail-biting 13–12 win over the Dodgers.

"It was Gillom who broke through and blocked the extra point to prevent the tie game," Brown said.

The Browns stayed on a roll the entire season, going 12-1-1 to win another Western Division crown and set up a rematch against the Yankees in the championship game. Graham again starred for the Browns, as the coach's hand-picked passer put together a remarkable season yet again. Graham finished with 2,753 passing yards, 25 touchdowns, and just 11 interceptions for a 109.2 rating. Even by today's standards, those would be considered good numbers, especially over a fourteen-game season. But consider how remarkable that kind of production was at a time when pro football still revolved around the running game.

Graham was not only physically gifted, but his ability to see the field and have a feel for how plays developed was remarkable. It was something even Brown couldn't teach, that kind of innate sense of when to throw, when not to throw, when to tuck the ball and run, and when to take a chance.

Graham had also built up remarkable rapport with his receivers, particularly Dante Lavelli. Brown remembered, in a game against the

Yankees, calling a play for Lavelli to run to the right corner of the end zone. "The Yankees' defense sensed the pass and set itself to stop it even before the ball was snapped," Brown said. "But then, in the middle of his pattern, Dante suddenly broke the pass route and headed in the opposite direction toward the goalposts. Otto's arm was already in motion to throw the ball toward the corner, but amazingly he changed the direction of his throw without a hitch and passed to Dante for a touchdown. Otto came skipping off the field yelling, 'Did you see what that crazy son of a gun just did?' "

How good was Graham? Better than anyone that ever played football, according to Brown.

"As far as I'm concerned," Brown said, "Otto Graham was the greatest player in the game's history."

It was still early in Graham's career when he led the Browns to their second straight AAFC championship game—a rematch of the previous year's game against the Yankees—and more fans came out to watch the game—61,879—at Yankee Stadium than any previous pro football championship game ever.

Yes, the NFL was taking note of a league that posed an unmistakable threat to its own popularity. In fact, the Browns-Yankees game in the regular season drew even more fans—70,060.

According to unofficial estimates, around a third of the crowd was African-American, drawn in large part by the presence of Motley, Willis, and now Gillom from the Browns and the first Black player to join a New York pro team: Buddy Young.

"There is a lesson for anyone who takes the trouble to see it in that huge turnout," *New York Amsterdam News* columnist Dan Burley wrote in a piece about the Browns-Yankees championship game. "It is apparent that something has happened to transform large portions of the Negro population in northern cities into sports fans almost overnight."

Burley cited the presence of the four Black players as evidence of the surge in popularity among African-American fans.

The regular season matchup was a thriller, as the Yankees raced to a 28–0 first-half lead before the Browns scored their first touchdown just before intermission. As the teams left the field, some Yankees players derided the Browns for their poor play—a big mistake, in hindsight.

"They got us upset, got us angry," Graham told reporters. "Finally we got mad as a team and said, 'We'll show these guys,' and we started playing football."

The Browns came out of the locker room and played with passion and purpose. Graham got the passing game going, Motley ran for two touchdowns in the third quarter, and Jim Dewar scored in the fourth quarter before Lou Saban, filling in for injured kicker Lou Groza, kicked the extra point. The game ended in a 28–28 tie.

"That game, more than any other to date," Brown said, "helped establish Otto as football's premier passer."

Even though they didn't win, Brown was ebullient afterward.

The championship game rematch was a far less dramatic affair, mostly because it was played in frigid conditions on a slick field at Yankee Stadium. That worked to the detriment of the Yankees, who relied on the speed of Young and dual-threat runner-thrower Spec Sanders, as the Browns defense shut down the New York offense in a 14–3 win.

Motley again keyed the Cleveland offense, running for 109 yards and setting up Graham's 1-yard touchdown run in the first quarter with a 51-yard run. Motley also was instrumental on the team's other touchdown drive.

"Motley battered the Yankees' defense so badly with his running," Brown said, "that they were easy bait for Edgar Jones's 4-yard trap play that scored the second touchdown."

Gillom was a star, too, averaging 45 yards on his five punts and blunting New York's normally superior return game.

* * *

As great as the Browns were in 1947, the 1948 season elevated the team to a different level.

An historic level.

With the off-season additions of running back Parseghian, linebacker Agase, and defensive back Tommy James, Brown also traded for Dub Jones, a defensive back and halfback who eventually became a terrific flanker in the Cleveland offense.

One other player the Browns acquired: quarterback Y. A. Tittle, who was signed out of LSU. Unfortunately for Brown, he was forced to allow Tittle to join the Baltimore Colts out of concerns for competitive balance. Brown had designs on making Tittle the heir apparent to Graham but had to give up that plan, making him eventually wonder just how long his team might have dominated pro football.

The Browns raced out to a 9-0 record with more fine performances, including wins over the Yankees, Colts, Bills, and Los Angeles Dons. But they had competition this time around, as the San Francisco 49ers, featuring quarterback Frankie Albert, halfback Johnny Strzykalski, and fullback Joe Perry, had a 10-0 record heading into their first matchup of the season against the Browns.

A packed house of 82,769—the most to attend a pro football game to that point—showed up at Municipal Stadium. The home team did not disappoint, as the Browns gutted out a 14–7 win behind rushing touchdowns from Graham and Edgar Jones to give the 49ers their first loss of the season. The win didn't come without a cost, though, as several Browns players, including Willis, Speedie, Graham, and guard Weldon Humble suffered an assortment of injuries.

The Browns now faced a critical three-game stretch; over the course of an eight-day span, from November 21 to 28, the Browns would play three games. All on the road:

At the Yankees in New York on Sunday.
At the Dons in Los Angeles on Thanksgiving.
At the 49ers in San Francisco the following Sunday.

Never before—and never since—has one football team been asked to play that many games in such a short period of time.

The schedule was the brainchild of Branch Rickey, whose baseball background with the Brooklyn Dodgers convinced him that having the Browns play three games within a week would continue to help grow the sport. Rickey, who was now running both the baseball and football Dodgers, got intense pushback from Brown when he first broached the idea in the off-season. But Rickey had convinced enough owners that Brown's protests were overruled.

It was a torturous schedule for any team. Even one as good as the Browns. And with the 49ers now challenging the Browns for the Western Division lead, there were playoff implications.

"With his baseball background, he thought that a football team could play more than one game a week," Brown said of Rickey's idea. "Compounding the problem was a schedule that began on Sunday in New York, followed by a 16-hour flight to Los Angeles, where we played on Thanksgiving Day, and ending on Sunday in San Francisco. Our preparation time was literally sliced in half, and we were given almost no time at all for any injuries to heal."

Brown's plan was to try and build early leads in as many of the games as possible and rest his starters once the outcome was assured. That wasn't a problem in the game against the Yankees, thanks to Motley's superb efforts. The big running back showed his versatility when he turned a short pass from Graham into a 78-yard touchdown in the first quarter, and Motley allowed Brown to take his starters out after a 12-yard touchdown run in the third quarter made it 34–14. The Browns won, 34–21.

The cross-country trip was exhausting, and with such a short week to prepare for a Thursday game, Brown cut corners where he could. Things were going well in the Thanksgiving game against the Dons, with the Browns breaking the game open with a 17-point third quarter in a 31–14 win. But Graham was hit while attempting a pass and suffered stretched knee ligaments that caused him to hobble off the field.

Brown was deeply concerned that Graham wouldn't be able to play against the 49ers in three days, in a game that would, for all practical purposes, decide the divisional championship. And likely the league title, since only the divisional winner advanced to the one-game playoff.

Brown had his team stay north of San Francisco in Sonoma, and there were mineral baths near the team hotel. Graham and most of his teammates bathed in the waters, and actually seemed to feel better. Still, Brown expected that he'd have to use Cliff Lewis to face the 49ers, who went into the game at 11-1, a game behind the 12-0 Browns.

Graham warmed up before the game at Kezar Stadium, still limping badly, and he went up to Brown and said he could play. Brown confided that he didn't want to have Graham play and injure himself further, but Graham was insistent. The players thought Lewis would start, so when they saw Graham hobble onto the field, they were stunned.

The 49ers took a 21–10 lead into the third quarter, and it looked as if the Browns' perfect season—and possibly a playoff bid—would be ruined.

But the Browns scored 21 unanswered points, with Motley scoring a 6-yard touchdown off a Graham pass and then Dub Jones and Edgar Jones scoring off two more passes from the hobbling quarterback. The Browns pulled off the epic comeback and held on for a 31–28 win to remain unbeaten and clinch the division.

"That was one of the doggondest games I ever did see," Brown told reporters afterward. "It was obvious from the start that the 49ers were going to make it a scoring duel. We, fortunately, did the most scoring."

Incredibly, the Browns played a fourth straight road game to finish the season, as they beat Rickey's Dodgers, 31–21, at Ebbets Field to complete a perfect season at 14-0.

Two weeks later, the Browns drubbed the Bills, 49–7, to win their third straight title. And it was Motley yet again serving as the engine for the offense, scoring three touchdowns and further enhancing his legacy as one of pro football's most accomplished runners.

Motley, who led the league in rushing with 964 yards, and Willis, whose defensive dominance was again instrumental in the team's success, had won their third AAFC championship. Willis gave Brown exceptional versatility on defense, thanks to his speed, range, intensity, and an uncanny knack for anticipating where plays would go. While Graham and Motley were often the focus of attention on offense, the understated Willis was at the heart of the defense's exceptional play, with attributes that allowed Brown to employ alignments that hadn't been used before. Willis would become an eventual prototype for a traditional middle linebacker; while effective near the line of scrimmage, his ability to play off the ball and be in position to make plays to either side was a game-changing skill set.

For Motley and Willis, the latest title was an astonishing feat for two men who only three years earlier thought their dreams of playing professional football might never happen.

Let history show that the Browns became the first team in professional football history to finish a season unbeaten and untied, a feat matched only by the 1972 Miami Dolphins. But that piece of history was bittersweet for Brown, because the NFL has not recognized that season in its record books.

* * *

The first sign of trouble for the AAFC came in the 1948 championship game in which the Browns completed their unbeaten season. It was nothing that happened on the field itself, but in the stands.

They were virtually empty.

The team had drawn monstrous crowds during the season, but perhaps because the Bills were only 7–7 and a Cleveland victory seemed all but assured, only 22,981 showed up for the championship game. They were treated to another dominant performance by the league's best club, but Brown began to understand that being such a powerful team might be working against the best interests of the league.

Today's NFL is the country's most popular sport, in large part because parity allows just about any team in any given year to compete for a playoff berth and ultimately the Super Bowl. But Brown's AAFC team was almost too good.

"I learned that for a league to succeed, each team must be given the means to become as competitive as possible," Brown said.

For the first time since the AAFC's formation in 1946, there were informal merger talks with the NFL, as Browns owner Mickey McBride discussed a potential alliance with Giants owner Tim Mara and Steelers owner Art Rooney. NFL commissioner Bert Bell was at least listening to the proposals, if not ready to act on them. But one owner firmly opposed a merger: Washington's George Preston Marshall.

Marshall thumbed his nose at the league, once suggesting the NFL's worst team could beat the AAFC's best.

Brown preferred that the AAFC and NFL join forces to create a two-conference league similar to baseball, with the American League and National League. But the NFL wasn't ready to agree to such a sweeping plan.

Both leagues began to struggle financially in 1949, in large part because they were competing for players and salaries were escalating to unaffordable levels. The AAFC reduced its regular season to twelve games from fourteen, and the NFL had lost its Boston franchise in 1949 after the Yanks left town and the New York Bulldogs were added.

While the owners of both leagues were at a crossroads, public appetite grew for some sort of competition between the NFL and AAFC. A championship game seemed to be the most logical idea, something that was floated by Eagles owner Alexis Thompson after Philadelphia won the NFL title. Thompson and McBride at one point agreed on a playoff, but his fellow owners scuttled it, and Bell chastised Thompson for bringing up the idea, since the NFL seemed determined to outlast the AAFC.

With no breakthrough for a merger, the 1949 season proceeded in much the same fashion as the previous three—with the Browns dominating. They did struggle to force a 28–28 tie with the Bills in the opener, as Graham led a 21-point comeback in the fourth quarter. But they lost only once—to the 49ers at Kezar Stadium—and finished 9-1-2 to again win the Western Division over the rival 49ers.

Interest in the league continued to falter, however, and where the Browns had regularly drawn crowds of sixty thousand and more, attendance dwindled to below thirty thousand for many of its home games. The only game that attracted significant attention was against the 49ers, as 72,189 fans showed up at Cleveland Stadium and were treated to a thrilling 30–28 Cleveland win. But only 16,506 attended the following week's game against the Chicago Hornets, yet another sign that the league was in trouble.

There was a two-round playoff this time, with the Browns beating the Bills and then the 49ers in the championship game. Still, only 22,550 were on hand for the Browns' fourth straight AAFC title, as they beat the 49ers, 21–7. Helping to key the win: a 68-yard touchdown run by Motley in the third quarter.

The Browns agreed to play against a team of AAFC all-stars in Houston in what Texas oilman Glen McCarthy dubbed the "Shamrock Bowl." McCarthy had hoped to get an AAFC franchise, but with the league's imminent shuttering, he believed that staging a well-attended event would cast him in a favorable light with the NFL once it was ready to expand to Texas.

The game was a bust, as only 10,000 fans showed up to see the Browns lose to the all-stars, 12–7. There were also problems beforehand, when it was uncertain whether the Browns' three African-American players—Motley, Willis, and Gillom—as well as all-stars Joe Perry and Buddy Young would be allowed to play. There was also debate about whether Black fans would be able to purchase tickets.

They were eventually allowed in, albeit under dubious circumstances.

"When the powers that be decided to let in a few hundred Negro fans in a Jim Crow section of Rice Stadium to attend the Shamrock Bowl... it was no act of democracy by any means," according to an article in the *Alabama Tribune* on December 30, 1949. "It was really an act afforded by lagging ticket sales at $15 a ticket for every seat in the house. Negroes were put in the east end of the stadium—the farthest corner in the park in a spot where they could not see the scoreboard."

The article from the Associated Negro Press went on to say that "another sidelight to their admittance was the fact that in the announcement, no mention was made of the Rice charter which allegedly bars Negroes from the stadium. Unfortunately, this game set a sad stage for the finale of the All American conference, which actually emancipated the Negro football player from oblivion after college."

Motley said years later he was initially denied entrance into Rice Stadium and had to stand in the pouring rain before stadium employees eventually let him in. And none of the Black players were allowed to stay at the hotel where white players stayed—a hotel owned by McCarthy.

All these troubles were foreshadowing the league's demise: The Shamrock Bowl was the final AAFC event in the league's four-year history, as the NFL decided to accept three of the league's teams—Cleveland, San Francisco, and Baltimore—to begin play in 1950.

* * *

Paul Brown understood that nothing his team had done during its four-year run of championships in the AAFC would convince the NFL the Browns were a legitimate threat now that they had been incorporated into the more established league.

In fact, that sentiment from Marshall's comment about the NFL's worst team being able to beat the AAFC's best—aka the Browns—was shared by many of his fellow owners. They simply didn't blurt it out obnoxiously like Marshall.

But make no mistake; that kind of doubt only served to fuel Brown's competitive temperament.

"I didn't mind the challenges, because we had a few things to prove ourselves after being ridiculed and taunted [by the NFL] for four years," Brown said. "We had only one thing at stake: our honor."

The Browns added several key players in the off-season, including guard Abe Gibron, halfback Rex Bumgardner, defensive end Len Ford, tackle John Sandusky, and fullback Emerson Cole. Ford, who went on to a Hall of Fame career, and Cole were African-American, giving the Browns five Black players—nearly a third of the total in the entire league.

Brown would get the chance to see how his team measured up to the NFL right from the start; commissioner Bert Bell scheduled the Browns to face the NFL's defending champion Eagles at Philadelphia Municipal Stadium.

And Motley and Willis would continue to play central roles in Cleveland's first foray in an NFL that had been highly selective in choosing just the Browns and 49ers from the AAFC to join the more established league. Motley remained one of pro football's most impactful runners, the perfect inside runner with a terrific combination of size, speed and power, and also a team-first temperament that made his bond with Graham so strong.

While Motley was known mostly for his great running skills, it was his blocking that also helped set him apart. He was fierce in protecting Graham, and the quarterback avoided a lot of unnecessary punishment because Motley fended off defensive linemen with the same ferocity that made him such an impactful runner.

Even legendary Browns running back Jim Brown, often considered the greatest player in NFL history, singled out Motley for his all-around ability.

"Playing with Otto Graham, Marion didn't have the same opportunities to carry the ball as the rest of us," Brown said. "But he was a devastating blocker. He was the complete package when it came to blocking and running. On that level, he stands alone."

Willis was the unquestioned leader on defense, and not just because of his speed, quickness, and tackling ability. He was one of the team's most popular players, a man who could earn your trust with a simple smile yet who would sacrifice just about anything for those around him.

"Some athletes are all about themselves, but my father wasn't like that," Bill Willis Jr. said. "Whether you were the chairman of the board of a company or swept up at night, he treated you just the same."

And that was the way he was with his teammates and coaches. He carried out his assignments with the kind of precision that Brown demanded, which was a big reason he had always been one of the coach's favorite players, going back to their days at Ohio State. Brown also didn't like players who drew attention to themselves, and Willis was about as self-effacing a player as there was.

"He didn't want to toot his own horn, and he never did," Mike Brown said of Willis. "He didn't want the spotlight, he didn't feel he was anything special. He never bragged about his role, yet he was the leader and the one who set the pace."

Despite the talent that Brown had on his team heading into its first NFL season, very few people thought the Browns could keep up with the Eagles. Philadelphia coach Greasy Neale was one of those people, and he rarely passed up a chance to publicly deride the Browns as the best team in a minor-league operation.

"We've been taunted and disparaged about playing in an inferior league," Brown told his team. "We've heard that the worst team in the NFL can beat the best in the All-America Conference. There is not only this coming season at stake but four years of our achievement as members of the AAC. I'm asking that you dedicate yourselves more than ever to preserve the reputation the Browns have made."

The Browns had five preseason games to prepare for the start of the regular season, and Brown's regulars played most of the way in every game—a far cry from today's NFL, when starters barely play in the preseason. They won every game over the summer, and Brown had his team playing at a high level even before the games started to count.

His intensity was remarkable.

In a 35–14 win over the Lions in the third exhibition game, the Lions had extended their lead to 28–0 on Motley's 41-yard touchdown run in the third quarter. Brown took his starters out, but after the Lions scored twice in the fourth quarter, Brown put his starters back in. Graham threw a touchdown pass to seal the win.

Still, Neale did not take the Browns seriously. In fact, he didn't send any scouts to the Cleveland preseason games, choosing instead to prepare for the season opener by watching game film from the Browns' 1949 season.

Brown, meanwhile, studied the Eagles' defense in minute detail and came up with an ingenious plan to take advantage of what he saw as some significant weaknesses. First, he sent Bumgardner in motion to force the Eagles into single coverage on the Browns' receivers. That meant that Dub Jones, who had flourished in Brown's offense and become a favorite target of Graham, would have single coverage—a huge advantage for the six-four, 202-pound flanker.

Next, Brown had his offensive linemen spread out the Eagles' defensive line by moving the guards and tackles out—inches at a time—on successive plays. That meant there would be additional running room when the Browns used their inside trap play and the draw, which had become favorites for Brown, especially with the hard-running Motley hitting the gaps.

The Eagles failed to adequately adjust, and the Browns took full advantage.

Late in the first quarter, with the Eagles up 3–0, Graham and Jones went to work. After Jones ran a series of short routes, he told Graham he was ready to beat single coverage on a deep pattern. After running to the outside for what seemed like another short pass, Jones raced upfield, forcing All Pro cornerback Russ Craft to get his feet tangled up. Jones was wide open for Graham's 59-yard pass, which gave the Browns their first touchdown.

"When [Jones] caught Otto's pass," Brown said, "he was 10 yards behind the Eagles' defensive back and easily ran for our first touchdown."

A 21-yard screen pass to Motley on the Eagles' next possession set up another Graham touchdown pass—this time to Lavelli on a play that would never happen in today's NFL. Because the goalposts were on the goal line and thus in the field of play, receivers would occasionally use the posts as part of their patterns. On this play, Lavelli swung around the right post to get away from his defender, and Graham found him wide open in the end zone.

Motley was a star on defense, too. On one Eagles drive deep in Cleveland territory, Brown put Motley in as an extra linebacker. He tackled the Eagles runners on three straight plays, forcing a fourth-and-goal. Motley prepared for what he thought would be another running play, but the Browns felt the Eagles might pass, so the coaches yelled to Motley from the sidelines, "Loosen up, Marion! Loosen up!" They wanted him to play off the line just a bit.

Motley heard the coaches, hesitated a moment and "did the neatest body shimmy I had ever seen because he thought we meant he was too tight and we wanted his muscles looser," Brown said. The coaches cracked up, but it helped ease the tension. The Eagles were stopped once again on fourth down.

Willis was another relentless presence on the Browns' defense, as his speed and strength thwarted an Eagles running attack that was admittedly weakened by the absence of injured star Steve Van Buren.

It was a remarkable performance all the way around, as the Browns outclassed the defending NFL champions in a 35–10 rout.

"Every phase of our offense and our defense was devastating that night," Brown said.

NFL commissioner Bell, who'd once coached and owned the Eagles, visited Brown in the locker room and congratulated the coach, telling Brown he was glad the Browns won because it added credibility to the NFL that a former AAFC team had been so good. Bell told him he'd never seen a team as prepared as the Browns were for that game.

Neale was humiliated, especially after casting so many doubts about the Browns beforehand and taking them far too lightly in his preparations. "Why, all they do is pass and trap, and they're like a basketball team the way they throw the ball around," Brown recalled Neale saying.

"You are the greatest team to ever play football," Bell told Brown afterward.

This was the start of another special season for the Browns, perhaps even more than their unbeaten season two years earlier. With Motley enjoying his best year in the NFL with a league-high 810 yards and fellow offensive stars Graham, Jones, Speedie, and Lavelli playing at the tops of their games, the Browns went 10-2 to finish in a tie with the Giants atop the American Conference. Willis was the team's only defensive player to be selected for the Pro Bowl.

Neale had another crack at beating the Browns in a late-season matchup in Cleveland, but Brown got the better of him once more in a 13–7 win. Neale was fired before the start of the 1951 season.

A week after beating the Eagles, the Browns beat Washington at Griffith Park, 45–21, but not before Motley was ejected after throwing a punch at linebacker Gene Pepper. Motley was fined by the NFL, but Brown paid it and was furious about the circumstances surrounding the incident.

"They can fine Motley all they want, but he won't have to pay. I'll take care of it," Brown said. "How in the world could they put him out of the game when there was a melee involving several players. Motley did take a punch at Pepper and we should have been penalized 15 yards. Motley throughout the first half of the game had been the victim of a number of stray knuckles and elbows, and I can't blame him for losing his temper."

It was also reported that Motley had been subjected to several racist taunts from some of Washington's white players.

Since the Browns and Giants both finished at 10-2, a one-game playoff was held to determine which team would face the National Conference winner in the Championship Game.

The Browns won a coin toss to gain home field advantage, although the windy, frigid conditions at Cleveland Stadium made the going tough for both teams. In a defensive struggle played on a mostly frozen field, the Browns took a 3–0 lead into the fourth quarter when the Giants appeared headed for a victory on a drive deep into Cleveland territory.

At the Browns 36, quarterback Charlie Conerly took the snap and handed off to Gene "Choo Choo" Roberts, who broke into the open field after running around right end. He appeared headed for a sure touchdown, and Willis feared the Browns' playoff hopes were slipping away.

"All I could think of was that number on Roberts's back represented the championship running away from me," Willis said.

"Suddenly, there was no one between [Roberts] and the goal line," Brown said. "Our closest player was 15 yards away, and I was sure Roberts would score. Incredibly, Willis ran him down in the last 20 yards."

Willis got there just in time, tackling Roberts at the Browns' 4.

With more fine play from Willis and his defensive teammates as the series continued, the Browns held the Giants to a field goal to make it 3–3.

On Cleveland's next drive, Brown changed his tactical approach, using a heaping dose of quarterback draws to move the ball down the field. After rushing for 45 yards to get to the Giants' 22 with 58 seconds to play, Groza kicked a 28-yard field goal to make it 6–3.

In the final seconds, Willis and Jim Martin applied heavy pressure on Conerly, who was sacked in the end zone. The Browns won, 8–3, to qualify for the NFL Championship Game against the Rams, who had beaten the Bears in a playoff to decide the National Conference winner.

"The entire game and indeed, the season," Brown said, "had boiled down to Willis's catching Roberts from behind and preventing a touchdown."

There was more excitement to come.

It was the Rams' first visit to Cleveland since the team left the city after the 1945 season, as Dan Reeves's team looked to avenge the previous year's 14–0 loss to the Eagles in the NFL Championship. The Rams' offense was among the best in NFL history, with quarterbacks Bob Waterfield, who'd won a championship for the Rams in their final season in Cleveland in 1945, and Norm Van Brocklin averaging an astonishing 309 passing yards per game. Matched up against Graham, whose reputation was now firmly entrenched after leading the Browns to the title game in his first season in the NFL, this had the makings of an NFL classic.

It was.

The Rams held a 14–13 lead at halftime, and they looked as if they would win the title by building a 28–20 lead heading into the fourth quarter. But Graham engineered an epic comeback, leading the Browns to a touchdown and setting up Lou Groza's game-winning 16-yard field goal with 28 seconds left in a 30-28 victory.

After four straight AAFC titles, the Browns now stood atop an NFL that had once thumbed its nose at what was considered to be an inferior team.

Not anymore.

"It was," Brown said, "the most satisfying football experience of my life."

A few days after winning the title, Brown received a letter from Branch Rickey, his old rival in the AAFC and the man who saw Brown's signings of Motley and Willis as a forerunner to Jackie Robinson breaking baseball's color barrier.

"I want you to know how happy I am that you won the championship," Rickey wrote, "partly because it vindicated the claims of our old league, but mostly because it was you who did it."

* * *

The incredible ride for Motley and Willis continued after that championship run in 1950. They played three more seasons with the Browns, and Cleveland went to the championship every year, albeit losing each time in the title game.

This was the golden age for the Browns franchise, one of the most remarkable runs for any professional team, even if their time in the AAFC might not be fully appreciated. Then again, the fact that the

Browns dominated the NFL after being incorporated into the league in 1950 reflects well on their time during that remarkable four-year run of championships in the rival league.

The Browns won the National Conference every year from 1950 to 1955, and Brown went back to the championship game twice more before being unceremoniously fired by Art Modell after the 1962 season. Brown transformed the game with his visionary concepts on offense, and Motley and Willis were critical components in how that plan was executed.

Motley rushed for 4,720 yards, averaging an incredible 5.7 yards per carry. He scored 31 rushing touchdowns, led the NFL in rushing in 1950, won four titles in the AAFC, led that league in rushing in 1948, and was a member of the NFL's 1940s All-Decade Team, the 75th Anniversary All-Time Team, *and* the 100th Anniversary All-Time Team.

In 1968, he was inducted into the Pro Football Hall of Fame. Right there in his hometown of Canton, Ohio, next door to the high school where he started it all: Canton McKinley.

"The greatest all-around football player there ever was," former 49ers running back Joe Perry said of Motley.

"He was, in my father's opinion, the best all-around fullback ever," Mike Brown said. "He was a great runner, very fast, had a very high yards-per-carry average, but he was also a great pass receiver. He had incredibly soft hands, and with Otto Graham, he was used effectively on screen passes. He was a great pass protector, and he was willing. He didn't back off like some of the guys who tend to think of themselves as great runners."

Legendary *Sports Illustrated* writer Paul Zimmerman once called Motley "the greatest player I'd ever seen" and offered a unique perspective on how his career ought to be viewed.

In his book *A Thinking Man's Guide to Pro Football*, Zimmerman wrote about how hard it was to quantify just how great Motley was.

"There's a statistical table at the end of this chapter detailing the numbers that made up Motley's professional career, but it's a kind of meaningless way of evaluating this remarkable player," wrote Zimmerman, who attended many of Motley's games against the Giants at Yankee Stadium. "It would be like trying to describe a waterfall in terms of gallons per second, or a sunset in terms of light units. Never has there been a set of statistics to measure the force and intensity of a man's hitting power, or his effectiveness as a pass blocker, unless you use a seismograph."

Motley's impact began to wane as the years went on, with age and knee problems gradually diminishing his effectiveness and Brown using Jones and Ken Carpenter for much of the ground game in 1951. Motley was limited to just 273 yards and a touchdown that season, and it was Graham who again starred in an 11-1 first-place run that featured 11 straight wins after an opening-game loss to the 49ers.

In a rematch of the 1950 NFL Championship Game, this time it was the Rams who outlasted the Browns, 24–17, as Motley was held to just 5 carries for 23 yards. The wear and tear was clearly evident.

Motley had a decent year in 1952, running for 444 yards and a touchdown with a 4.3 yards-per-carry average and was still effective in the passing game with 213 receiving yards and 2 touchdowns, as the Browns again advanced to the championship game before losing to the Lions. Motley had his least productive year in Cleveland with just 161 yards in 1953.

Motley showed up at training camp the following year, and the knee problems persisted, to the point where Brown let it be known that this once-great fullback wouldn't be kept on the roster when cuts were made. But just before Brown finalized his team, Motley announced that he would take the year off, figuring time would allow him to recharge if he wanted to keep playing the following year. It was a quasi retirement of sorts, at least as far as Brown was concerned. His comments reflected the notion that Motley was stepping down for good.

"Marion realized that his knee was weak and did not feel that it was coming around," Brown said. "He was one of the truly fine fullbacks in his prime, the type that comes along once in a lifetime. I certainly will never forget some of his runs, and I imagine Cleveland football fans feel the same."

But a year later, at age thirty-five, Motley wanted one more shot, convincing Brown to let him prove there might still be a place for him. As training camp went on, Brown realized Motley simply wasn't the same player and was ready to move on without him. He tried using him at linebacker to make up for the knee problems that were limiting him as a running back, but knew that wasn't much better.

Instead of releasing him outright, Brown found interest from the Steelers, who dealt fullback Ed Modzelewski to Cleveland in exchange for Motley. It was an unceremonious parting, one that left bitter feelings on Motley's part and regret for Brown.

"The way it was done, it left a bad taste in my mouth," Motley said. "Paul Brown was the greatest coach I ever saw, and I liked him. He taught me a lot about life, but I felt he could have handled my trade to Pittsburgh a little different."

Brown never told Motley directly that he was being traded, something he felt badly about for years. Especially because he had known Motley for so long. The same with two other Browns players he'd known since coaching them at Massillon—Horace Gillom and Tommy James.

"I didn't handle the situation well, because I didn't have the courage to tell Marion firsthand that we had traded him," Brown said. "Before I could think of a better solution, he found out from another source, deeply hurting him. Letting him, and later James and Gillom, go were the most difficult things I ever had to do in pro football, and I handled their situations badly. I just could not bring myself to tell these men, whom I had known since they were boys, that their careers were over."

Brown eventually admitted his failures to Motley and his former teammates.

"I know that Tommy would have broken down and cried, and I would have cried right along with him," Brown said. "It would have been better, however, had I suffered those emotional consequences, rather than carry the regrets with me for so long. All these players understand my feelings, and I told them how sorry I was for that action, but it didn't make it any easier at the time."

* * *

Bill Willis made one of the most important tackles in Browns history when he chased down Clarence "Choo Choo" Coleman in the 1950 playoff game against the Giants, helping to secure a place for Cleveland in the championship game against the Rams and allowing the Browns to capture the title in their first year in the NFL.

It was the type of play only an elite performer of his caliber could make, and it was in keeping with Willis's stature as a Pro Bowl selection that year. The Cat had a combination of speed and quickness never before seen at the highest level of the sport, and Willis's decision not to follow in older brother Claude's shoes as a running back surely paid dividends.

Willis remained an integral part of the Browns defense over the following three seasons, earning first-team All Pro status all three years. He helped revolutionize the game as a middle guard, a position that had previously been reserved for bulkier linemen to do the dirty work on the inside running game, as he added a unique dimension with his speed, which is now one of the most highly sought-after qualities in today's interior linemen. Willis was also a forerunner of the middle linebacker position when Brown would back him off the line and allow him to use his range to track down runners.

"I'm a great admirer of Bill Willis, just so impressed at how effective he was at nose guard at his size," said former Bears running back Bobby Watkins. "He was about 215, 220, not a big guy for a nose guard, but his forte was his quickness. He moves so fast that guys who were almost 100 pounds bigger couldn't handle him. He was almost unstoppable, he was so quick."

It was an unconventional journey to the NFL for Willis, who thought in 1946 he was resigned to a career as a coach or, at best, as a Canadian Football League player. But after Brown invited him to join his fledgling AAFC team, it was a perfect match. And even Brown might not have realized just how good a player Willis would become.

In the end, he was one of the team's best, most reliable, and most accomplished players. His teams went to the championship every single year he played from 1946 to 1953, and he was selected as an All Pro or Pro Bowl player every year of his career.

"In my opinion, Bill ranks as one of the outstanding linemen in the history of professional football," Brown said when Willis retired. "He was certainly the fastest, and many coaches use his technique as a model in teaching line play."

Willis was still at the top of his game in his final season in 1953, although a knee injury late in the season had limited his effectiveness. He was again selected first-team All Pro, but at age thirty-two, he felt it was time to step away.

Willis had prepared for this moment. With three young sons—Bill Jr., Clement, and Dan—he felt the time was right for the next phase of his life. He took a job as the assistant director of the Cleveland city recreation department, where he had worked on a part-time basis since 1948. He would go on to earn a master's degree in education.

Brown called the decision "the best for him and his family."

"It's a rather big decision to quit," Willis said in announcing his retirement on March 16, 1954, "but we realize we can't play the game forever."

Chapter 19

LEGACY AND REDEMPTION

Fifteen years after Washington, Strode, Willis, and Motley became the first African-American players to play professional football, there was one last holdout among NFL owners.

George Preston Marshall, who was at the heart of the ban on Black players from 1934 to 1945 and made no secret of his refusal to integrate his Washington franchise, remained staunchly opposed to the idea until his hand was forced by the highest reaches of the United States government.

Just months after John F. Kennedy had been inaugurated on January 20, 1961—when he delivered his famous speech that included the iconic appeal, "And so, my fellow Americans: Ask not what your country can do for you, ask what you can do for your country"—Marshall faced pressure unlike any he'd experienced before.

There had been steady criticism and derision about his refusal to draft or sign Black players. A lot of it. Many in the African-American press consistently took Marshall to task for his policy, and his stubborn reputation as a segregationist had also spilled over into more mainstream media.

Longtime *Washington Post* sports editor and columnist Shirley Povich often tweaked Marshall, whose team was a laughingstock on the field with a combined five wins from 1959 to 1961. The Browns would regularly pummel Marshall's club during the days when Jim Brown starred with Cleveland, and Povich once wrote, "While the Redskins steadfastly refuse to employ Black athletes, their end zone was being integrated four times by Jim Brown." Povich also called the team's colors "inflexibly burgundy, gold and Caucasian."

In 1957, the NAACP staged two-day protests outside a league meeting to draw attention to Marshall's ban on Black players. Influential African-American sportswriter Sam Lacy of the *Baltimore Afro-American* called for a boycott, writing in 1956 that Washingtonians "should now hang their heads in shame" over the all-white team.

Browns Hall of Fame quarterback Otto Graham spoke in 1949 at the Washington Touchdown Club—years before he coached Washington at a time when Marshall was unable to operate the team because of an illness—and referenced the team's refusal to integrate. He suggested that if "the people of this country and the world had the philosophy of our [integrated] Cleveland football team, the prejudiced people could take a tip from our success."

Not Marshall.

The criticism was unrelenting, especially in the late 1950s. Yet Marshall remained unyielding.

Prominent African-American leader Lawrence Oxley, who'd previously worked in the Franklin D. Roosevelt administration as a close advisor to the president, once remarked, "When Dixie is played instead of the Star-Spangled Banner at a football game or any other place, we know what the score is."

Cleveland-based writer Gordon Cobbledick said the team was "spotting their rivals the tremendous advantage of exclusive rights to a whole race." And Black leader E. B. Henderson called for a boycott, saying, "When we note the thousands of young people throughout the South risking life and limb and going to jail rather than submit to the indignity of racial discrimination, why should we be able to deny ourselves the luxury of supporting Marshall's racism?"

Marshall remained defiant.

Before a preseason game against the Rams in 1961, columnist Ridgely Cummings addressed the topic in a piece that appeared in the *Lincoln Heights (CA) Bulletin-News*. In a column written before Washington was due to play the Rams in a preseason game in Los Angeles, she approached Marshall's lead football executive, longtime general manager Dick McCann. She referenced an article in the *Eagle*, a Black-owned weekly newspaper that urged a boycott of the game because Marshall didn't have any African-American players. "I'd known Dick since the days when he was publicity man for the team and had less hesitancy about opening a tender subject," Cummings wrote.

"We won't break the law," McCann said in answer to Cummings's inquiry about whether the team would integrate. "If they pass a law saying we have to have a Negro on the squad, we'll get one."

Cummings then referred to the team's dismal record in recent seasons and suggested that a willingness to sign Black players might help their fortunes on the field.

"There's enough room to go around," McCann replied. "You say there are a lot of good Negro players. Well, there are a lot of good Catholic players, but you don't see them on the Southern Methodist team. There are a lot of good Protestant players, but very few of them go to Notre Dame. Don't worry, if they pass a law, we won't break it."

The backdrop for Cummings's column and other criticism was the increasing pressure brought to bear on Marshall's team by the Kennedy administration, with Interior Secretary Stewart Udall demanding that the club be integrated. Udall sent a letter to Marshall on March 25, 1961, and wrote that the owner was in for "a moral argument with the President and the administration"—and even potential criminal prosecution—if his team continued to practice discrimination.

Udall wrote the letter after issuing a new National Park Service rule to prohibit discrimination by teams using the newly built D.C.

Stadium, located on land leased from the Park Service. The team was due to move to the new stadium in October.

Marshall bristled when he received the letter, and he asked Udall to arrange a meeting with President Kennedy. When asked later if he planned to hire any Black players for the 1961 season, Marshall told reporters, "Our roster is closed. The draft is over."

Udall told Marshall in the letter that the Interior Department was changing its regulations "to harmonize our contract policies with the general anti-discrimination policy enunciated by the President a few days ago."

Marshall had thus met up with a foe he hadn't encountered before: the federal government. Udall had backed Marshall into a corner. Race relations around the country were at a boiling point, with activists using "Freedom Rides" to test a 1960 U.S. Supreme Court ruling that prohibited segregation in bus-terminal restaurants, bathrooms, and waiting areas. In Alabama, one of the buses used as part of the protest was hit with a smoke bomb and activists were beaten by white supremacists.

The NAACP and Congress of Racial Equality (CORE) picketed outside the D.C. Stadium site as well as at the team's exhibition games outside of Washington. Black residents in Washington picketed at the stadium, with some carrying signs that read, "People who can't play together can't live together." Kennedy himself refused an invitation to attend a game at the new stadium.

By July, when Marshall hadn't answered to his demands from the March letter, Udall wrote again demanding Marshall relent. Some of Marshall's business partners with the team, including minority stakeholder Jack Kent Cooke (who would eventually take over as owner), lobbied Marshall to yield to Udall's demands. And owners from other teams urged commissioner Pete Rozelle to intercede. Rozelle initially declined, but after Udall made it clear the government would not change its stance, he went to work trying to convince Marshall to concede. After Rozelle met with Marshall in August, a deal had been brokered. Marshall announced that his team had "no policy against the hiring of football players because of their race" and would consider taking Black players in the draft in December. He suggested Syracuse star running back Ernie Davis as a potential consideration.

Udall agreed to allow the team to play at D.C. Stadium for the 1961 season with the understanding that they would begin to integrate the roster starting in 1962.

Marshall had finally backed down.

His team finished with the worst record in the NFL—1-12-1—and had been a miserable 2-21-3 over the previous two seasons. Washington was assured of the first overall pick in the 1962 draft (which was held on December 4, 1961, in Chicago), and Davis, who had broken Jim Brown's records at Syracuse, was indeed the choice.

But the man who had played a key role in integrating pro football more than fifteen years earlier, and who had made no secret of his enmity toward Marshall, was also interested in Davis.

Paul Brown wanted two former Syracuse stars in his backfield in Cleveland (the other being the legendary Jim Brown). He and Marshall—who had widely divergent views on African-Americans deserving the chance to play in the NFL—held secret talks about a trade. Brown didn't even tell the team's new owner, Art Modell, who had purchased the team less than eleven months earlier for $4 million.

Brown and Marshall, together with Washington head coach and general manager Bill McPeak, worked out a trade: The Browns would acquire the rights to Davis, and Washington would receive running back Bobby Mitchell, who'd already established himself as a fine player, and running back Leroy Jackson, the Browns' eleventh overall pick that year.

Modell said he never knew about the trade until Marshall phoned him.

"I got a call from George Marshall asking me about the deal," Modell once told longtime Cleveland columnist Terry Pluto.

"What trade?" Modell said.

"Mitchell and your No. 1 pick for our No. 1 pick," Marshall said.

Modell was silent.

"Art, aren't you running that franchise?" Marshall said.

"George . . . well . . . I don't know," Modell said.

"Art, never let that happen again," Marshall told him. "You are the owner. You own the franchise. It's yours."

The incident set off a chain of events that would eventually prompt Modell to fire Brown after the 1962 season.

Davis never played for the Browns. He was diagnosed with leukemia in the summer of 1962 and died May 18, 1963. His condition briefly improved during the 1962 season, and Modell found doctors who would clear Davis to play. But Brown refused out of concern for the player's health.

A few games into the season, Modell again pressed the issue with Brown and urged him to put Davis in a game. Brown was so concerned that he called Rozelle, who agreed with Brown. Modell finally relented, but the damage was done.

"From that time forward," Brown said, "the Paul Brown–Art Modell relationship really went into the deep freeze."

On January 7, 1963, Modell fired Brown.

And as for Marshall's former general manager, Dick McCann, who became executive director of the Pro Football Hall of Fame in 1962: The Professional Football Writers of America had named its career achievement award—the highest honor for a writer—after McCann since 1969, two years after his death. After being informed in April 2021 of McCann's affiliation with Marshall and his pushback against pressure for the team to integrate sixteen years after the first Black players rejoined the NFL, the PFWA decided to take McCann's name off the award. The honor is now named after former longtime *Pittsburgh Courier* columnist and editor Bill Nunn Jr., who went on to become a valued personnel executive with the Steelers.

(Keyshawn here: Congratulations to Bob for winning this lifetime achievement award in 2021!)

* * *

After Marshall finally backed down from his pledge to never hire African-American players, Washington showed improvement with the additions of Mitchell and Jackson. The team had also signed other Black players, including Ron Hatcher, who had been the first African-American player to sign with Washington, and guard John Nisby, a former Steelers standout who immediately improved his new team's line.

Mitchell developed into a star, helping his team improve to 5-7-2 in his first season and going on to a Hall of Fame career and an eventual role as the team's assistant general manager.

It was a difficult transition for Mitchell, though, as he dealt with "a great deal of racial discrimination from the fans and the Washington community." He didn't put himself at the same level as Jackie Robinson—"I wasn't quite as tough as Jackie," he said, but added that the racist comments "affected me greatly, and I haven't forgotten them."

Mitchell, who died in 2020, referred to Marshall as "a nice man" and said he "never came across to me as a bigot or showed any behavior in that manner."

Nisby had a different take. "I never appreciated that man at all because of the stand he took on Blacks prior to my arrival here," he said. "My relationship with the front office wasn't really that great."

Marshall's health went into decline soon after his team was integrated. He underwent hernia surgery in August 1962, suffered a cerebral thrombosis, and later developed a heart condition, diabetes, and arteriosclerosis. Marshall was unable to operate the club on a day-to-day basis after 1963. He died at age seventy-two on August 10, 1969.

* * *

The team Marshall left behind would be unrecognizable to him if he were to see it today.

For starters, the team's bigoted nickname is gone; it is now simply the Washington Football Team after years of protests convinced current team owner Daniel Snyder, who once vowed never to change the name, to do just that.

The monument erected for Marshall was torn down and his name was stripped from the team's Ring of Honor at FedEx Field. The stadium's lower seating bowl is no longer called the George Preston Marshall Level. It is now called the Bobby Mitchell Level.

Before the 2020 season, the team hired head coach Ron Rivera, who is of Puerto Rican and Mexican heritage. He became the first minority coach in team history.

Martin Mayhew, a former Washington defensive back, was named general manager in 2021, becoming the first African-American to hold that position with the club.

Doug Williams, now a team executive, is forever known as a hero to Washington Football Team fans for becoming the first African-American quarterback to win the Super Bowl, as he led Coach Joe Gibbs's team to victory over the Denver Broncos in Super Bowl XXII after the 1987 season.

It would have been simply unimaginable for Marshall to have a Black quarterback on any of his teams.

And perhaps even more unlikely: On August 17, 2020, Jason Wright was named the WFT's president, becoming the first African-American team president in NFL history.

* * *

Jason Gomillion Wright was on a Zoom call with his client, friend and mentor, Dr. Michael Lomax, CEO of the United Negro College Fund. The two were discussing a variety of business matters, with Wright acting in his role as a management consultant with McKinsey & Company.

The subject turned to Wright's middle name, by which Lomax almost always referred to him.

"Whether you like it or not," Lomax told him, "this makes you a permanent part of any movement on race in this country, and you're going to have to own that. You can't run from it."

Weeks later, Wright became president of a team once owned by an avowed segregationist.

Wright was given the middle name Gomillion in honor of Charles Gomillion, a Tuskegee University professor who was a plaintiff in a landmark voting rights case. Gomillion helped lead a boycott in 1957 after an Alabama state senator, Samuel Martin Engelhardt Jr., the executive secretary of the White Citizens Council of Alabama, drew up legislation that drastically changed the boundaries of voting districts that heavily skewed toward white candidates—a process known as gerrymandering. The move excluded most Black residents from being able to vote. After the dismissal of Gomillion's challenge, a decision that was upheld by the Court of Appeals in the Fifth Circuit in New Orleans, Gomillion took his case to the nation's highest court.

The Supreme Court ruled in favor of Gomillion, striking down the redistricting as illegal and paving the way toward the landmark Voting Rights Act of 1965.

Many of Wright's relatives were educators and civil rights activists, and carrying the middle name of such an important figure has always kept Wright mindful of his and his family's legacy.

One of the people Gomillion impacted most: Lomax.

"I learned way more about Charles Gomillion through Dr. Lomax than I had before," Wright said. "I learned more about who he was as a person, how he mentored and developed people, how he saw Dr. Lomax as someone worth investing in, and that is a very inspiring thing for me."

Football and race intersected in a profound way early in Wright's life, and the team once owned by Marshall was a central part of it.

"My knowledge of this franchise went back to Doug Williams as the first Black Super Bowl winning quarterback, and it's tied to my personal history," he said. "My dad is from east Texas, my whole family is from Dallas—generations of civil rights activists and Black college and high school educators there. They were also devoted Cowboys fans growing up, and that's a rabid rivalry."

That all changed when Joe Gibbs anointed Williams as his starting quarterback before the 1987 NFL playoffs.

"My family switched allegiances that season once Doug Williams became the starting quarterback for the team, which anyone who is part of that rivalry understands that's a big deal," Wright said. "What he represented for them in terms symbolically of opportunity for Black folks came at a time when doors were just starting to crack open in many different industries and many different areas of the country. You could now live and work and breathe as a Black person safely—or feeling more safely. Something was taking place in the culture at the time, and my family orienting around that is as far back as I go with this club."

Wright grew up in southern California and was a running back at Diamond Bar High School, where he broke many of the rushing records set by… Kenny Washington's grandson, Kraig. Wright went on to play at Northwestern and then had a seven-year career in the NFL. After his career ended, he earned his master's in business administration at the University of Chicago Booth School of Business and became a consultant at McKinsey & Company.

It wasn't until he was hired by the Washington Football Team that he understood just how far back the roots of racism went in the franchise.

"I learned about the deeper history, going back to Bobby Mitchell being the first Black player on this team, but us being the last team to integrate across the NFL and the political machinations that put pressure to make it happen," he said. "It wasn't like the light came on and we decided to jump in. I learned about the deep bravery of Bobby Mitchell and that first set of folks here and what Bobby Mitchell ended up representing for this city—a very Black city—at that moment. I got acquainted with the richer, deeper, more complicated history."

One of Wright's most trusted advisors: Doug Williams, who has been an executive with the team since 2014.

"My dad is so excited for me, but the thing that he's most excited about is that I get to talk to Doug Williams," Wright said.

Williams's experience has been invaluable to the team's president.

"The strength that he drew from the Black community, the way he found his own personal resilience against that seen and unseen pressure of people hoping he would fail, his ability to navigate the media with grace and poise and integrity," Wright said. "It's that depth of wisdom that I absolutely need to help the Washington Football Team be the sort of franchise we want to be."

While there might appear to be extraordinary pressure on Wright in his new role, that's not what weighs on him.

"If I were to feel any pressure because of being the first Black president of an NFL franchise," he said, "I would feel it because my ancestors were slaves in this nation and gave their very lifeblood to give opportunities to the next generation. My parents sacrificed their opportunities to do the same. The history of the team, that's not putting any additional pressure on me. Someone else can absorb that pressure."

Wright does, however, find it interesting how very different things are with Washington now than they were under Marshall.

"I think God and the universe have a way of orchestrating things," he said. "I think it provides an interesting opportunity for a narrative of redemption and what it means to quickly accelerate from the back of the pack to the front."

Chapter 20

THE SINS OF THE GRANDFATHERS

More than sixty years after his first—and last—season as a two-way tackle with the then Pittsburgh Pirates, Ray Kemp had returned to the sidelines of the iconic Steelers team for a pregame coin toss. The Steelers were honoring their 1933 team to commemorate their first season in franchise history, and Kemp, at age eighty-six and one of the three surviving members of the team, served as a Steelers captain.

Art Rooney II, the grandson of Steelers founder Art Rooney Sr., was there to meet Kemp at Three Rivers Stadium for the ceremony, and the two shared a warm exchange.

The subject of what happened to Kemp after that season never came up.

"I wasn't able to sit down and have a heart-to-heart conversation, but he never expressed any kind of animosity to me," Rooney said. "I'm sure it wasn't something he felt good about, but it didn't seem like he had any lingering animosity toward the team or the family. In fact, he was really appreciative of being part of that when we brought him back."

Kemp was indeed appreciative of the honor.

"I was the first Black to be on a new NFL team [and] I have to pat Art

Rooney [Sr.] on the back for giving me an opportunity to be a pioneer," Kemp said in an interview with Ed Bouchette of the *Pittsburgh Post-Gazette.*

Kemp was far less understanding when he was not asked back in 1934. Kemp and Cardinals running back Joe Lillard were the last two African-Americans to be on NFL rosters in 1933, and there were no Black players in the league until 1946, when public pressure led the Rams to sign Kenny Washington and Woody Strode.

"I was upset at the time," Kemp said in a 1978 interview. "It wasn't the fact that I was going to be out of professional football that hurt. Back then, pro football was pretty loosely organized and you could only make about a hundred dollars a game. In fact, people used to look down at you for being a football player. What hurt me, though, was that I couldn't participate."

Time softened Kemp's anger and frustration, and when he met with Rooney's grandson in 1994, there was no ill will. But for the Rooney family itself, there had been a stain on NFL history.

"My grandfather, in the one glaring mistake of his career, did not challenge the unofficial agreement among NFL owners to ban Black players," Jim Rooney wrote in his 2020 book, *A Different Way to Win: Dan Rooney's Story.* He added, "The desperation generated by the Great Depression had undoubtedly given rise to an increase in racism...That long detachment from Black players was a marked incongruity for my grandfather, who otherwise had a history of working with the Black sports communities in baseball and boxing."

The ban on Black players, though never formally approved or codified in the league's constitution, is nevertheless an undeniable truth. And a blight on the league's legacy, especially for a sport in which approximately 70 percent of the current players are African-American.

But for the family-owned NFL franchises that were a part of the twelve-year ban on Black players, their awareness of and yearslong response to an era defined in large measure by institutional racism have resulted in a push toward inclusiveness and diversity. It is not a coincidence that Rooney was appointed by NFL commissioner Roger Goodell as chairman of the league's Workplace Diversity Committee; the Rooney family name is synonymous with the league's emphasis on improving diversity hiring, even if there is still much work to be done, particularly in the hiring of Black, indigenous, and people of color (BIPOC) head coaches.

It was Rooney's father, Dan, architect of the Rooney Rule that, beginning in 2003, requires all teams to interview BIPOC candidates for head coaching positions. The measure has since been expanded over the years to include lead football executives, team presidents, and offensive and defensive coordinators.

Dan Rooney also made one of the most important hires in franchise history, a move that helped set the course for the team's 1970s dynasty period, during which they won four Super Bowl titles. One of the most frequent critics of the Steelers, particularly Art Rooney Sr., whose teams struggled for years, was *Pittsburgh Courier* sports editor and columnist Bill Nunn. The *Courier* was one of the most influential African-American newspapers in the country, and Nunn routinely pushed the professional leagues—particularly baseball and football—to use more Black players.

Nunn had paid particular attention to football programs at historically Black colleges and universities around the country, and started a "Black College All-America" team in 1950. The Rooney family, particularly Art's oldest son, Dan, took note of the extensive coverage Nunn provided, and the two met in 1967. Nunn told Rooney in no uncertain terms that the Steelers—as well as almost every other NFL team—were missing out on a deep pool of talent. Rooney agreed and hired him as a scout, giving him a full-time job two years later.

Nunn relied on his extensive contacts at the HBCUs and went to work casting a net for players who could help the perennially underachieving team. And he wasn't beyond a little trickery when he needed it. Like the time he and a handful of other scouts went to Alabama A&M for wide receiver John Stallworth's predraft workout in 1974. It was a rainy day, and Stallworth ran a disappointing 4.7 in the 40-yard dash—slow by any measure for a wide receiver.

But after watching film on Stallworth that his coaches provided, Nunn pretended to be ill and told scouts from other teams who often traveled together to go on without him. He also kept the film, promising he'd make copies to distribute to the other scouts.

Well, he never did copy that tape, and Pittsburgh took Stallworth in the fourth round. He enjoyed a fourteen-year career with the Steelers, helping them win four championships and earning induction into the Hall of Fame in 2002.

Stallworth wasn't alone in a Class of '74 that had Nunn's fingerprints all over it. Wide receiver Lynn Swann, linebacker Jack Lambert, and center Mike Webster were also in that draft class. And it was Nunn who convinced undrafted free agent safety Donnie Shell to sign with the Steelers the same year. And Hall of Fame defensive end "Mean" Joe Greene was drafted in 1969, Nunn's first year as a full-time Steelers executive.

"Bill was certainly a major force in really shaping the team that became the great team of the 1970s and won all those Super Bowls," Art Rooney II said. "That's part of our history. That's an important part of our history."

In many ways, Dan Rooney learned from his father, Art Sr., what *not* to do in building a team. Which meant creating a more diverse culture, which Art Sr. had failed to do, in part because of pressure from other owners who would not use Black players in the 1930s and '40s.

"The Chief [Art Sr.] did things that were important, but he did them because they were the right thing to do, whereas my dad didn't mind pushing it a step further," Jim Rooney said. "[Dan Rooney] didn't get in your face and tell you you were wrong, but he wasn't afraid to say no, this is what we need to do and this is the right thing to do. The Chief went along with the NFL and put his time and energy into other things.

"The Chief was a boxing promoter, and in those days, boxing was brutal for Black fighters," Rooney said. "Black fighters were getting killed. It was merciless. Art Rooney's promotions were considered to be some of the best for African-American boxers. They loved to fight under his promotions. He got referees that were fair and judges that were fair. There is ample evidence to show that he really missed the boat with [integration in] the NFL, but he really was a pioneer in sports that were much more relevant to the African-American community at the time."

Art Rooney II also noted that the Chief was heavily involved in Negro League baseball.

"He was a financial backer of the Negro League baseball teams in Pittsburgh," Rooney said.

But there were regrets about not having African-American football players on his Steelers teams.

"I knew he was comfortable having a Black player on the first team," Rooney said, referring to Ray Kemp, "and I'm sure it was a difficult time for him [not having Black players with the Steelers], just because of his background, being involved in the Negro Leagues and in boxing."

Joining Art Rooney II on the diversity committee: the grandsons of owners of the New York Giants (John Mara), Arizona Cardinals (Michael Bidwill), and Chicago Bears (George McCaskey)—three other flagship NFL teams that also had no Black players on their rosters for a prolonged period of time.

"I think we're not close to where we should be [with BIPOC head coach hires], given the makeup of the players in the league," Mara said.

"It's been an issue for the commissioner and the diversity committee for a number of years. I think we'll get there, just not as fast as many of us would like. There's certainly a good-faith effort to be more inclusive in the hiring decisions we make, not only with coaches and general managers, but assistant coaches as well."

While it is a fact that no Black players were in the NFL from 1934 to 1945, Mara questions whether there was any sort of agreement to disallow African-Americans from the league. "I know that it's been reported there was a tacit agreement, but I'm not sure that was the case, to be honest," he said. "I am not naïve enough to think there may have been some clubs that had their own policy, but I do not believe there was any such agreement in place across the board."

When Washington and Strode signed with the Rams in 1946, Giants founder Tim Mara, who had never had a Black player on his team since its founding in 1925, grasped the importance of what was about to happen and expressed a willingness to change, even if he was somewhat defensive about the league's exclusion of African-Americans between 1933 and 1945. "We can't lose on that move," Mara told *Pittsburgh Courier* columnist Wendell Smith in a June 1, 1946, article. "Both are good football players and both will prove to be real attractions. I am sure we will get thousands of more Negro fans to attend the games at the Polo Grounds this year because they will have an added interest in the league."

Mara added, "The signing of the two Negro stars couldn't be called sensational... Why, we have had Negro players in this league before. Joe Lillard, Paul Robeson, and Duke Slater were on teams in this league. They got along all right, too. I don't expect Washington and Strode to have any trouble. They will just be two more football players in the league."

Asked if he would be interested in signing a Black player, he responded, "I certainly am interested. In fact, I am interested in any good football player. I don't care what his color or nationality is."

Two years later, Mara signed the team's first African-American player—

defensive back Emlen Tunnell, who joined the team in 1948 and became the first Black player to be selected for the Hall of Fame in 1967. Tunnell played with the Giants from 1948 to 1958 and then with the Packers from 1959 to 1961 and was a six-time first-team All Pro who played in nine Pro Bowls. Tunnell, who served in the U.S. Coast Guard from 1943 to 1946, received the Silver Lifesaving Medal for heroism after rescuing a shipmate in a torpedo attack and rescuing another who had fallen into the ocean.

John Mara got to know Tunnell when the former defensive back served as a Giants assistant coach from 1963 to 1974.

"If I had to pick figures in our team's history, who my favorites were, Emlen Tunnell would probably be number one," Mara said. "He was everybody's favorite assistant coach. My brothers and I spent summers at training camp and we were ball boys and we'd be assigned to different position groups. He was so much fun to be around, just a very personable, warm-hearted, funny guy. He loved being a part of the Giants, and he had such a personable way about him. He was friendly to everyone he met. Nobody ever said a negative word about him."

Mara was one of the last people Tunnell spoke to before he died on July 23, 1975. He was just fifty-one.

"We were at training camp the night he died, watching television in the lounge," Mara said. "I remember him getting a soda out of the machine, and we sat there and watched TV. I went to bed, and later they told me he died. It was surreal. It took me a long time to believe that he was gone... just such a big part of our lives."

Tunnell died of a heart attack, his second in less than a year.

For George McCaskey, the grandson of Bears founder George Halas, promoting diversity in his organization is deeply meaningful. And he struggles with the team's past in trying to determine why there were no Black players on the Bears until running back Eddie Macon joined the team in 1952.

"We don't know all that went into the decisions they made and the reasons for those decisions," he said. "But what it comes down to for me with George Halas is that he could have signed an African-American player to the Bears roster, and why he didn't is a puzzle to me."

McCaskey admits he wonders what might have been.

"Could [Halas] have done more? Yes," McCaskey said. "But he did make some significant contributions to promote race relations."

As time went by, Halas integrated his team more fully, and the Bears became central to the issue of race relations when the owner-coach listened to an idea presented by his son-in-law, Ed McCaskey, who was married to Halas's daughter, Virginia.

Ed suggested before the 1967 season that running backs Gale Sayers and Brian Piccolo become roommates—a first in the NFL, which never had interracial roommates. Halas listened and agreed and then paired Sayers, the spectacular running back and kick returner out of Kansas, and Piccolo, the undrafted running back out of Wake Forest.

"[Ed McCaskey] took it to the Old Man [Halas], and the Old Man could have said, 'We're not going to do that,'" George McCaskey said, using his grandfather's nickname. "But he embraced it and endorsed it and implemented it, and it's well documented that Gale Sayers proudly said that he loved George Halas."

After a sometimes difficult adjustment period, Sayers and Piccolo eventually became best friends, driving one another toward becoming as good as they could possibly be and providing the NFL with an important example of how racial harmony could work.

During the 1968 off-season, as Sayers was recovering from a career-threatening knee injury, Piccolo helped him through a torturous rehab, and Sayers, determined to rush for 1,000 yards, did just that the following season.

Piccolo himself appeared healthy going into training camp in 1969, but he'd battled a persistent cough during the season. Tests revealed that Piccolo had embryonal cell carcinoma in a large tumor in his chest cavity. He would undergo surgery at Memorial Sloan-Kettering Cancer Center in New York the following week, and Sayers tearfully broke the news to his teammates.

The tumor was removed in a four-and-a-half-hour operation, and Piccolo underwent chemotherapy. He resumed working out in January 1970. But by February, he discovered a large lump on his chest, and an X-ray revealed spots in his left lung. He underwent further surgery, including the removal of his lung, but the cancer continued to spread.

McCaskey went to visit Piccolo in the hospital, and after breaking down in tears at his bedside, Piccolo said, "Don't worry, Big Ed, I'm not afraid of anything. Only [Ray] Nitschke."

On June 16, 1970, at age twenty-six and with a wife and three daughters, Piccolo died.

His story became the subject of a book, *Brian Piccolo: A Short Season*, by Jeannie Morris and was made into a feature film, *Brian's Song*. Gale Sayers wrote about Piccolo in his autobiography, *I Am Third*.

Less than a month before Piccolo died, Sayers was presented with the George S. Halas Courage Award by the Professional Football Writers of America at a banquet in New York. Sayers paid tribute to his gravely ill teammate.

"He has the heart of a giant and that rare form of courage that allows him to kid himself and his opponent—cancer," Sayers said. "He has the mental attitude that makes me proud to have a friend who spells out the word 'courage' twenty-four hours a day, every day of his life. You flatter me by giving me this award, but I tell you that I accept it for Brian Piccolo. It is mine tonight, it is Brian Piccolo's tomorrow.

"I love Brian Piccolo, and I'd like all of you to love him, too," Sayers said through tears. "Tonight, when you hit your knees, please ask God to love him."

George McCaskey has tried to further the vision his parents shared when he was growing up in the Chicago suburbs.

"I would say both of my parents were certainly progressives in race relations," McCaskey said. "When I was growing up, this was during the 1960s, a very difficult time in our country. They would have African-American players over to our house for barbecue or whatever to get them acclimated to Chicago and to make them feel welcome. It was a fairly regular thing for us as kids. A little bit of a curiosity for the neighborhood kids in our all-white neighborhood, but I think they recognized that kind of thing was important to do, and I think my dad recognized that it was an important thing for the Bears to do."

McCaskey is also a member of the NFL's Workplace Diversity Committee, and takes his mission seriously. That he collaborates with fellow third-generation owners is also significant.

"I don't know if it's one of those things that just happened to come about, but I'm honored to serve with those gentlemen, because I have the utmost respect for all of them and for the other members of the diversity committee," he said.

Michael Bidwill is the grandson of Chicago Cardinals owner Charles Bidwill, who had been part owner of Halas's Bears team before purchasing Chicago's other NFL team for $50,000.

The Cardinals won the league championship in 1947—the last time they've won an NFL title—but Charles never got to enjoy it; he had died of pneumonia months earlier. After his death, Violet Bidwill took control of the team, becoming the first woman to own a professional sports franchise.

It is that piece of history that provided a lasting imprint on her grandson, Michael. His father, William, was in high school when Charles died. William eventually took over as the team's principal owner.

"My father saw my grandmother become the first principal owner in the NFL, and she ran the team for the next fifteen years," Michael Bidwill said. "I think from his perspective, this was sort of normal, that anybody could do things if given the opportunity, and then I saw that growing up."

The Cardinals became the first team in NFL history to simultaneously have an African-American coach—Dennis Green—and a Black general manager—Rod Graves. Adele Harris was one of the first women to serve in an executive capacity for an NFL team. Michael Bidwill hired attorney Bob Wallace, the first African-American to negotiate contracts in NFL history.

Michael was given the Paul J. Tagliabue Award in 2019 by the Fritz Pollard Alliance for his work on promoting workplace diversity; the award is named after the former NFL commissioner. "I was blown away and really honored, because Paul Tagliabue is another person who led in this area, and as a young lawyer coming into the league, he was a mentor," Bidwill said. "We've had several conversations about how important his voice was and how he handles the room. There were a lot of complex issues that he was able to navigate the league through."

Bidwill acknowledges there is work to be done to improve the diversity record, especially with BIPOC head coach hirings. It's one reason he instituted the Bill Bidwill Fellowship, which awards internships to BIPOC coaches with an offensive specialty to try and build a stronger pipeline that will ultimately result in more African-Americans finding opportunities as quarterbacks, coaches, offensive coordinators, and ultimately head coaches.

Bound together by history, the four third-generation owners—whose grandfathers are all in the Pro Football Hall of Fame—share a collective sense of responsibility to do what is right. And while they weren't responsible for one of the darkest times in NFL history, they push for the common good moving forward.

"I think all four of us take a very long view of the game of football," Bidwill said, "and our responsibilities for making sure this game is great, but also making the right types of decisions."

* * *

The video message from Roger Goodell was posted on the NFL's Twitter account on June 5, 2020. It was an unexpected message from the longtime commissioner, yet it produced shock waves around the sports world as the words came out of his mouth.

"We, the National Football League, condemn racism and the systematic oppression of Black people," Goodell said. "We, the National Football League, admit we were wrong for not listening to NFL players earlier and encourage all to speak out and peacefully protest. We, the National Football League, believe Black Lives Matter."

The video was posted less than twenty-four hours after more than a dozen of the league's most successful African-American players, including Chiefs All Pro quarterback Patrick Mahomes, the reigning Super Bowl MVP, delivered a powerful video message of their own. The players pushed the owners—and Goodell—to acknowledge past wrongs—starting with the peaceful protests of players bringing attention to police brutality and systemic racism in America. That movement had been initiated by former 49ers quarterback Colin Kaepernick's decision to kneel during the National Anthem in 2016. Mahomes was joined by Texans quarterback Deshaun Watson, Browns receiver Odell Beckham Jr., Giants running back Saquon Barkley, Cardinals receiver DeAndre Hopkins, and others to draw further attention to the issue in the aftermath of the brutal killing of George Floyd by a Minneapolis police officer. Another player in that video: Saints All Pro receiver Michael Thomas.

"It's been ten days since George Floyd was brutally murdered," Thomas said at the start of the seventy-one-second video.

"How many times do we need to ask you to listen to your players?" Chiefs safety Tyrann Mathieu said.

"What will it take?" Cardinals receiver DeAndre Hopkins then asked.

"For one of us to be murdered by police brutality?" Browns receiver Jarvis Landry said.

Many of the players then ask:

"What if I was George Floyd?"

They invoke the names of other Black men and women killed by police, including Breonna Taylor, Ahmaud Arbery, and Eric Garner.

The video closes with a message from the players that they "will not be silenced." And they demanded that the NFL condemn "racism and the systemic oppression of Black people... We, the National Football League, admit wrong in silencing our players from peacefully protesting... We, the National Football League, believe Black lives matter."

Thomas initiated the video after getting in contact with Bryndon Minter, a member of the NFL's social media team who helped produce the piece.

On May 25, Floyd was killed during an arrest after allegedly passing a counterfeit $20 bill. Derek Chauvin, a white officer, knelt on Floyd's neck for nine minutes and twenty-nine seconds. The forty-six-year-old Floyd repeatedly told Chauvin, "I can't breathe," and at one point called for his mother. "Please, please, please," he begged the officer.

Floyd was pronounced dead at Hennepin County Medical Center ninety minutes after the encounter.

The murder led to protests around the country and around the world, with millions of people taking to the streets to express their outrage. The video posted by the players was another expression of that grief and anger, but also a direct challenge to the league to do more about drawing attention to racism in America.

That Goodell responded so swiftly and so apologetically for the league's insensitivity during the early period of Kaepernick's protest triggered a severe backlash among many fans—up to and including President Donald J. Trump, who constantly criticized players for taking a knee during the anthem and had previously prodded team owners to "get that son of a bitch off the field."

In some respects, this was one of the most transformative moments in NFL history, even though it had nothing to do with what happened on the field.

Much has changed in pro football since the fledgling days of integration in the modern NFL, but Goodell's admission that the league had failed to take the players more seriously when they first addressed racial injustice was an unmistakable shift in the league's attitude moving forward.

Goodell, who told none of his fellow owners about his plans to make the video answering the players' call for him to make the Black Lives Matter acknowledgment, expanded on his mea culpa with a public apology to Kaepernick.

"I wish we had listened earlier, Kaep, to what you were kneeling about and what you were trying to bring attention to," Goodell said. "We had invited him in several times to have the conversation, to have the dialogue. I wish we had the benefit of that, we never did. We would have benefited from that, absolutely."

Kaepernick was shunned by the NFL after his release from the 49ers in March 2017, and it wasn't hard to know the reason why. No coaches, general managers—or owners—were willing to take a chance at inviting more polarizing reactions.

In fact, the owners had passed a measure in 2018 requiring players to stand for the anthem or else face a fine. That decision was roundly criticized by players and eventually led to discussions between the two sides that led to the league investing millions of dollars in social justice initiatives.

But it was a long and contentious awakening before Kaepernick's original message was truly understood. Look back now at what he said were the roots of his protest, and it makes sense.

Not then, however.

"People don't realize what's really going on in this country," Kaepernick told reporters in August 2016, explaining his decision to protest during the anthem. "There are a lot of things that are going on that are unjust. People aren't being held accountable. And that's something that needs to change. That's something that this country stands for: freedom, liberty, and justice for all. And it's not happening for all right now. There's a lot of things that need to change. One specifically? Police brutality. There's people being murdered unjustly and not being held accountable. People are being given paid leave for killing people. That's not right. That's not right by anyone's standards."

He made it clear then that his protest wasn't intended as a criticism of the military, even though many Americans took it that way.

"I have great respect for the men and women that have fought for this country," he said. "I have family, I have friends that have gone and fought for this country. And they fight for freedom, they fight for the people, they fight for liberty and justice, for everyone. That's not happening. People are dying in vain because this country isn't holding their end of the bargain up, as far as giving freedom and justice, liberty to everybody. That's something that's not happening. I've seen videos, I've seen circumstances where men and women that have been in the military have come back and been treated unjustly by the country they have fought for, and have been murdered by the country they fought for, on our land. That's not right."

Goodell eventually understood and accepted the deeper meaning behind players taking a knee or raising a fist in the air during the anthem. He understood that the entire meaning behind Kaepernick's protests and similar ones used by other players was to focus on the very reasons behind the killing of George Floyd and other African-Americans in confrontations with police. It didn't change the fact, however, that Kaepernick never received a meaningful chance to play again.

"It is not about the flag," Goodell said. "The message here, and what our players are doing, is being mischaracterized. These are not people who are unpatriotic, they're not disloyal, they're not against our military. In fact, many of those guys were in the military, and they're a military family. What they were trying to do was exercise their right to bring attention to something that needs to get fixed."

The protests that erupted throughout the country after Floyd's killing intensified the league's push to find common cause with the players.

"It was horrific to see that play out on the screen," Goodell said of Floyd's death. "There was a part of me that said, 'I hope people realize that's what the players were protesting.' And that's what's been going on in our communities. You see it now on television, but that's been going on for a long, long time. And that's where we should have listened sooner."

While Goodell's video response to the message delivered by many of his star players was stunning in its own right, especially considering the league's clumsy handling of the anthem protests, it was not a difficult decision for the commissioner. He was at his vacation home in Maine when the players' video was posted, and the next day, he told some of the league's executive vice presidents during a regularly scheduled Zoom call that he was going to address the players' video with one of his own.

He knew it would be criticized by many of the league's fans, especially those who spoke out against the players' protests during the anthem. That included President Trump, the loudest critic of those forms of expression.

But he learned at an early age that making unpopular decisions was a risk worth taking when the cause was just.

"My father had a huge influence in my life, and I spoke about it with my employees that day [when making the video]," he said. "I told them I grew up in Washington, DC, during the 1960s and civil rights were a big part of the '60s, a big part of my father's life. It's a big part of who I am, and to me, it's very natural. I believe in people. I believe in respect and making sure people are treated correctly. I just don't see a place for hatred."

Charles Goodell was a four-time U.S. congressman from upstate New York who was appointed by Gov. Nelson Rockefeller to serve the remainder of the term of Robert F. Kennedy, who was murdered on June 5, 1968. A moderate Republican, Goodell went against his party in calling for an end to the Vietnam War, a decision he knew might have serious ramifications on his political career.

"When he was in the Senate and he was about to introduce legislation to end the Vietnam War, he knew that he was going to have a tremendous reaction to this from the Nixon administration," Roger Goodell said. Charles gathered his sons for a conversation about the impending legislation.

"The bottom line is that this may very well end my political career," he told them. "But it's the right thing to do."

"I think that had an impression on all of us," Roger said. "And that is to stand up and do the right thing, regardless of the consequences. The right thing to do is the right thing to do, and you do it."

In 1970, Charles Goodell was defeated in the Senate race by conservative James L. Buckley.

"You're going to be judged on what you do and don't do, and they both speak volumes," Roger Goodell said. "Living our values and talking about our values and respect for everyone is something that is important in everything we do. That was not difficult. Having people speak up, whether it's President Trump or others, standing up for what we believe in is totally natural and something we're capable of doing. We don't normally jump into political debates, but speaking of our values or principles is something we're comfortable in doing.

"In fact, the last several years, in working with our players, we've been deeply involved in these issues and understand them a lot better than we did four or five years ago," he said. "We've done a lot of work to try to address this, so we felt we were speaking from a position of strength there."

Floyd's death prompted some owners to dig deeper into the roots of systemic racism, with McCaskey entering into a monthslong period of soul searching. It also prompted him to try to gain a better understanding of why pro football didn't have a Black man on a roster for more than a decade before Washington, Strode, Willis, and Motley played in 1946.

"If I had to point to one thing, it would be that video, and thank God the woman kept recording," McCaskey said, referring to Darnella Frazier, who was seventeen years old at the time she recorded Floyd's killing. "You can't watch that video and not think, 'What on earth is wrong with us?' What struck me is [Chauvin's] indifference that one human being could have for another. How does that happen? The worst thing that could happen would be if this thing just fades into the background, if this is just another death of an African-American at the hands of a white police officer. We need to keep having these discussions. We need to keep examining what we're doing and how we're doing it and how we can do things better. I'm certainly not the first one to say this, but we're better than this."

* * *

From the beginnings of NFL reintegration in 1946, there has been an uneven record of progress over the years. Yes, the color barrier was broken when Washington and Strode joined the Rams and Willis and Motley signed with the Browns. But it wasn't as if the floodgates suddenly opened and there was equal opportunity for African-American players.

"No doubt, for Black players the integration process that began in 1946 was a significant accomplishment," Dr. Charles Ross wrote in *Outside the Lines: African Americans and the Integration of the National Football League*. "However, by the end of the decade, only twenty-six Blacks had played in the NFL or AAFC. Many had only one-year careers, and were merely tokens on their respective teams... At the end of the 1949 season... only three teams—the LA Rams, Detroit Lions, and NY Giants—had Black players on their rosters."

In the 1950s, NFL rosters remained predominantly white, with Brown remaining the big exception among coaches willing to have Black players on their rosters. By the end of the 1951 season, only seventeen Black players were employed, according to Ross. And it wasn't until 1955 that the Lions became the last team other than Marshall's Washington club to integrate.

Even after Marshall reluctantly bowed to pressure from the Kennedy administration and integrated his team beginning in 1962, it was not a straight line toward the NFL's current threshold of approximately 70 percent Black players, as well as the addition of dozens of Asian-American and Pacific Islanders and other players with descendants from other countries, including Europe, Mexico, and Vietnam. From a virtually all-white league in the 1930s and '40s, the NFL may now be the most diverse professional sports league in the world.

One of the key pressure points for integration was the success of the American Football League in the 1960s. Many owners from the upstart league, including Lamar Hunt of the Dallas Texans (now the Kansas City Chiefs), had no hesitation in hiring Black players, in part because they needed to draw from as many talent pools as possible to field competitive teams. But also because Hunt believed players ought to be judged by their talent.

"Lamar was the kind of guy who started eight Black players on his defense in the 1960s, when some NFL teams didn't have eight Black players on their entire roster," said Chiefs Hall of Fame linebacker Willie Lanier, a major contributor in the team's Super Bowl IV victory. "You didn't see that in college, and I think we were the only ones doing that in professional football."

Jets star quarterback Joe Namath, who gave credibility to the AFL like no other with his victory guarantee and colossal upset of the Colts in Super Bowl III, was also instrumental in fostering a welcoming environment for Black players. Even if he did so quietly.

"He really got along with the Black guys," *Sports Illustrated*'s Paul Zimmerman told Mark Kriegel in his biography of the Jets quarterback, *Namath.* "He'd come off the cafeteria line with his tray and go straight for the Black table, integrating it. I saw him do that so many times I know it wasn't an accident. He was way ahead of his time."

"Namath was like, 'I have an understanding of Black culture, and I'm not afraid of it. I'm comfortable with it,'" Ross said. "If white people in American are able to understand the differences and be comfortable, we'd all be a lot better off."

The 1960s were also a time when other prominent African-American athletes, including Muhammad Ali, had an impact that was felt throughout the sports world, including the NFL. Cleveland teammates Jim Brown and guard John Wooten in 1966 formed the Negro Industrial Economic Union—later named the Black Economic Union—to help African-Americans become competitive in the business world. Ali—then known as Cassius Clay—became an active partner.

"What a lot of people don't understand is the relationship between the Champ and our group," said Wooten, who went on to become the first executive director of the Fritz Pollard Alliance to promote diversity in NFL hiring practices. "All of us—doctors, lawyers, councilmen, just the entire community—were hanging out at a social gathering at the Sir John Hotel, and that's where we met Cassius Clay. He's down there [in Miami] to fight Sonny Liston. We helped our communities economically. When we had closed-circuit TV for Ali's fights, Ali said we had to be available in certain areas, particularly the inner city. Ali was our leading guy for this."

It was Wooten who'd carried the message with him he'd first heard from Paul Brown when he was drafted by Cleveland in 1959.

"Paul Brown wasn't a publicity guy, but he was strong in terms of race relations, and I feel very fortunate with that," Wooten said. "I'm not saying he's a great civil rights person, but I am saying that what he did for us was very important. Bill Willis, Marion Motley, those guys were at practice a lot. We never had a problem, never any racial slurs. Why? Because Paul Brown gave this message at training camp every year: 'We don't have any Black Browns. We don't have any white Browns. Everybody here is a Cleveland Brown, and if there's anybody who has trouble with that, let us know and we'll get you on your way.' When you have a leader that stands up and speaks that way to a team, you're not going to have any problems."

The AFL-NFL merger in 1970 that signaled a new alliance among the once-rival leagues also led to more opportunities for African-American players, and NFL teams that might have been reluctant to sign Black players were realizing that hiring the best athletes—regardless of race—was beneficial to their product. Nunn, the acerbic sportswriter turned Steelers personnel executive, played a crucial role in bringing players from HBCUs into the NFL, a trend that other teams eventually followed.

But while the jobs increased for African-Americans, stereotypes persisted, especially many of the key positions on the field and on the sidelines.

Black players had very few opportunities at what Hall of Fame linebacker Harry Carson calls "the thinking man's positions," including quarterback, center, and middle linebacker. He said of his switch from defensive line to middle linebacker:

> I remember my [linebackers] coach, Marty Schottenheimer, told me flat out [because I was a rookie] that there were going to be people who are going to doubt whether I can make the transition. This was the first time he sort of alluded to me that there are people within the business that consider the center, the quarterback and the middle linebacker position to be thinking men's positions. With those three positions, you didn't see a whole lot of Black guys—probably because most coaches in the NFL assumed that those are positions that they needed white guys who are the "smart guys" to play there. When you're the guy who becomes the quarterback of the defense, that's asking a lot and perhaps they didn't trust the guys who probably could have made the transition, so they stuck with what they considered safe.

There may still be resistance to using Black players, particularly at quarterback, but the greatest challenge for the league now is a lack of diversity at the head coaching position.

"As far as players are concerned, when you look at where the league is, it hasn't had much of a choice [in using Black players], because the thing that fuels it is college football," Ross said. "They're still trying to hold on to the quarterback position in which clearly athleticism is becoming a factor in how you evaluate this particular position, because there's an argument that can be made that athletic ability was something you almost didn't want at quarterback. You wanted to have someone that could read defenses and stay in the pocket. But the running aspect of the position that has taken place in the last fifteen to twenty years is putting pressure on owners and general managers."

Tom Flores broke down barriers as the NFL's first Latino starting quarterback, and he made history once again as the only Latino coach to ever win a Super Bowl. In fact, he won two with the Raiders and was selected for Hall of Fame enshrinement in 2021.

Art Shell's hiring in 1989 as the first African-American coach in the modern NFL seemed to provide a breakthrough, and his appointment by Raiders owner Al Davis was met with near-universal praise.

"When I watched Art Shell play, I always felt he would make a good coach and a good head coach," John Madden said of the Hall of Fame offensive lineman. "He's a very bright, studious person who not only played the game physically, but knew everything about what he did, what everybody else did and why... Some players never think about anything but their own jobs, but Art always thought about everybody."

But progress would be slow for African-American coaches, a problem that continues today.

"We're just asking a great game to live up to its greatest potential, and we can't be proud of it," Fritz Pollard executive director Rod Graves said of the lack of diversity among head coaches. "This is an area that is one of the black eyes that we carry. At the end of the day, in order to make the progress that's necessary, it's got to be an intentional effort by the owners."

Goodell continues to push for more opportunities for BIPOC coaches, with the league now offering draft choice compensation for teams that develop coaches and front-office executives.

He does see a path forward that will lead to more diversity at the leadership positions in his sport, but he acknowledges that much more needs to be done.

He also understands that the roots of the league's racist past run deep. Yet he owns up to what once was.

"It's part of our history, and you don't change history," he said. "All you can do is change what you do going forward by learning from history, and I think the NFL did. It's dramatically different now than it was in those days."

Goodell also believes it's critical that the legacies of Washington, Strode, Willis, and Motley never be forgotten.

"I think it's incredibly important to think about what those players did, and what Paul Brown did," he said. "They broke the color barrier and started the integration of the NFL. What they did is very significant."

They helped pave the way for those who came after, even if their legacies have largely been overlooked.

"The pioneers of anything, anyone who has invested anything or been the first of anything or broken down any barrier, they should be heralded," veteran NFL safety Logan Ryan said. "It took a lot of courage and bravery and heroic feats. That's how you grow society and grow the game. Now the league is 70 percent African American, and it shows you where they broke down that barrier for us.

"Our job is to move it even further so kids thirty, forty years from now have it even better, grow the game even more, open it to people of all colors, all races, all religions, all creeds," he said. "That's really the goal. It wouldn't be possible without those people before us."

Chapter 21

THE COULD-HAVE-BEENS . . .

By the time Washington was signed by the Rams in 1946, NFL offenses had undergone a significant transformation. Gone was the single wing alignment that Washington thrived in at UCLA, where he did the bulk of the running *and* passing, even though he was called a halfback. For all practical purposes, he performed the duties of a quarterback, and he was one of the country's best.

But the T-formation had replaced the single wing, and when Washington began his NFL career, Bob Waterfield was the Rams quarterback, having come off an NFL championship as a rookie when the team was in Cleveland. Waterfield and Washington had a kinship as former UCLA star players, and it was Waterfield who played an instrumental role in welcoming Washington to the Rams and making him feel a part of the team.

It was also Waterfield who helped Washington understand the new concepts and was prepared to have the former UCLA star as his backup.

While history may proclaim that Willie Thrower, who was signed by Halas as a quarterback, was the first African-American quarterback to throw a pass in an NFL game—on October 18, 1953—there is a case to be made that Washington should hold that distinction.

"Kenny played quarterback at the beginning of the 1946 season," pro football historian and author Dan Daly said. "He came up in the single wing, but the Rams were one of the T-formation teams in 1946. [Coach] Adam Walsh had Kenny working with the quarterbacks."

Case in point: In the Rams' final preseason game before their debut in Los Angeles against the Eagles, it was Washington who started—at quarterback—against a team of Pacific Coast League all-stars at Balboa Stadium in San Diego.

"Washington has been announced as the starting quarterback ahead of Bob Waterfield and San Diego fans are pleased to learn that they will see Kenny in his first real test with a major league team," read a story in the *Valley Times.*

When the regular season opened against the Eagles, Waterfield suffered a chest injury in the third quarter and was replaced by... Kenny Washington. The Eagles lost the game, 25–14, but let history show that Washington played quarterback. He had just seven pass attempts and one completion as a rookie, and finished with 14 passes for his career.

And while press reports indicate that an injury had forced Waterfield out of the game, Strode suggested otherwise when he told his son, Kalai, later in life about the incident.

With Washington sitting on the bench for the entire game, Strode said the crowd became increasingly restless, especially with the Rams trailing. Chants of "Put Kenny in! Put Kenny in!" could be heard.

After Waterfield was tended to on the field by team doctors and he returned to the bench, Strode said the quarterback told him, "I'm OK."

"You were never injured, were you?" Strode asked him.

Waterfield looked at Strode and said, "Go Bruins," a nod to the UCLA team all three played for.

"You crazy son of a gun," Strode said.

A few minutes later, Walsh came over to Waterfield.

"How you feeling now, Bob?"

"Better," Waterfield told him.

He went back in the game, and Washington returned to the bench and sat next to Strode.

"He wasn't injured," Strode said of Waterfield.

"What?" Washington exclaimed.

"He faked it to get you in the game."

* * *

It certainly makes you wonder: If Washington had come out of UCLA in recent years with his rare skill set, would he have been considered a quarterback? Or at least been given the chance?

Remember this, too: While Baker Mayfield is credited with throwing the longest completed pass in the air in NFL history—70 yards, in a December 14, 2020, game—Washington once threw a ball 72 yards in the air when he played with the Hollywood Bears in 1945. And after he joined the Rams, he once threw a ball 100 yards.

Really.

In a short film featuring Waterfield—which is now part of the NFL Films library—Washington is filmed throwing a pass from one goal line toward the other. The cameraman is situated near midfield, with yard markers placed every 10 yards, and he captures the ball in midflight, arcing high in the air toward the other goal line. At the last moment, the ball hits the 100-yard marker on the opposite goal line.

True story. It's on film.

With that kind of arm strength, and with his incredible mobility that made him such a dangerous runner, there's simply no question he'd be considered a quarterback prospect in today's game. For that matter, Walsh did use him at quarterback when the two were together in 1946.

But progress was painfully slow to come for Black quarterbacks. The first African-American to start a game at quarterback was Marlin Briscoe with the Broncos in 1968.

It wasn't until a year later that a tall, strong-armed quarterback from Grambling broke through as the first African-American starter on a full-time basis. James Harris was an eighth-round pick of the Bills in 1969, and he won a seven-way training camp competition as a rookie.

Acceptance came grudgingly.

Harris received hate mail—and sometimes worse.

"There were death threats," Harris said. "People write to you and tell you what they're going to do to you. I'm from the segregated South, so I understood segregation. I rode on the back of the bus. I went to the school where we got books from other schools. I grew up knowing that you had to be careful when you left your neighborhood."

He was shocked when he'd read the letters. "I'd open them, and it surprised me," he said. "It kept coming, and so much of it when I ended up starting the opening game."

He'd become the first African-American quarterback to start a season in the NFL, but his tenure didn't last long. After just one game, he was replaced by Jack Kemp, and he started just two more games before being released in 1972. Harris signed with the Rams in 1973, and this time he would blossom into a playoff quarterback, becoming the first Black quarterback to start a postseason game in 1974.

It was another Grambling quarterback and protege of Hall of Fame coach, Eddie Robinson, who broke the color barriers for quarterbacks. After the 1987 season, Doug Williams became the first African-American quarterback to win a Super Bowl when Washington beat the Denver Broncos in Super Bowl XXII in San Diego. Williams was the game's MVP, rewarding the faith that legendary coach Joe Gibbs placed in him.

The legacy of that game cannot be minimized; Williams had achieved what once was unthinkable in a league that simply had not given Black quarterbacks the kind of opportunities afforded white passers. And while it would be years before teams would shed their reluctance to entrust their teams to Black quarterbacks, Williams's accomplishment was an undeniable line of demarcation. All he'd asked was that the color of a quarterback's skin shouldn't determine whether he got the chance to play.

"The mentality of ownership and coaches is a lot different than it was a few years ago, and there is a belief that you can win with a Black quarterback," Williams said. "If you don't have an opportunity, you never do it. That's the bottom line."

Hall of Famer Tony Dungy believes the acceptance of Black quarterbacks has come a long way from his days as a player and coach.

"With people recognizing culturally that there's no issue, that African-Americans can be leaders, can lead the whole team, we've gotten past that," Dungy said. "It's better for the NFL. We're seeing exciting football that twenty-five years ago we might not have seen."

Dungy experienced the double standard during his football career. A standout quarterback at Minnesota in the late 1970s, he went undrafted and was urged to switch positions if he wanted to play in the NFL. He made the Steelers roster as a defensive back in 1977. After two seasons, he was traded to the 49ers, where he played under Bill Walsh in 1979, also as a defensive back.

Dungy played at Minnesota at the same time Warren Moon starred at the University of Washington, where he won MVP honors in the 1978 Rose Bowl. Moon also was undrafted and played six seasons for the CFL's Edmonton Eskimos before joining the Houston Oilers in 1984. He played seventeen NFL seasons and in 2006 became the first Black quarterback enshrined in the Pro Football Hall of Fame.

"I'm leading the Big Ten in passing, Warren is leading the Pac-8 and goes on to be MVP of the Rose Bowl, and neither one of us got drafted," Dungy said. "Our options were to change positions or go to Canada."

Stereotypes didn't change easily.

"It was an unwritten rule that the reason Blacks weren't playing quarterback was because we weren't smart enough," Harris said. "We couldn't lead. There was some concern about character. Throughout the country, there was that issue. We just didn't have Blacks getting the opportunity to excel.

"All anybody ever wanted was a chance," he said. "When you grow up and you want to play professional football and you want an opportunity to play your best position, I think all you can ask is that the best players play. That hasn't always been the case."

While much progress has been made, there still are many who believe there is an inherent bias against African-American quarterbacks. Among the most critical: former Eagles quarterback Donovan McNabb.

"It's still an issue," said McNabb, the second overall pick in 1999. "It's always a question of the ability—can [African-American quarterbacks] play in a pro-style offense? How about why don't you draft him and build an offense around him? It's questions like that that really still keep us in the same path that we've been in for years. I'm excited to see there are opportunities for some of these young quarterbacks so that more will have the opportunity going forward in the coming years."

And the opportunities are undeniably increasing. At the start of the 2020 season, for instance, ten teams had African-Americans as their starting quarterbacks. Lamar Jackson was selected as the NFL's MVP after the 2018 season, and Mahomes won the award in 2019.

But even Williams acknowledges that despite the increase in and acceptance of African-American quarterbacks in the NFL, things can still improve in the years ahead.

"When we get to the point that it's not an issue," Williams said, "then we're not having this conversation."

* * *

A decade after Marion Motley's playing career had ended, he issued a lengthy statement to the press on February 4, 1965, decrying the Browns for what he perceived as their unwillingness to hire him for a coaching position.

He made it clear he felt he was being prohibited from rejoining the team as a coach because of his race.

"I believe that Modell has doubts as to whether I have the knowledge and qualifications of knowing a football player," he said.

Motley divulged that he'd first asked Paul Brown about a coaching job shortly after retiring in 1955 following a one-year stint in Pittsburgh. Brown said there was no room on his staff and told Motley, "Have you tried the steel mills?"

Motley had no interest in returning to the job he'd once held before Brown gave him the chance to start his professional playing career in 1946.

"Then about one year ago, I inquired at the Browns' front office about a coaching job and was told there were no vacancies," he said. "When I heard of the hiring of a new assistant, I began to wonder if the full reason is whether or not the time is ripe to hire a Negro coach in Cleveland on the professional level."

Motley had also inquired with his former teammate, Browns quarterback Otto Graham, when Graham was head coach in Washington from 1966 to 1968. No opportunity there, either.

"I know Otto wanted to give him an opportunity, but he knew he would be jeopardizing his own job had he given Motley this opportunity for a chance to coach," said Tony Motley, the Hall of Fame fullback's grandson.

Motley was so eager to find a role in the NFL coaching community that he coached a women's semipro football team for a year.

"It was unheard of for Black players to get an opportunity to coach back then," Tony Motley said. "If anyone would have given him the chance, it would have been Otto—a running backs coach or receivers coach or something. But Otto pretty much caved in to the moment of the racial tensions that were still going on in the NFL at the time. There was a belief that Black people didn't have the knowledge and the know-how to coach. But if you played the game and you're professional, why wouldn't you? Those were the barriers back then."

And to a significant degree, those are still barriers, particularly when it comes to NFL head coaching opportunities. While it is no longer uncommon to see African-American assistant coaches—many of them former players like Motley—there remains a dearth of Black head coaches. From 2018 to 2021, there were twenty-seven head coach openings; just five positions went to BIPOC candidates.

Motley's protestations, which came more than sixty years ago, were clearly a sign of the struggle yet to come. And while there is much more attention being paid now to giving BIPOC coaches more opportunities, Motley's public anger was stunning and proved prescient.

Modell bristled at Motley's criticisms.

"My position on Negroes needs no defense, nor does the record of the Browns over the years," he said.

Motley never got the chance to coach, something that bothered him the rest of his life.

"Marion Motley died of a broken heart," George Taliaferro once told *USA Today*'s NFL columnist, Jarrett Bell. "He should have been the first African-American coach in the NFL. But Marion didn't get his degree. No team would hire him to coach. Allegedly, he didn't have the intellect to contribute anything, beyond what he did as a player. That was tragic."

Jim Rooney is quite certain his father would be disturbed about the lack of advancement by BIPOC coaches in today's NFL.

"[My father] would have great empathy and frustration and this feeling of disturbance related to the fact that so many guys set out to be involved in this business—minorities and African-Americans, in particular—and they're clearly experiencing a ceiling," Jim Rooney said. "You can't get away from that fact."

While the Rooney Rule has helped many African-American coaches—including Mike Tomlin, who was hired by Rooney in 2007 to coach the Steelers and has won seven divisional titles and made it to two Super Bowls, winning one—the NFL has come under justifiable criticism for its continued lack of diversity hiring in recent years.

"My father never set a quota or a number," Jim Rooney said. "Individuals have the right to make the final say within their hiring process. It's thirty-two different companies, and that was one of the challenges. But I certainly feel like he would be clear that there had been progress and there is not progress now."

Dan Rooney, in consultation with prominent lawyers Johnnie Cochran and Washington-based Cyrus Mehri, as well as Fritz Pollard Alliance executive director John Wooten, eventually came up with the framework of hiring practices for all head coaching positions. The rule has since been expanded to include general manager positions, team president, and other top front-office jobs.

To those who say all would-be head coaches are treated the same, regardless of race or background, Mehri would argue otherwise. Not only that, but it's in the best interests of the NFL's long-term health to cast a wide net when hiring the most important person for every team's on-field success.

"In the end, as we reflect on the league now, it's important that the owners buy into what's best for the game, best for the league, best for the long-term success of this game to be better on the diversity issues," Mehri said. "If we didn't have the Rooney Rule, many of these coaches might never have had a chance."

Mara, the Giants president and co-owner and member of the NFL's workplace diversity committee, believes part of the problem stems from the current trend toward hiring offensive-minded head coaches.

"Because so many coaches are getting hired from the offensive side of the ball, that's where we need to focus on getting more diverse candidates and eventually get them to be offensive coordinators, because that's who most people are hiring now," Mara said. "There's just not enough diverse coaches in those areas, so we [on the diversity committee] have talked about trying to increase the hiring at the lower levels of the offensive side. Eventually, those guys can become coordinators."

Mara's hiring of Joe Judge, a thirty-eight-year-old special teams coordinator with the Patriots who has no previous head coaching experience, created questions about the Giants commitment to diversity—especially given that they had interviewed minority candidates Kris Richard and Eric Bieniemy.

"Loved Bieniemy," Mara said of his interview. "He was terrific."

So why take Judge over Bieniemy?

"This guy [Judge] made such an impression on us," Mara said. "He was our guy. We picked the guy that we felt was the best guy."

Former Bengals coach Marvin Lewis, who interviewed for the Cowboys job in 2020 that went to former Packers coach Mike McCarthy, said convincing owners to hire diverse candidates is the toughest part of the equation.

"You keep beating your head up against the wall," Lewis said. "But I would say—and again, this is somebody's business, this is somebody's franchise, and nobody is going to tell them who to hire. But if we can just somehow open the process a bit more and provide more opportunity. The decision-makers are gonna favor people they know that way, and they don't know the minority coaches as well."

Jim Rooney agreed that ownership bears the ultimate responsibility for creating a more diverse workforce, not only among head coaches but at all levels of their organizations. Though there are no African-American owners, he believes the presence of an increased number of women owners might help.

"Look, we really don't have strong racial diversity in the ownership room, but for the first time ever, you have women sitting at the table in decision-making roles," he said. "You have Dee Haslam [in Cleveland], Kim Pegula [in Buffalo], Gayle Benson [in New Orleans], Sheila Ford Hamp [in Detroit], Katie Brown Blackburn [in Cincinnati]. You now have some diversity at the table in a way that you never had before.

"Not that their experiences are the same as a Black coach, but that's one place where they can really make a difference, providing something similar to what [Dan Rooney] did."

Washington Football Team president Jason Wright believes the NFL is on the right track, and that corporate America would benefit greatly by following its example.

"I think the awareness in the NFL is incredibly high," he said. "It's not about having the homer line because I'm part of the league and the leadership structure. It's my objective opinion, based on having worked in private industry across multiple different industries. I don't know if there's any industry that is more aware of it than professional sports, and in particular the NBA and the NFL. Part of it is because so much of the on-field talent are Black men. But I would also say that in the league office, they care deeply and are invested in making progress and are not satisfied with the progress."

Wright said he has seen intense pushback on diversity in private companies for applying the Rooney Rule. "Oh, my gosh, you should have seen the tantrums that people had," he said. "They're like, 'No, that's stacking the deck in the other direction. That is reverse discrimination.'"

Not true, he said, and companies would benefit from increased diversity.

"All the research says that we make better decisions, that companies that are more diverse outperform others over time," he said. "The companies with the most gender-diverse leadership teams are 25 percent more likely to be outperformers and those that are the most ethnically diverse leadership teams are 33 percent more likely to be top performers in their business. That's across all industries, all places around the globe."

Bill Belichick, the most accomplished coach in the game's history, provided a stark reminder about the slow progress of accepting Black coaches in the opening game of the Patriots' 2020 season against the Miami Dolphins. He affixed a patch to his visor with the name "Fritz Pollard," a tribute to the NFL's first African-American coach—in the one hundredth season since Pollard became the first Black coach in the league's history.

"What [Pollard] did, the courage that he showed as a player in the NFL and then later as a player-coach, and then later, when he left the NFL and after the NFL banned all Black players, he continued to work with professional teams, all-Black teams and have them compete. They just weren't in the National Football League," Belichick said. "Really honored to have worn this, and I appreciate the opportunity to recognize Fritz Pollard for all he's done and what he represented and what he worked so hard for."

Even so, a century after Pollard coached and nearly two decades after Dan Rooney created the rule bearing his name to increase opportunity, there is more work to be done. Just as the NFL's increasing openness to giving Black quarterbacks more of a chance on the field has led to greater opportunity for some of the best athletes in the game, increased diversity on the sidelines someday may lead to greater representation among coaches.

That day hasn't come yet.

That day when the next Marion Motley can share his passion for football and live his dreams of inspiring young players in the game they love.

Chapter 22

WOODY STRODE: A PIONEER SEVERAL TIMES OVER

The first time Woody Strode left football, the choice wasn't his, and he was personally devastated. Even suicidal, according to his family. He'd been released by the Rams after just one season in 1946, the year he and Kenny Washington broke the NFL's color barrier once and for all. He simply didn't know where to turn.

But after playing two-plus years with the CFL's Calgary Stampeders, winning a Grey Cup title as part of an unbeaten run in his first season, Strode knew it was time to go.

"I loved football, and I probably played longer than I should have," he said, "but when you start getting injured like I did toward the end, that's a sign to hang 'em up."

Shoulder and rib injuries were the signs that told him it was time.

"At the start of the [1950] season, I got hit in midair as I was going for a pass," he said. "I must have been three feet off the ground when this guy went right through me and busted two ribs over my heart."

He walked off the field and told Les Lear, his former Rams teammate who'd brought him to Canada, "That's it. I'm through."

"What the hell, Woody, you're in better shape than anybody on the field," Lear told him.

"What do you think I was doing out there?" Strode told his coach. "I was listening for the footsteps."

Strode said he'd been asked many times how you know it's time to quit football, and he'd tell them, "You just run out of guts."

But Strode didn't run out of opportunity when his playing career ended. In fact, it just started.

Truth be told, Strode couldn't have imagined the journey he was about to take, one that would take him around the world and lead to a stint in professional wrestling and then a film career that would last the rest of his life.

After his first season with the Hollywood Bears, Strode was looking for extra work to supplement his income and went to see a friend, Cal Eaton, who ran the Olympic Auditorium in Los Angeles, to see about making some money in boxing. Eaton suggested he consider wrestling instead, since he'd absorb less punishment.

Eaton introduced him to a sixty-five-year-old wrestler named Baron Ginsberg.

"I'm going to teach you how to wrestle," Eaton told him. "When you can pin him, we'll cut you loose."

Considering the age difference, Strode figured this wouldn't take long.

"He kicked my ass for eight months before I could pin him," Strode said.

Strode went on tour before the next football season, appearing in San Bernardino. Strode was always cast as a "good guy" in the ring.

"I could not play the villain," he said. "If I came into the ring and my opponent was a nice, clean white boy and the first thing I do is punch him in the eye, now he's walking around blind...They would have hung me in the ring. I dress all in white: white trunks, white shoes. I was the clean colored boy."

He put his wrestling career on hold until after his CFL days had ended, but once he returned to Los Angeles, he wrestled sometimes every night of the week and traveled throughout California, the Midwest, the South, Hawaii, and Canada. One of his opponents was a man who helped Strode improve his own visibility and make him some decent money: "Gorgeous George," an infamous villain who wore sequined capes to the ring and was attended by valets spraying perfume as he sauntered around in an exaggerated manner. "Gorgeous George" became one of wrestling's biggest draws in the 1940s and 1950s, ushering in an era that led to the sport's worldwide popularity.

Strode was billed as the Pacific Coast Heavyweight Wrestling Champion and the Pacific Coast Negro Heavyweight Wrestling Champion and later was a tag-team partner of Bobo Brazil.

Strode eventually transitioned into the acting business when a producer, Walter Mirisch, saw one of his matches and cast him as an African warrior in the 1951 film *The Lion Hunters.* Strode's familiarity with motion pictures from his days at UCLA came in handy. Back then, Bill Ackerman had gotten Strode and Washington jobs in the service department at Warner Bros., and the two star football players worked as porters for the likes of Bette Davis, Jimmy Cagney, Ann Sheridan, and Olivia de Havilland. And chances are the actors knew Strode and Washington.

"I remember walking up to Errol Flynn and him saying, 'Oh, you and Kenny, I just love watching you guys play,'" Strode said.

Working in that environment made Strode more comfortable as he accepted film roles, and the jobs came regularly enough that he transitioned away from wrestling entirely. Strode appeared in eighteen movies in the 1950s—including a small role in Cecil B. DeMille's *The Ten Commandments* in 1956. But it was in 1960, when he was cast for the title role in the movie *Sergeant Rutledge* by legendary director John Ford that Strode achieved a breakthrough as a serious actor.

The movie centers on a Black cavalry regiment that was assigned to keep the frontier regions in the American West safe. Strode's character was falsely accused of a double murder and the rape of a teenaged white girl. Worried about being subject to prejudice during his trial, Rutledge runs away from the cavalry unit.

"But the Indians were about to trap my men, and for me, it was either freedom for myself or save them from the trap," he said in a 1971 *New York Times* interview.

> "You never seen a Negro come off a mountain like John Wayne before," Strode says, standing to demonstrate how he rode down the side of a mountain with a nine-pound gun hoisted in the air. "I had the greatest Glory Hallelujah ride across the Pecos River that any Black man ever had on the screen. And I did it myself. I carried the whole Black race across that river."

He forged a lifelong relationship with Ford. Strode, who called Ford "Papa," stayed with the director after he'd fallen ill, spending the last four months of Ford's life with him, sleeping on the floor to keep him company.

"John Ford told me I should have received an Academy Award nomination for *Sergeant Rutledge*," Strode said. "I've never gotten over *Sergeant Rutledge*. That was a classic. It had dignity. John Ford put classic words in my mouth."

Strode's other signature role was in the movie *Spartacus*, starring Kirk Douglas. Strode played the role of Draba, an Ethiopian gladiator who is forced to fight Spartacus (Douglas) to the death. Draba wins the fight, but instead of killing Spartacus, he attacks the Roman military official who set up the fight. Draba is killed, and a rebellion among the gladiators erupts.

Legendary director Stephen Spielberg called it one of the most memorable scenes in cinematic history.

"You can't beat the fight between Kirk Douglas and Woody Strode, the first fight in the arena," he said in a 2012 interview. "They're not supposed to fight to the death, but they made an exception in this case. That was a pretty amazing sequence of the long pitchfork and the net against the short sword. It was a brilliant scene."

Another memorable role came in 1968, when he played the lead role in *Black Jesus*, an Italian drama based on the final days of Patrice Lumumba, the prime minister of the Democratic Republic of Congo. And his role in *The Professionals* was on a par with Burt Lancaster, Lee Marvin, and Robert Ryan, although he wasn't given the same billing.

Box office fame never truly materialized for Strode, despite a remarkable body of work in sheer volume and quality. In many ways, his film career was like his football career—he was an underappreciated man before his time.

"I'm a ghost," he once said of his film legacy.

Some of Strode's most enjoyable—if not cinematically memorable—times came when he made several movies in Italy called "Spaghetti Westerns." He grew to adore his time in Italy, and he once partnered with Hall of Fame quarterback Joe Namath in *The Last Rebel*.

"I made a two-hundred-yard run, jumped from my horse to the runaway horses and reined in that six-horse team," said Strode, who was an excellent horseman and did all his own stunts throughout his career. "Joe sat there watching me and couldn't believe it. I was fifty-seven years old, and it was the first time I had ever done that. If you ever run across Joe, ask him about how old Woody caught that stagecoach."

We did ask him.

"What a wonderful guy," Namath said of Strode. "I can see him riding that horse ramrod straight. It was beautiful. It was magnificent. It was one of the greatest treats of my life to be able to be close to him. We would work together six, seven days a week, and we all stayed relatively close to one another. I was amazed at his physique, his athleticism, the way he handled those horses. He was the nicest cat you'd ever want to be around."

Like Strode, Namath had once played for the Rams. After his twelve-year career with the Jets, Namath's final injury-plagued season was with Los Angeles in 1974.

But the two didn't talk much football on the set. And Namath never realized that Strode had joined Washington as the men who had broken the NFL's color barrier in 1946.

Strode didn't make Hollywood's gossip columns much, but there was the time he created a ruckus in Las Vegas in 1966, when he and Lee Marvin were shooting *The Professionals.* After a night of drinking, Marvin mentioned that he wanted to shoot an arrow into the gaudy thirty-foot neon sign of a cowboy called "Vegas Vic" that stood outside a casino. After Marvin had passed out in his room, Strode and a friend did just that from their sixteenth-floor room at the Mint Hotel. Police noticed this session of target practice and ran into the hotel. Strode then took his bow and arrow, knocked on Marvin's door, and told him to hide them.

Press reports indicated Marvin had been the one to shoot the arrow, when in fact it was Strode.

"That crazy son of a bitch got so excited he fired a shotgun out his window," Strode said of Marvin. "The cops came and found the bow in his room. Lee was so proud. It got to be the biggest joke in town."

Strode also nearly came to blows with John Wayne. During a scene in the filming of Ford's movie *The Man Who Shot Liberty Valance,* Wayne had trouble controlling the horses leading his stagecoach, and Strode came over to help. Wayne brushed Strode's hand away when he went to grab the reins. When the horses finally stopped, Wayne fell to the ground, and Strode stood above him, ready to fight.

"Woody, don't hit him!" Ford shouted. "We need him!"

Years later, when Wayne was being treated for cancer at the UCLA

Medical Center in 1979, he often wore a UCLA baseball hat and when he passed people in the hallway, he'd tip his cap, only to show a USC hat. Before he changed his name to John Wayne for his movie career, Marion Morrison went to USC on a football scholarship as an offensive tackle in 1925.

Morrison had been a football star at Glendale High School—just a short drive from Strode's ranch in Glendora, which he'd bought with his earnings from pro wrestling and football.

Before getting sick with what was later believed to be mesothelioma—possibly due to previous exposure to asbestos—Woody Strode had kept up a prolific pace with his acting. He appeared in dozens of movies and television shows in the 1980s and was inducted into the Black Filmmakers Hall of Fame in 1980. His last film was *The Quick and the Dead,* starring Gene Hackman, Leonardo DiCaprio, and Russell Crowe. The film came out in 1995 and was dedicated to Strode.

Strode lived his final days on his ranch after being diagnosed with cancer in 1994. No longer the strapping actor who'd enjoyed a life playing football before going on to delight crowds as Woody Strode the wrestler and then the actor, he spent hours each day talking to his son, Kalai, now grown and enjoying his own career as an assistant director in television and the movies. Just as Woody had moved in with director John Ford in his final months, Kalai lived with his father until his death on December 31, 1994.

"Woody wanted Kalai to know his entire life story in the time he had left," said Kalai's widow, Pam Larson Strode. "They'd walk together, sit outside in two chairs, bring their ukuleles and they'd sit in the sun and talk and Kalai would write notes and they'd go back and forth with his whole life story."

A few years after Woody's death, Pam, who'd appeared in an episode of the television series *Diagnosis Murder* that Kalai had helped direct, gave him a gift after the two had fallen in love. It was Mitch Albom's

Tuesdays with Morrie, the story of Albom making a series of visits with a former professor as he was dying of ALS. Kalai would spend time between takes reading the book, and Pam saw that he often cried uncontrollably. She thought she'd made a horrible mistake giving him the book.

That wasn't it.

"In reading the book," she said, "that's exactly what he'd done with his father."

The two were married on December 31, 1999—to coincide with the fifth anniversary of Woody Strode's passing. Kalai died of cancer in 2014.

Strode's legacy as a football player, a professional wrestler, and an actor might not have led to the kind of fame it undoubtedly deserved, but he is at least a part of American culture in a very big and very meaningful way.

You know the lead characters in the animated film series *Toy Story*? Well, Buzz Lightyear, played by Tim Allen, is named after the former astronaut, Buzz Aldrin.

And Sheriff Woody, played by Tom Hanks?

He's named after Woody Strode.

And that hat he wears in the movies? A replica of the one Woody wore in the dozens of Westerns he'd made.

So next time you see Sheriff Woody Pride, think of his fascinating namesake.

Chapter 23

BETTER DAYS

There may have been no finer all-around fullback in NFL history than Marion Motley, who not only averaged more yards per carry (5.7) than any other runner in pro football history but was one of the game's greatest blockers, too.

Otto Graham, the Hall of Fame quarterback Motley played alongside, once said Motley was without peer. And that included the legendary Jim Brown, who broke Motley's records with Cleveland.

"There is no comparison between Jim Brown and Marion Motley," Graham once said. "Motley was the greatest all-around fullback."

Former Browns head coach and longtime Paul Brown assistant Blanton Collier took it a step further.

"He was the greatest all-around football player I ever saw," Collier said.

But Motley's post-football life was far less kind to the big fullback, who did far more than he'd ever dreamed on a football field, but experienced much heartbreak and disappointment after his career ended.

He'd desperately hoped to become a coach but was rebuffed by Paul Brown, and later by Graham when he was the head coach in Washington. He tried again with Cleveland, only to have the door closed. And when he saw that the team had gone outside the organization to hire Bob Nussbaumer to become ends coach and do some additional football operations work, he'd become furious.

The three-page letter that he'd publicly released was taken by many in the Cleveland market as the rants of a frustrated ex-player, but his accusation that the team wasn't ready to hire an African-American for a coaching position was actually a harbinger of a league-wide problem that continues to resonate in today's NFL—especially at the head coaching position, where the hiring of African-Americans continues to lag.

His impassioned conclusion to the letter, which was printed in full by then–*Pittsburgh Courier* columnist Bill Nunn—yes, the same Bill Nunn who went on to join the Steelers in a front-office position and help draft players who'd formed the core of their 1970s dynasty—eloquently stated his case.

"After playing for Paul Brown and playing with such great players as Otto Graham, Lou Groza, Ray Renfro, Lenny Ford, Bill Willis and a host of others," Motley wrote, "I have no doubt that I am qualified to teach the game of football."

> In writing this, I am not begging or asking for charity, but like Jim Brown, I, too, have something to get off my chest. I hope this will not lead to the hiring of me or any other Negro without thought being given to qualification and knowledge of the particular sport, because I am not writing this for sympathy but only for the hiring of whomever it may be for their knowledge and not their color.

Motley never did get the chance to coach in the NFL, and while there might have been college opportunities he could have pursued, his dream was to coach in the league for which he'd once played.

Like many former players of his era, Motley couldn't retire on his NFL earnings, which were minuscule, certainly by today's standards. He earned $4,000 as a rookie, and his highest annual salary was $15,000. He wasn't eligible for the league's pension, which players had to fight for during contentious collective bargaining agreement negotiations.

"They were ready to let me run the ball, but they weren't ready to pay me—or let me think," Motley once told students at a high school assembly in New York.

He said he didn't harbor frustration over the players who would go on to earn much larger salaries, but there was at least some envy about how the money game worked as time went on.

"I don't have any feeling of resentment toward the players who are making big money," he said. "The thing that upsets me is the fella who gets $100,000 before he comes to camp. My bonus was $400. That was what I got, and I didn't get it until I got to camp."

After his career ended, he approached the Cleveland Recreation Department about a job, but a department official said he didn't think the organization could meet his asking salary requirements. Motley remained in northeast Ohio to be with his family, and ended up working at the Cleveland post office for four years, then as a safety director for an Akron-based construction company for eight years. He spent ten years with the Ohio Lottery, and then worked with the Ohio department of youth services in Akron before retiring.

But life after football wasn't without its joyful moments, and there was none bigger than August 3, 1968, when Motley was given the greatest individual honor of his sport. Just a few hundred yards from where he starred at Canton McKinley High School to begin what would become an unforgettable and legendary career, Motley was inducted into the Pro Football Hall of Fame.

By his side to present him at the ceremonies: Bill Willis.

"I am extremely proud to be a part of this program, and to have the privilege of presenting to you the greatest all-around football player in professional history," Willis said. "It gives me a great deal of pleasure to present to the fans of Canton their own Marion Motley."

Willis then offered a brief reminiscence of the beginnings of Motley's professional career:

> Whenever you think of the Cleveland Browns, you must think of Paul Brown—really. Whenever you think of Paul Brown, you think of Marion and you think of Otto Graham. But you can neither think of Otto Graham or Paul Brown or the Cleveland Browns without thinking of Marion Motley. He was truly a complete football player... So, it gives me a distinct pleasure to present to the Hall of Fame the greatest fullback of all times, Marion Motley.

An emotional Motley stood before the assembled crowd, many of whom had seen him play high school football all those years ago and others who'd witnessed his breathtaking career with Cleveland. One of pro football's most important pioneers accepted his sport's greatest recognition.

"I look out over this crowd, and I see many faces that I know that I've gone to school with," Motley said.

> And it makes a person being from his hometown, of being presented into the Hall of Fame, in the hometown—it's a wonderful feeling. I've been asked many times in the last two or three days as to how you feel, or what will be your feeling. Well, trying to express or say how you feel about this, going into the Hall of Fame, it's rather hard. I'd like to thank the many teammates that I've played with that helped me to be the so-called player that I was at that particular time. Fellows like Bill Willis, Lin Houston, Cliff Lewis, Dante Lavelli, and

> many others that I could go on and name, but it would take quite a while. But I'd just like to say again, I'd like to thank everyone for coming and thank the people that inducted me into the Hall of Fame.

Short. Simple. To the point. Just like Motley on a football field.

"I was fortunate to be able to be one of the few to excel at something I liked to do," Motley said. "I felt proud to be a Black American. Just as Martin Luther King had a dream, let me tell you, without a dream, you can't accomplish anything."

He was a role model to so many, including another little kid from northeast Ohio who grew up watching him play.

"Not only was I a tremendous follower of my hometown team, but certainly of Marion Motley," Paul Warfield, who grew up to be a Hall of Fame receiver for the Browns and Dolphins, said in the 2021 PBS documentary *Lines Broken: The Story of Marion Motley*. "He was a superlative player who made great plays for the Cleveland Browns, an integral part of their winning, and he looked like me."

Motley took one more bow for the fans in Canton at the Hall of Fame's thirtieth anniversary celebration of his Class of 1968. One final curtain call for those who witnessed a splendid career that began at the epicenter of where Hall of Fame greatness now resides.

"This is a guy who did so much for pro football," said longtime Hall of Fame executive director Joe Horrigan. "If he did it in New York, there'd be a building named after him, a highway named after him. In Canton, Ohio, he was just Marion."

On June 27, 1999, after suffering from prostate cancer, Marion Motley died at age seventy-nine.

Chapter 24

FINDING MEANING AFTER FOOTBALL

Bill Willis was ready for the next part of his life. The more important part of his life, as far as he was concerned.

Willis enjoyed a superb career with the Browns, and he never shirked his responsibility of setting an example for other African-Americans who would follow the trail that he and Motley blazed as the team's first Black players. Truth be told, he could probably have played another two or three years at the time he announced his retirement in 1953; after all, he'd been an All Pro or Pro Bowl selection in all eight of his professional seasons.

But Willis felt there was another purpose to be served. And while he helped the players in his own locker room and others who followed in his footsteps, he wanted to help a different group of athletes now that his playing days were over.

He wanted to help the children of Cleveland. Particularly troubled youth.

Willis took a job as Cleveland's assistant recreation commissioner and in 1957 was selected as chairman of the Ohio Youth Commission—a position he held for twenty-five years before retiring.

"Bill Willis's football career was phenomenal, but his contributions to the development of schooling for disturbed young people in Ohio is equally or more important," former Ohio State teammate Don Steinberg said of Willis in his book, *Expanding Your Horizons.* "We had great satisfaction watching his play on the football field for fifteen years. We can take more satisfaction knowing of his contributions to young people that have covered twenty-five years."

Forget about the respect he commanded as a football player; Willis was one of the most widely appreciated people in Ohio. He carried himself with class for the Browns, helping them win four AAFC titles and an NFL championship, but he also made a lasting impact on the greater Cleveland community with his dedication to the area's young people.

And he did it with the kind of ingenuity that helped make him a dominant player, adjusting to situations with a collaborative approach.

"He would use his celebrity as an ex-football player to solicit funds to supplement different programs, to start leagues for young kids," said Clem Willis, one of Bill's three sons.

Clem pointed to a local football program that had teams sponsored by various businesses in the community.

"They would give out uniforms, but there was nothing for the little kids," Clem said. "So my dad went to [Browns owner] Art Modell, and the Browns footed the bill."

But there was a catch.

"The one caveat was that all the teams had to be named after a current Browns player at the time," Clem said. "I played for the 'Jimmy Ray Smiths,'" Clem said of the team named after the Browns guard. "But the team to beat was the 'John Wooten' team."

Bill Willis knew what it was like to be shunned, to face discrimination not because of who he was but because of the color of his skin. He knew he wanted to give back, in part because of how he'd been helped by others.

"The same discrimination I had in high school and college was still in the professional leagues," he said. "Oftentimes, Marion Motley and I had to stay with friends in the Southern cities when we played in the All American League. But after a lifetime of slanted social overtones of racial bias, the acceptance of Black people into the social fabric of our country was beginning. The first acceptance was through Paul Brown's unwavering attitude that the best players should play on his team regardless of any other factors. I always maintained my self-respect without surrendering to the injustices I felt so often. We led the way and had broken the barriers against Black athletes in America. I feel that I had made the right choices and I was truly able to lead the way and help my people."

It was a steely resolve that helped Willis get through his career, and it was that same reliance on his principles that made him so impactful through his work in the Cleveland recreation department and with the Ohio Youth Commission.

"There were three common values for my dad—teamwork, being a positive influence, and the power of persistence," said Bill Willis Jr. "For him, teamwork was the secret sauce of how you improved race relations. He worked with his teammates so they would be a successful team and they could work together despite the social injustices they confronted."

His emphasis on education—not only for his three sons, Bill Jr., Clem, and Dan, but for the youth he helped in his postcareer life—was uncompromising.

"He was smart enough to realize after his football career that one of the things that holds Black kids back is not having a degree," Bill Jr. said. "He teamed with judges all around the state to make sure kids would earn their diplomas while incarcerated, so that when they came back, they wouldn't be a burden on society. He encouraged us to do that, to be a positive influence."

And then there was persistence.

"Just not being deterred," Bill Jr. said. "Not giving up. Always doing the best you could with what you had. Always looking forward and being focused on the goal, keeping your eye on the prize."

The challenge of helping troubled youth never waned as Willis got older.

"My master's degree in education was extremely important as we were dealing with hundreds of boys and girls with social problems who were unable to function in normal society," he said.

He served three governors during his tenure and was lauded by all.

The crowning achievement of Willis's pro career came on July 30, 1977, when he was inducted into the Pro Football Hall of Fame. He was part of one of the most celebrated groups that also included running backs Gale Sayers and Frank Gifford, quarterback Bart Starr, and offensive tackle Forrest Gregg.

Where Motley chose Willis to present him for enshrinement, Willis selected the coach who gave him the chance to play pro football. The coach who himself was selected for the Hall of Fame a decade earlier.

"We were at camp at Bowling Green and I had an idea so I called Paul Horning, the sports editor of the *Columbus Dispatch*, and I said, 'Would you please try to find the deacon and bring him to Bowling Green and all you have to do is just have him ask for a tryout,'" Paul Brown said in reminiscing how he brought Willis into the AAFC. "I had him get hold of Marion Motley, and just come up and ask for a try-out. Well they did and the rest of it is history. I say this to you, so we understand each other, this was no social idea. I am looking for guys to play football for people who are men among a bunch of men, and this guy really measures up."

And Willis measured up. Oh, how he did.

"You have heard these people talk about playing different positions today," Brown said. "This guy played offensive tackle, offensive guard, and defensive middle-backer. He probably rewrote the book on how you take a ball from center and make a ball exchange because centers couldn't cope with him when he played over their head and we all had to get down to brass tacks in pro football and find a better way to get the quarterback out of there before it got upended."

With Browns fans who made the short trip from Cleveland there to celebrate his Hall of Fame moment, Willis expressed his thanks and eloquently described a football life—and life after football—so well lived.

"This is a great, great day for me. I am very thankful I have been blessed in many, many ways for the love of my dear wife, Odessa," he said. “She has given me inspiration and encouragement in her very strong love through the years. We have been blessed with three very fine sons. We are extremely proud of them.”

He thanked his high school coach, Ralph Webster, who was instrumental in getting him into Ohio State at a time when few Black players enrolled there. And then he thanked Brown.

“Paul, I am honored to have you to be my presenter today, because after all that’s the way it began, thirty-three years ago,” he said. “I have often said that Paul Brown saved my life, and if it had not been for PB, I am certain I would not be here receiving this honor today. Because it was he who afforded me the opportunity to play pro football, when it was not the popular thing to do. I was the first Black to play in the All-American conference and Paul Brown arranged for me to play. Without fanfare, he simply gave me the opportunity to make that ball club of his and in his own quiet way, he did have to defend his actions in those days, and it was a week later that he brought Marion Motley to camp. And Marion Motley as you know, did prove to be the best the pro football game has ever seen, in my opinion.”

And he thanked his great friend and teammate.

“Motley and I became fast friends because we had to be fast friends,” he said. “We had to go through a lot together and we had to depend upon each other. However, we not only depended on each other, we had our teammates to depend upon. And I would like to say to all of my teammates who are here today and those who are not here today, that I am deeply grateful for the companionship, for the friendship, for the togetherness we shared in those days.”

* * *

Harry Carson sat next to Bill Willis on the bus ride to a meeting of the Fritz Pollard Alliance. It was 2004, and Willis was there to share his experiences with an organization dedicated to promoting diversity hiring in the NFL.

Carson, who produced a Hall of Fame career with the Giants from 1976 to 1988, listened intently as Willis spoke of the struggles he endured as one of pro football's first Black players beginning in 1946.

"He talked about how guys would step on him with their cleats, how these guys were subjected to tremendous racism, and they had to take it," Carson said. "You're in a pile, and guys are punching you under the pile. You couldn't get angry. You just had to take it."

Carson had no idea about what Willis went through.

"When you look at him and speak to him, he was a guy who played football, but you don't envision him as a guy who was subjected to so much discrimination," Carson said. "He was that person that everybody should have been talking to to get his history. I felt so privileged to be able to speak to him and hear his stories. I think if everybody knew that story about the reintegration of the NFL, they would have a much different perspective in playing the game, understanding what their history is."

Willis always tried to pay it forward, a legacy the Browns have honored with the introduction in 2020 of the Bill Willis Coaching Fellowship. The program provides opportunities and experience to minority coaches who have historically faced barriers in their pursuit of entry-level positions and promotions. There could not be a more fitting tribute.

On November 27, 2007, a little over three years after he shared his story with Carson and others from the Fritz Pollard Alliance, Bill Willis died of complications from a stroke. He was eighty-six.

"My dad wasn't an eye-for-an-eye person," Bill Willis Jr. said. "He was a very smart guy in that he understood the consequences of acting the way people were trying to get you to act. He was too smart for that. That's part of his rock-solid character for him to be successful as a player and to endure."

Chapter 25

GONE TOO SOON

Every year on April 15, Major League Baseball honors the legacy of Jackie Robinson, whose first game with the Brooklyn Dodgers was played on that date in 1947. Players, managers, and coaches all wear No. 42 to honor the legacy of a man who has become a transcendent figure in the history of pro sports and the push for racial equality.

It's not all that far-fetched to wonder if Kenny Washington could have been celebrated for this momentous accomplishment.

After all, the Dodgers had their eye on him, too, albeit under different circumstances than Robinson.

"The Dodgers came to [Washington] before they came to Jackie to be a part of the organization," said Kraig Washington, Kenny's grandson.

But there was a catch.

"They asked him if he would go to Puerto Rico for a year and then come back here as if he was Puerto Rican," said Kraig, who explained that it would have been more acceptable back then for a Hispanic player to join the team than an African-American. "But my grandfather didn't want to pose as a Puerto Rican ballplayer, so he said no."

A case can be made that Washington was the better baseball prospect than Robinson. After all, Washington, who was the first Black player on the UCLA baseball team, hit .457 in 1937 and .397 in 1938 with 4 homers and 17 RBI to lead the team. He once hit a ball 437 feet against Stanford. In Robinson's only year on the Bruins baseball team in 1939, he hit just .097.

But for better or worse, Washington stuck with football, and after being turned away by the Bears in that brief flirtation after the 1940 College All-Star Game, he made decent money with the Hollywood Bears and rejoined Woody Strode. It was a circuitous journey that finally brought him to the NFL in 1946 as the league's first African-American player.

It lasted three years in Los Angeles, and Washington walked off the Coliseum field one last time on Kenny Washington Day at the end of the 1948 season. At age thirty, after five knee surgeries, it was over in football.

But his baseball dreams didn't flicker out entirely, and he pursued one more unlikely dream.

A year after retiring from the NFL, Washington got a tryout with the New York Giants and showed up for spring training in Phoenix. He thought maybe, just maybe, the lack of wear and tear on his knees in a more physically forgiving sport like baseball might give him a chance to make it. And some of his former teammates, including Rams running back Tom Harmon, urged Washington to give it a shot.

Giants manager Leo Durocher welcomed Washington to what might have been the most unusual circumstance for a rookie in Major League history.

"We only got eight outfielders on the roster, and I'll only carry seven during the season, so he stands a good chance," Durocher said of Washington. "I'm anxious to see Kenny play. I hope he can make it."

But once again, timing worked against Washington.

He didn't see the pitches quite like he used to, he was a step slower in the outfield after so many years of football. Durocher knew it wasn't meant to be, so he offered Washington a spot on the team's minor league club in the Pacific Coast League.

Washington hung around for a few games, but his heart—and his body—simply weren't in it.

Finally, his sports career had ended.

Regrets? Maybe a few.

"I think he was deeply hurt over the fact that he never had become a national figure in professional sports," Strode said. "Many of us who were great athletes years ago grow old with that hurt. It's a shame that people have forgotten about Kenny Washington." It was Robinson who became the focal point for integrating pro sports when he played for the Dodgers, and, yes, there were times when Washington was frustrated.

"Next to me, Jackie was the best competitor I ever saw," Washington once said. "But when he became a baseball star, it kind of shook me. I outhit him by at least two hundred points at UCLA."

Even Robinson acknowledged that "Kenny's future in baseball seemed much brighter after his brief exposure to the college game than did mine."

And Robinson expressed remorse that Washington had been largely overlooked.

"I'm sure that he had a deep hurt over the fact that he never had become a national figure in professional sports," Robinson wrote. "Many Blacks who were great athletes years ago live with this hurt. It would be a shame if he were to be forgotten. I know I will never forget him."

But Washington rarely expressed disappointment so publicly. Even to his family.

"My dad said he didn't complain much," Kraig Washington said. "He went through it and gave all he could. I think it was more frustrating to my dad. He was more like, 'This is wrong. Let's do this the right way to honor him.'

"My grandfather knew when to keep his mouth shut, and maybe

he shut it for too long," Kraig said. "But at some point, there's a responsibility of the league or the organization that is promoting good and fairness. They should do what they're supposed to do. Take a blueprint from baseball the way they honor Jackie Robinson and piggyback off of that."

There's no telling how good Washington might have been in baseball had he made a different career choice. Just as his football legacy was diminished due to circumstances beyond his control.

"I've seen Washington play," said Adam Walsh, his first coach with the Rams, "and I am thoroughly convinced that here is a man who, if given an even shake by the breaks of the game, [would have] gone down as one of the great players of the National Football League."

Life after football and his brief dalliance with baseball was an eclectic mix of endeavors for Washington. He worked for a Los Angeles-based food market and was a representative for Cutty Sark, a liquor company.

And there were several roles in movies and on TV, including the 1950 film *The Jackie Robinson Story*. Other appearances included a two-part episode of *Tarzan*, *The Reformer and the Redhead*, *Pinky*, and *Easy Living*.

Washington's future daughter-in-law met him in the 1950s and could tell right away that there was something special about him.

"I was working at a vegetable stand in Los Angeles, and he was a sales rep for Cutty Sark," Marvel Washington said. "He came by there one day and says, 'Hi, how are you? Do you know my son?' I said, 'No.' He says, 'His name is Kenny.' That's how we got to know each other."

Marvel and Kenny Washington Jr. eventually married.

Washington also became involved in politics, and developed an unlikely relationship with California Republican Richard Nixon. He supported Nixon in his 1950 U.S. Senate campaign, and the night before Nixon defeated Congresswoman Helen Douglas, Nixon spent time at Washington's home.

"He supported Nixon and I know that a lot of his Italian friends appreciated the fact that he supported him," Kraig Washington said. "He was that staunch guy who, if he backed something, he was going to stick with it."

By the 1960 presidential election, Washington had a change of heart; he voted for John F. Kennedy over Nixon and mostly voted for Democrats the rest of his life.

While Washington remained close with many of his Rams teammates, he drifted away from the organization after his career. But he did stay close with baseball and was named a part-time scout for the Dodgers in 1958. He remained with the organization for years, and his son later played with the team's minor league club.

Washington was awarded one of college football's highest honors when he was inducted into the National Football Foundation Hall of Fame in 1956, the same year his No. 13 jersey was retired at UCLA. It was the first number retired in school history.

If Washington's once-gigantic public profile had diminished over time, he remained an immensely popular person in what had now become a smaller circle of friends and relatives. He was a devoted father to Kenny Jr. and daughter, Karin, who was adopted by Washington and his wife. And Washington did for the kids in the neighborhood what the older athletes had done for him when he was growing up in Lincoln Heights.

It wasn't unusual for Washington to drive by a local park where his son and friends were playing football or baseball.

"He had a lot of respect in the neighborhood," said Kenny Norwood, who was close friends with Kenny Jr. "I was at his house just about every day. A lot of guys were there. We'd play table tennis in his garage. His wife, June, such a very nice lady. She'd get all the kids together, form a social club to keep them busy, keep them off the street."

Washington once saw Norwood playing football with the

neighborhood kids at a park on Rodeo Road (now called Obama Boulevard).

"He stopped, got out of the car, went to the gate and came onto the field, and watched us play a little touch football," said Norwood, who was sixteen at the time. "I was always the quarterback, and he liked the way I passed. But he wanted to show me something, so he took off his suit coat and laid it on the ground, rolled up his sleeves and said, 'Let me show you a better way to do that.'"

Washington told one of the kids to run down on a pattern, maybe thirty or forty yards.

"He never had to warm up his arm, and he would throw the ball on a rope," Norwood said. "He threw five or six passes and showed me how to step back and move. I could not believe how strong his arm was. He made us look wimpy. We were like, just wow."

Willard Love will never forget the time Washington showed up at the 1958 Los Angeles city championship game between Love's Dorsey High team and San Fernando. Willard and Kenny Jr. were teammates and close friends, and "Big Kenny," as they called the elder Washington, was there to show support.

For Love, it was a moment that offered a lasting impression.

"I had not expected to play that day because I was playing behind a couple of players," Love said. "But I got in, and I came up to bat and I remember Mr. Washington standing behind the backstop. He let me know that I was a good hitter to give me the confidence to do well."

Love drew a walk that scored a run on his first at-bat.

The next time he came to the plate?

"I hit a three-run homer," he said. "He really encouraged me with my self-confidence."

Dorsey won, 18–5.

(Keyshawn here: Talk about a small world. Mr. Willard was my principal when I went to Dorsey High.)

Washington also taught life lessons to his son and his friends. Like the time he came home one day to see Kenny Jr. and his buddies playing dominoes and shooting craps for money. Washington put away his coat and walked over.

"Mind if I join you guys?" he said.

"Guys had their paychecks with them, their rent money," Norwood said. "Kenny got in the game and, needless to say, after the game, he'd won and he picked up the money—even the checks before they were cashed—and put on his coat again and walked out the door."

Norwood and his friends were stunned.

"Guys were going crazy," he said. "What are we going to do?"

A little while later, Washington walked back into the house.

"He gave everybody their money back, and then he gave us a little chat, a little lesson about gambling," he said.

There were two things.

"Number one, don't gamble in his house," Norwood said. "Number two, don't gamble."

* * *

Jim Tunney Jr. barely recognized Kenny Washington when he ran into him at a Dodgers game during the 1970 season.

Tunney, the son of Washington's high school coach, first met the legendary athlete when Tunney was just a small boy and Washington already seemed like a larger-than-life figure. But now, he looked thin, frail. His smile was still there, but just barely. Tunney knew something was wrong.

"He just didn't look good, and he was really down," Tunney said. "His whole being was depressed."

Washington, just fifty-one, was suffering from polyarteritis nodosa, a rare disease affecting small and medium-sized blood vessels that damages vital organs.

Tunney knew he needed to do something. So he, Mike Frankovich, the former UCLA quarterback turned actor and producer, and others arranged a benefit at the Hollywood Palladium to honor Washington and help raise funds to defray his medical expenses.

More than a thousand luminaries from sports, the movie and television industries, and other businesses showed up to support Washington. The event raised thousands of dollars for Washington, who seemed to be doing better by the time the benefit was held in September.

Letters were read from well-wishers, including Bears owner George Halas, the man who'd tried but failed to bring him to the Bears in 1940. And there were in-person tributes—including one from actor Eddie Albert, who said "Kenny Washington was a two-way athlete. He was a player on and off the field, a grand man." At the end of the night, Washington was given a standing ovation.

Overcome with emotion, Washington addressed the crowd, "In reverse, this tribute to Kenny Washington," he said, "ought to be a tribute from Kenny Washington to you."

When Strode had heard about his friend's situation, he returned from Italy, where he was making a film.

"I couldn't believe how skinny he'd gotten," Strode recalled. "It took all the guts I had to hold the tears back. I wanted to take him back to Rome with me. I said, 'Why don't you come over and we'll sip some wine on the Via Veneto.'"

Over the next several months, Washington's condition worsened, and by May, he'd returned to UCLA Medical Center for further treatment.

"I've been in and out of here so many times, I guess I'll stay here this time until it all comes out," he told Associated Press reporters Bob Myers from his hospital room. "I can take a little exercise, walking around, but I get tired pretty easily."

Washington never got better, though.

Kenny Jr. and his dear friend, Kenny Norwood, visited him and knew the prognosis was grim.

"He grabbed my hand and said, 'Kenny, you look out for my son,'" Norwood said.

On June 24, 1971—after having done so much for so many, even if he'd never gotten the chance to flourish the way he would have if opportunity and timing had been different—Kenny Washington was gone.

He was just fifty-two.

* * *

Hall of Fame quarterback Bob Waterfield was one of Washington's pallbearers at his funeral, a final testament to a friendship between the two legendary UCLA players that began when they were teammates with the Rams and lasted until Washington's final days.

As far as Waterfield was concerned, there was never another player like Washington, either before or since.

"Kenny was the best football player I ever saw in my life, and that includes everybody I ever knew," Waterfield said. "If he had come into the National Football League directly from UCLA, he would have been, in my opinion, the best the NFL had ever seen."

Washington never got that chance because the NFL was not ready for him in 1940, when he was at the height of his athletic brilliance. Not until the wear and tear of five knee surgeries and years of punishment with the Hollywood Bears would the league finally welcome him—and only then after fierce pressure when the Rams moved to Los Angeles.

He didn't enjoy a legendary Hall of Fame career in his three seasons with the Rams, but he did help transform the NFL as a pioneer in his own right. As did Woody Strode, his best friend and the man he demanded be by his side; they were the first Black players to reintegrate the NFL after more than a decade-long ban.

But on this, the seventy-fifth anniversary of Washington's first NFL season with the Rams and fifty years after his passing, he deserves a place in football immortality for his historic journey that has benefited so many who have come after. As does Strode, who was with Washington since their days at UCLA, then with the Hollywood Bears pro team and the Rams before helping Calgary to the only unbeaten season in CFL history.

The Pro Football Hall of Fame is reserved for those who made lasting contributions to the game, and the impact that Washington and Strode had was simply incalculable. They deserve a place alongside Willis and Motley.

May they never be forgotten.

ACKNOWLEDGMENTS

The story of the first four players to break the color line in professional football could not be told without the help of so many who took the time and effort to share their knowledge, insight, experiences, and analysis. We thank all of you for your efforts.

The families, friends, and other acquaintances of all four players were incredibly helpful. Bill Willis Jr. and Clem Willis are proof that Bill Willis was as good a father as he was a football player. Kraig Washington and Marvel Washington, your help in telling the Kenny Washington story was invaluable. "Uncle" Kenny Norwood and Willard Love, your recollections of Washington made it seem like it all happened yesterday, not more than half a century ago. Jim Tunney Jr. first met Kenny Washington when he was a star for his father's Lincoln High School team in the 1930s, and his stories from that time were incredibly detailed. Upton Bell was just a boy when his father, former NFL commissioner Bert Bell, took him to see Kenny Washington and Woody Strode in their first training camp with the Rams in 1946. Thank you for all your insights.

Pamela Larson Strode, you carry your family's name with great pride and dignity, and your time and attention to detail were extraordinary.

Mahalo. Thanks to Tony Motley for sharing thoughts of your grandfather's legacy. And to you too, Joe Horrigan and Shaun Horrigan, for your vast knowledge of these players and their historical significance.

Paul Brown was a central figure in the integration of pro football, and his signing of Willis and Motley was vitally important. Brown's son Mike, now the Bengals' owner, offered remarkably vivid personal recollections of his dealings with both players and provided extraordinary insight into Paul Brown's thinking. His participation is greatly appreciated.

The absence of African-American players is a blight on the NFL and the owners from that era. Four families still run teams from that era, and the willingness of George McCaskey, Art Rooney II and Jim Rooney, John Mara, and Michael Bidwill to reflect on that time is greatly appreciated. NFL commissioner Roger Goodell also offered an unvarnished assessment and acknowledged the importance of owning up to the league's failures.

Jason Wright is making history with the Washington Football Team—a team whose history of bigotry was at the center of the previous ban on African-American players—and his reflections on the past, present, and future were extraordinary.

Paul Brown's willingness to give Willis and Motley a chance others would not is central to the story of NFL integration. His son Mike Brown was an eyewitness to that era of history, and his insights and recollections of Willis, Motley, and Paul Brown were exceptional. Thanks also to Bud Grant, a former teammate of Motley's, who played for Brown in the service.

John Wooten played for Brown and knew Motley and Willis quite well, and his memories and analysis were greatly appreciated. His lifetime spent trying to increase opportunities for African-American coaches offers a lasting and important legacy. Harry Carson carries on that work for the Fritz Pollard Alliance, and his help in bringing this story to life was most appreciated. Thanks also to Fritz Pollard III for his remembrances of his grandfather, another true pioneer of professional football. And to Rod Graves, who continues the heavy lifting in Pollard's name.

Joe Namath is immortalized for his work as Super Bowl III champion, but he also contributed to better race relations during his time with the Jets. He also got to work in the movies with Woody Strode, and sharing those memories was an unexpected bonus.

Thanks to Doug Williams, James Harris, Tony Dungy, Donovan McNabb, and Logan Ryan for your insights.

The insights of sports historians Damion Thomas, Dr. Charles Ross, Professor Rob Ruck, Jon Kendle, Dan Daly, Larry Phillips, and Len Shapiro provided important texture and perspective. Shout-out to Chris Murray for his help on Motley's time at Nevada.

With great appreciation to Brandon Faber, Peter John-Baptiste, Emily Parker, Pete Abitante, Julie Jensen, Joanna Hunter, Artis Twyman, Mark Dalton, Pat Hanlon, Jennifer Conley Escobar, Steve Rourke, and Tim Tessalone.

Many thanks to Mike Ibara and Robert Granados of Lincoln High School.

Thanks to California-based librarians Marilyn Smithson and Elena Smith.

To everyone at Grand Central Publishing, thank you for your patience, wisdom, and support. Rachel Kambury, Bob Castillo, and Kamrun Nesa, so greatly appreciated.

And Sean Desmond: Words don't do justice to your faith and willingness to have this story told. We cannot thank you enough for all you've done.

FROM KEYSHAWN

To my family: My wife, Jennifer Johnson; and my kids, Maia, Keyshawn, London, Vance, and Shyla. Thank you for putting up with my work commitments. Love all you guys so much. I wouldn't be able to do any of this without you in my life.

Special relationships: Shelley Smith, Jerome Stanley, Chris Ellison. Thank you for putting up with me.

Brothers and sisters: Sandra Thomas, Kimberly Thomas, Denise Thomas, and Michael Thomas.

And all my family members I didn't name: Love all of you.

Special thank you to my ESPN crew: Norby, Stephanie, Seth, Greg, Justin, Dave, Amanda, Evan, Zubin, Jay Will, Alan, and all the radio production crew.

My OG *NFL Countdown* crew: Boom, TG, CC, Coach. No one could touch us, period!!

My *NFL Live* crew: Laura, Spears, Dan, Mina, RC. Again, no one can see us, and ESPN is blessed to have us. Thank you for putting up with me.

Thank you to my wife for dealing with me, for holding me down, loving me unconditionally, and being so beautiful. Thank you for marrying my pain in the ass. I love you so much.

To Bob: Thanks a million for this great collaboration you put together with me. Without your insight, none of this would have happened. Thanks again, my friend.

FROM BOB

To Calvin Lawrence and Hank Winnicki, thank you for believing in this project. Pat Dolan, thank you for saving *Newsday*. You did, and your colleagues can never repay you.

To an amazing *Newsday* staff of writers and editors, a privilege to work next to you.

Thanks to the Pro Football Writers of America, just an extraordinary group of writers dedicated to bringing the story of the NFL to our readers.

Special thanks to the Board: Lindsay Jones, Mike Sando, Dan Pompei, Jenny Vrentas, Charean Williams, Mike Jones, Calvin Watkins, and Jeffrey Legwold. And to Chris Pika, for some great research and advice.

Much gratitude to Jim Donovan, Ian O'Connor, Wayne Coffey, and Jon Eisenberg for your sage advice.

Judy Battista, Neil Best, Tom Rock, Kimberley Martin, Al Iannazzone, Steve Serby, Mike Giardi, Kimberly Jones, Mike Garafolo, and Darin Gantt, thanks for sharing all the insanity.

Mom and Sandy, Dad and Jackie, love you always.

Andrea Glauber: Your guidance, patience, and advice on this project have been priceless. I love you.

Emily Glauber: Thanks for all the suggestions, the edits, and for being an incredible sounding board. And thanks for the title! I love you.

Jutta Glauber: The shining light in my life. Always. None of this happens without you.

To Keyshawn: I could not have asked for a better partner to share such an important and worthwhile story. Your passion, belief, and trust were extraordinary. Thank you, my friend.

SOURCE NOTES

INTRODUCTION

Interviews with John Wooten, Bill Willis Jr., Mike Brown, Joe Horrigan; "'Most Underrated Team' Gives Fright of Season to 'Most Powerful Team,'" *Los Angeles Times*, Dec. 10, 1939; *Goal Dust: The Warm and Candid Memoirs of a Pioneer Black Athlete and Actor* by Woody Strode and Sam Young, 1990; 1940 NFL Draft Listing, Profootballreference.com; "Segregationist George Preston Marshall's Monument Removed from RFK Grounds," *Washington Post*, June 19, 2020; "George Floyd Death Ignited Protests Far Beyond Minneapolis," *Minneapolis Star-Tribune*, June 3, 2020; "UCLA 2020 Football Information Guide"; "Branch Rickey," Baseballhall.org; "UCLA Classic UCLA Bruins Rediscovered," May 20, 2014.

CHAPTER 1: INTO HIS UNCLE'S ARMS

Interviews with Marvel Washington, Kraig Washington, Jim Tunney Jr., Kenny Norwood, Robert Granados, Mike Ibara; LAPDonline.org; *Goal Dust: The Warm and Candid Memoirs of a Pioneer Black Athlete and Actor* by Woody Strode and Sam Young, 1990; "Edgar 'Blue' Washington," by Mark Perkins, Sabr.org; Blue Washington IMDB;

"Kenny Washington," *Encyclopedia Britannica*; "NFL Groundbreaker Kenny Washington Nearly a Forgotten Man," *Los Angeles Times*, Oct. 12, 2011; "Lincoln High Will Now Seat You," *Los Angeles Times*, Oct. 11, 1992; "The Kenny Washington Stadium Foundation"; Lincoln High School yearbooks 1934, 1935, 1936; *Forgotten Four: The Integration of Pro Football*, EPIX, documentary, 2014; "The NFL's Jackie Robinson," *Sports Illustrated*, Oct. 11, 2009.

CHAPTER 2: FROM "BEANPOLE" TO BRUIN

Interviews with Joe Horrigan, Pamela Larson Strode, Damion Thomas; *Goal Dust: The Warm and Candid Memoirs of a Pioneer Black Athlete and Actor* by Woody Strode and Sam Young, 1990; "Best Performance in Changing Sport," *Los Angeles Times*, March 26, 1991; Prep Cal Track results, Lynbrook Sports; Furlong Tract Community in Los Angeles, AAregistry.org; *The Black Bruins: The Remarkable Lives of UCLA's Jackie Robinson, Woody Strode, Tom Bradley, Kenny Washington, and Ray Bartlett* by James W. Johnson, 2017; *Hardballers: The Men Who Broke the NFL Color Barrier*, screenplay by Kalai Strode and Pamela Strode, 2009.

CHAPTER 3: THE BIG KID FROM CANTON

Interviews with Tony Motley, Shaun Horrigan, Joe Horrigan, Larry Phillips, Willie Jeffries, Chris Murray, Bill Robinson, Damion Thomas, John Wooten, David Jingo; Pro Football Hall of Fame luncheon taped interviews, Feb. 13, 1967; *Lines Broken: The Story of Marion Motley*, PBS Western Reserve, documentary, 2021; *Ohio's Autumn Legends* by Larry Phillips, 2016; *The Best Show in Football: The 1946–1955 Cleveland Browns* by Andy Piascik, 2007; *The New Thinking Man's*

Guide to Pro Football by Paul Zimmerman, 1984; *Legends by the Lake* by John Keim, 1999; *Gridiron Gauntlet: The Story of the Men Who Integrated Pro Football in Their Own Words* by Andy Piascik, 2009; *Forgotten Four: The Integration of Pro Football*, EPIX, documentary, 2014; "Bulldogs Take 48–6 Decision in New Rivalry; Motley Leads Drive," *Canton Repository*, Sept. 18, 1938; "McKinley Bulldogs Impressive in 54–0 Triumph over East Tech; Marion Motley Makes Fine Debut at Fullback," *Canton Repository*, Sept. 19, 1937; "Bruising Motley Could Do It All," *Canton Repository*, Jan. 27, 2002.

CHAPTER 4: OUT FROM HIS BROTHER'S SHADOW

Interviews with Bill Willis Jr., Clem Willis, Joe Horrigan, John Wooten, Damion Thomas; *Expanding Your Horizons: Collegiate Football's Greatest Team* by Donald Steinberg, 1992; *The Game That Was: The Early Days of Pro Football* by Myron Cope, 1970; "Blazing Through Barriers, Remembering Speedy Bill Willis, Who Helped Integrate the NFL," *Sports Illustrated*, Dec. 10, 2007; "Cleveland Browns Great Bill Willis Leaves a Lifetime of Memories," *Cleveland Plain Dealer*, Nov. 29, 2007; *PB: The Paul Brown Story* by Paul Brown with Jack Clary, 1979; *Gridiron Gauntlet: The Story of the Men Who Integrated Pro Football in Their Own Words* by Andy Piascik, 2009; "Bill Willis, Dominant Defender," *Coffin Corner*, vol. 16 no. 5, 1994; "Was Jesse Owens Snubbed by Adolf Hitler at the Berlin Olympics?" Brittanica.com; "Bill Willis: Speed, Quickness Carried Ohio Lineman to 2 Halls of Fame," *Richland Source*, Aug. 10, 2019.

CHAPTER 5: UCLA BECKONS FOR WASHINGTON AND STRODE

Interviews with Jim Tunney Jr., Pamela Larson Strode, Kraig Washington, Marvel Washington, Kenny Norwood; "The NFL's Jackie

Robinson," *Sports Illustrated*, Oct. 11, 2009; *Goal Dust: The Warm and Candid Memoirs of a Pioneer Black Athlete and Actor* by Woody Strode and Sam Young, 1990; *The Black Bruins: The Remarkable Lives of UCLA's Jackie Robinson, Woody Strode, Tom Bradley, Kenny Washington, and Ray Bartlett* by James W. Johnson, 2017; "Leni Riefenstahl," Wikipedia.org; "World War II," Britannica.com; "Down Front, with J. Cullen Fentress," *California Eagle*, Dec. 21, 1939.

CHAPTER 6: 50 BUCKS AND GET OUTTA HERE

Interviews with Willie Jeffries, Harry Carson, Tony Motley, Bill Hamilton, Joe Horrigan, Shaun Horrigan, Chris Murray, Damion Thomas; "Marion Motley Thanks Friends Whose Support Returned Him to U.N. Campus," *Nevada State Journal*, Nov. 9, 1940; "On 100th Birthday, Legacy of Nevada's Marion Motley More Important Than Ever," Nevadasportsnet.com, June 5, 2020; "Marion Motley's Secret," *Washington Times*, Sept. 19, 2012; "Marion Motley," Nevadawolfpack.com; *Ohio's Autumn Legends* by Larry Phillips, 2016; South Carolina State Plans to Retire Motley's Jersey," *Times and Democrat* (Orangeburg, SC), June 29, 1999.

CHAPTER 7: THE SCRAWNY QUARTERBACK TURNED COACHING LEGEND

Interviews with Mike Brown, John Wooten, Dan Daly, Larry Phillips, Cliff Guyon; *PB: The Paul Brown Story* by Paul Brown with Jack Clary, 1979; "Salute to Victors," *Baltimore Sun*, Dec. 2, 1934; "Paul Brown: Father of Ohio QBs Casts Shadow over Draft," Bengals.com, April 20, 2020; "Stark Icons: Paul Brown's Influence Still Extends Far Beyond Massillon," *Canton Repository*, March 27, 2016; "Brown Smiles as

He Reads Cutter Yarns," *Evening Independent* (Massillon, OH), Dec. 15, 1934; "Cradle of Coaches: A Legacy of Excellence: Paul Brown," MiamiOhio.edu, 2013; Collegefootballreference.com.

CHAPTER 8: BROWN AND WILLIS DOT THE I

Interviews with Mike Brown, Bill Willis Jr., Clem Willis, Dan Daly, Larry Phillips, John Wooten, Dr. Charles Ross; *A Thinking Man's Guide to Pro Football* by Paul Zimmerman, 1970; *Expanding Your Horizons: Collegiate Football's Greatest Team* by Donald Steinberg, 1992; *The Game That Was: The Early Days of Pro Football* by Myron Cope, 1970; "Hall of Famer Helped Break Color Barrier in Modern Pro Football," *Los Angeles Times*, Nov. 29, 2007; "Ohio State to Retire Bill Willis' No. 99," *Dayton Daily News*, Oct. 6, 2007; *PB: The Paul Brown Story* by Paul Brown with Jack Clary, 1979; *Ohio's Autumn Legends* by Larry Phillips, 2016.

CHAPTER 9: BLACK PLAYERS NOT WANTED

Interviews with Roger Goodell, John Mara, Michael Bidwill, George McCaskey, Art Rooney II, Jim Rooney, Fritz Pollard III, Rob Ruck, Joe Horrigan, Len Shapiro, Bruce Speight, Damion Thomas, John Wooten; "Fans Feel That Negros Should Play Football," *Atlanta Daily World*, March 26, 1946; "A History of Segregation in the NFL," *Atlantic*, Nov. 17, 2011; "For Pollard, Recognition Is Deserved," *Chicago Tribune*, Jan. 28, 2005; "Prejudice in Sports: It's as Old as Fritz Pollard, 82," *Los Angeles Times*, July 6, 1976; *Chicago Bears Centennial Scrapbook* by Don Pierson and Dan Pompei, 2019; *The League* by Jon Eisenberg, 2018; "Robinson, Star Dimmed by Bias, to Play on Army Team," *New York Amsterdam Star-News*, Oct. 17, 1942; "An Open Letter to Jimmie

Powers," *New York Amsterdam Star-News,* Oct. 14, 1939; "After Baseball Victory, Demands Negro in Professional Football Leagues," *Cleveland Call and Post,* Nov. 17, 1945; "Negro Pro Football Only Needs Money," *Atlanta Daily World,* Nov. 14, 1940; *Lost Champions: Four Men, Two Teams, and the Breaking of Pro Football's Color Line* by Gretchen Atwood, 2016; "Joe Lillard Becomes the Last Black Man in Pro Football," Vice.com, Dec. 3, 2015; *Halas by Halas: The Autobiography of George Halas* by George Halas with Gwen Morgan and Arthur Veysey, 1971; "The Man Behind Floyd of Rosedale," *Iowa City Press-Citizen,* Nov. 25, 1989.

CHAPTER 10: JACKIE, KENNY, AND WOODY

Interviews with Jim Tunney, Kraig Washington, Marvel Washington, Pamela Larson Strode; *The Black Bruins: The Remarkable Lives of UCLA's Jackie Robinson, Woody Strode, Tom Bradley, Kenny Washington, and Ray Bartlett* by James W. Johnson, 2017; "Los Angeles and the Reintegration of the NFL," Los Angeles Public Library, blog post, Feb. 3, 2017; *I Never Had It Made* by Jackie Robinson, as told to Alfred Duckett, 1972; *Goal Dust: The Warm and Candid Memoirs of a Pioneer Black Athlete and Actor* by Woody Strode and Sam Young, 1990; "Kenny Washington Hailed as Better Back Than Red Grange," *Afro-American* (Los Angeles), Oct. 28, 1939; "Robinson, Washington on Bruin 11," *Los Angeles Sentinel,* Feb. 23, 1950; "UCLA to Have 5 Negroes on Squad," *New York Amsterdam News,* Sept. 30, 1939; "The Black Player: Kenny Washington Was a Man to Remember," *Gridiron Magazine,* Nov. 8, 1971.

CHAPTER 11: BLUEJACKETS

Interviews with Bud Grant, Mike Brown, Tony Motley, Joe Horrigan, Larry Phillips; *The Game That Was* by Myron Cope 1970; "Marion Motley: Force of Nature, Complete Player," *Baltimore Sun*, Nov. 10, 1995; *PB: The Paul Brown Story* by Paul Brown with Jack Clary, 1979; Collegefootballreference.com; "Great Lakes Routs Notre Dame 39–7 for Smashing Upset," *Pittsburgh Press*, Dec. 2, 1945. "Tonight! All-Stars, Packers Collide," *Chicago Tribune*, Aug. 5, 1966; "Arch Ward Dead; Sports Editor, 58; *Chicago Tribune* Columnist Originated All-Star Games—Heard on Radio, TV," *New York Times*, July 10, 1955; *America's Game* by Michael MacCambridge, 2004; *The Best Show in Football: The 1946–1955 Cleveland Browns* by Andy Piascik, 2007; "The All-America Football Conference," *Coffin Corner*, vol. 2, 1980; "Thanks, Arch, for Being a Sportswriter," Knight-Ridder Newspapers, July 14, 1987.

CHAPTER 12: WHEN HOPE TURNED TO HEARTBREAK

Interviews with Kraig Washington, George McCaskey, Pamela Larson Strode, Dan Daly, Rob Ruck, Dr. Charles Ross, Damion Thomas, Joe Horrigan; "Fay Young: The Stuff Is Here, Past-Present-Future," *Chicago Defender*, Sept. 7, 1940; "Packers Open Drills for College All-Star Game," *Chicago Tribune*, Aug. 13, 1940; "Kenny Washington Biography," Biography.jrank.org; "Salute to a Star," *Pittsburgh Courier*, Dec. 23, 1939; "Your Answer, Gentlemen," *California Eagle*, Dec. 21, 1939; *Gridiron Gauntlet: The Story of the Men Who Integrated Pro Football in Their Own Words* by Andy Piascik, 2009; "Bulldogs, Bears Vie Today at Gilmore," *Los Angeles Times*, Oct. 13, 1940; "Pacific Coast Football League 1940–45," Profootballarchives.com.

CHAPTER 13: KENNY WASHINGTON BREAKS THROUGH THE LINE

Interviews with Joe Horrigan, Dr. Charles Ross, Damion Thomas, Rob Ruck; "The Black Athlete Makes His Mark," *Ebony*, May 1969; "How the Media Helped Overturn the NFL's Unwritten Ban on Black Players," *Los Angeles Times*, Jan. 28, 2017; "A Change of Opinion," *Los Angeles Sentinel*, Jan. 29, 1950; *Lost Champions: Four Men, Two Teams, and the Breaking of Pro Football's Color Line* by Gretchen Atwood, 2016; "Los Angeles Sports Scribes Opened NFL to Blacks in 1946," *Los Angeles Sentinel*, April 14, 1983; "Los Angeles Pro Eleven Signs Kenny Washington," *Afro-American* (Los Angeles), March 30, 1946; "Pro Grid Bias May Be Problem for Rams," *Pittsburgh Courier*, Jan. 19, 1946; "Pro Grid Champs Say They Want Buddy Young," *Pittsburgh Courier*, Jan. 26, 1946; "Prying Pye: Another Slap at Rams," *Los Angeles Sentinel*, Aug. 13, 1970; "Rams 'Freeze Out' All-America Team," *New York Times*, Jan. 30, 1946; "Rams Sign Kenny Washington," *Pittsburgh Courier*, March 30, 1946; "Rams Complete Washington-Strode Battery, Outmaneuver Pro Rivals," *Cleveland Call and Post*, May 18, 1946; "A Tribute to Halley," *Los Angeles Sentinel*, April 27, 1967.

CHAPTER 14: TRYOUTS FOR THE BROWNS

Interviews with Mike Brown, Bud Grant, Tony Motley, Upton Bell, Bill Willis Jr., Clem Willis, John Wooten, Joe Horrigan, Shaun Horrigan; "Marion Motley Joins Bill Willis at Browns' Pro Football Camp," *Cleveland Call and Post*, Aug. 17, 1946; "Black Players Mark 50 Seasons in Pro Football," *Los Angeles Sentinel*, January 1996; *A Thinking Man's Guide to Pro Football* by Paul Zimmerman, 1970; *The Game That Was: The Early Days of Pro Football* by Myron Cope, 1970; *Expanding Your Horizons: Collegiate Football's Greatest Team* by Donald Steinberg, 1992; "Willis-PB Made History, Not Hype," Bengals.com, July 11, 2000.

CHAPTER 15: GREAT EXPECTATIONS AND DASHED HOPES

Interviews with Upton Bell, Kraig Washington, George McCaskey, Pamela Larson Strode, Rob Ruck, Dr. Charles Ross, Damion Thomas; "Pro Elevens in Grid Titanic for Replay of World Championship," *Los Angeles Times*, Sept. 6, 1946; "Kenny Washington," Biography.com, April 1, 2014; "Forgotten Hero: Washington Broke NFL's Color Barrier in 1946," NFL.com, Feb. 17, 2012; *Goal Dust: The Warm and Candid Memoirs of a Pioneer Black Athlete and Actor* by Woody Strode and Sam Young, 1990; "Los Angeles and the Reintegration of the NFL," Los Angeles Public Library, blog post, Feb. 3, 2017; "Kenny's Knee Well, Exercising Again," *Valley Times* (North Hollywood), May 9, 1946; "Ken Washington Under Knife," Associated Press, April 11, 1946; "The Hyland Filing," *Los Angeles Times*, March 22, 1946; *Hardballers: The Men Who Broke the NFL Color Barrier*, screenplay by Kalai Strode and Pamela Strode, 2009.

CHAPTER 16: GREATNESS TAKES ROOT IN CLEVELAND

Interviews with Upton Bell, Bud Grant, John Wooten, Mike Brown, Bill Willis Jr., Clem Willis, Tony Motley, Dan Daly; "Bill Willis, Marion Motley to Encounter Dixie Bred Stars as Cleveland Browns, Miami Seahawks Open All-American [*sic*] Conference Play," *Cleveland Call and Post*, Sept. 7, 1946; "Brown Turned Cleveland into a Football-Crazy City," Thomson News Service, July 20, 1999; *PB: The Paul Brown Story* by Paul Brown with Jack Clary, 1979; *Gridiron Gauntlet: The Story of the Men Who Integrated Pro Football in Their Own Words* by Andy Piascik, 2009; "Bill Willis, Dominant Defender," *Coffin Corner*, vol. 16 no. 5, 1994; *The Game That Was: The Early Days of Pro Football* by Myron Cope, 1970; *A Thinking Man's Guide to Pro Football* by Paul Zimmerman, 1970; *Legends by the Lake* by John Keim, 1999;

The Best Show in Football: The 1946–1955 Cleveland Browns by Andy Piascik, 2007.

CHAPTER 17: SEPARATE WAYS

Interviews with Kraig Washington, Jim Tunney Jr., Pamela Larson Strode, Joe Horrigan, Dan Daly; "Kenny Washington Day Proclaimed," *Los Angeles Sentinel*, Dec. 9, 1948; *The Black Bruins: The Remarkable Lives of UCLA's Jackie Robinson, Woody Strode, Tom Bradley, Kenny Washington, and Ray Bartlett* by James W. Johnson, 2017; *Forgotten Four: The Integration of Pro Football*, EPIX, documentary, 2014; Profootballreference.com; "Dream Backfield Haunted by Nightmares as Inspired Ram Team Rolls to Easy Triumph," *Valley Times* (North Hollywood), Oct. 20, 1947; "Cards Whip Rams, 17–10; Washington Goes 92 Yards," *Chicago Tribune*, Nov. 3, 1947; "Still the Kingfish," *Los Angeles Times*, Nov. 7, 1947; "Salute to Kenny," *Pittsburgh Courier*, Nov. 15, 1947; "Aerial Offensive Leads Esk Attack," *Calgary Herald*, Sept. 5, 1950; "Woody Strode: Calgary Stampeder and Hollywood Stalwart," Albertahistoricplaces.com, February 2018.

CHAPTER 18: A DYNASTY IS BORN

Interviews with Upton Bell, Bud Grant, Mike Brown, Bill Willis Jr., Clem Willis, Joe Horrigan, Dan Daly, Larry Phillips, John Wooten; *The Game That Was: The Early Days of Pro Football* by Myron Cope, 1970; Profootballreference.com; *PB: The Paul Brown Story* by Paul Brown with Jack Clary, 1979; *Gridiron Gauntlet: The Story of the Men Who Integrated Pro Football in Their Own Words* by Andy Piascik, 2009; "Bill Willis, Dominant Defender," *Coffin Corner*, vol. 16 no. 5, 1994; *Lost Champions: Four Men, Two Teams, and the Breaking of Pro Football's*

Color Line by Gretchen Atwood, 2016; *Return to Glory: The Story of the Cleveland Browns* by Bill Levy, 1965; *Expanding Your Horizons: Collegiate Football's Greatest Team* by Donald Steinberg, 1992; *Forgotten Four: The Integration of Pro Football* EPIX, documentary, 2014.

CHAPTER 19: LEGACY AND REDEMPTION

Interviews with Jason Wright, Joe Horrigan, Len Shapiro, Dan Daly, George McCaskey, John Mara, Jim Rooney; *Civil Rights on the Gridiron: The Kennedy Administration and the Desegregation of the Washington Redskins* by Thomas G. Smith, 1987; "Shirley Povich Dead at 92," Associated Press, June 7, 1998; "Ram-Redskin Boycott Backed by Local NAACP," *California Eagle,* Aug. 3, 1961; "Of Football: Civic Center Spotlight," *Lincoln Heights-Bulletin News* (Los Angeles), July 30, 1961; "Bobby Mitchell, Redkin Extraordinaire, RIP," *Fredericksburg Free Lance-Star,* April 8, 2020; "Redskins' Past Owner Marshall Was No Saint," *Murfreesboro Post,* June 29, 2014; *The League* by Jon Eisenberg, 2018; "As Red Sox Confront Their Former Owner's Racist Legacy, the Redskins Should Follow," *Washington Post,* Aug. 17, 2017; "Granddaughter of Former Redskins Owner George P. Marshall Condemns Team Name," *Washington Post,* July 23, 2014; "Dead Man Giving," *Washington City Paper,* May 7, 2004.

CHAPTER 20: THE SINS OF THE GRANDFATHERS

Interviews with Roger Goodell, George McCaskey, John Mara, Michael Bidwill, Art Rooney II, Jim Rooney, Fritz Pollard III, Joe Horrigan, Damion Thomas; "Bill Nunn Blazes Another Trail," Profootballhof.com, Feb. 17, 2021; "Confidentially Yours: Dan Burley," *New York Amsterdam News,* Sept. 20, 1947; "Football Again: NFL vs. the AAC," *New York*

Amsterdam News, Sept. 27, 1947; "Negro Fans Converted for Pro Football," *New York Amsterdam News*, Dec. 20, 1947; *Dan Rooney: My 75 Years with the Pittsburgh Steelers* by Dan Rooney as told to Andrew Masich and David F. Halaas, 2007; *A Different Way to Win: Dan Rooney's Story* by Jim Rooney, 2019; "Meet Four Men Who Broke the NFL's Color Line," NFLPA.com; "Black Players Mark 50 Seasons in Pro Football," *Los Angeles Sentinel*, January, 1996; *Brian Piccolo: A Short Season* by Jeannie Morris, 1971.

CHAPTER 21: THE COULD-HAVE-BEENS…

Interviews with Doug Williams, James Harris, Tony Dungy, Donovan McNabb, Tony Motley, Roger Goodell, Art Rooney II, Jim Rooney, John Mara, Jason Wright, Cyrus Mehri, Logan Ryan, Dr. Charles Ross, Joe Browne, Dan Daly, Pamela Larson Strode; *Outside the Lines: African Americans and the Integration of the National Football League* by Charles Ross, 2001; *Hardballers: The Men Who Broke the NFL Color Barrier*, screenplay by Kalai Strode and Pamela Strode, 2009; "NFL Films: Los Angeles Rams," footage from 1946; "Motley Raps Browns, Charges Team Ignores Negroes," Associated Press, Feb. 5, 1965; Bill Belichick press conference, Sept. 13, 2020; *Dan Rooney: My 75 Years with the Pittsburgh Steelers* by Dan Rooney as told to Andrew Masich and David F. Halaas, 2007; *A Different Way to Win: Dan Rooney's Story* by Jim Rooney, 2019; *Namath: A Biography* by Mark Kriegel, 2004; "Tony Dungy Pens Powerful Letter to NFL Owners About Black Coaches," Firstandpen.com, Feb. 5, 2021; "Rams Will Try Kenny Washington at Quarterback Post in Start of Season," *California Eagle*, July 25, 1946.

CHAPTER 22: WOODY STRODE: A PIONEER SEVERAL TIMES OVER

Interviews with Joe Namath, Pamela Larson Strode, Joe Horrigan, Thomas Nittmann; "Woody Strode: He Wasn't the Star, but He Stole the Movie," *New York Times*, Sept. 9, 1971; "Steven Spielberg interview on 'Spartacus,'" July 1, 2012; "Woody Strode Centennial Memorial," by Kalai Strode, YouTube video, July 24, 2014; "Toy Story: 10 Bizarre Facts You Never Knew About Woody," Screenrant, July 10, 2020; "2 American Stars Got Start in Italy," Associated Press, Jan. 3, 1975; "Toy Story: All the Pop Culture That Inspired Pixar's Classic Series," *Atlantic*, June 19, 2019; "On Field and Screen, His Strength Brought Us Together," Woody Strode profile, https://optimism.ucla.edu/profiles/woody-strode/.

CHAPTER 23: BETTER DAYS

Interviews with Tony Motley, Shaun Horrigan, Joe Horrigan, Dan Daly, Larry Phillips; "Jim Brown: Motley the Best Ever," *Lancaster (OH) Eagle-Gazette*, June 30, 1999; Marion Motley, Hall of Fame Induction Speech, Aug. 3, 1968; Bill Willis, Hall of Fame Presentation Speech, Aug. 3, 1968; "Motley Raps Browns, Charges Team Ignores Negroes," Associated Press, Feb. 5, 1965; "Marion Motley's Greatness Should Not Be Forgotten," *USA Today*, Feb. 17, 2013; "A Change of Pace," Bill Nunn column, *Pittsburgh Courier*, Feb. 20, 1965; "Motley Could Do It All," *Akron Beacon Journal*, July 28, 1968; "In Motley's Memory, Pro Football Still Hurts," *Pittsburgh Post-Gazette*, Feb. 27, 1982; *Lines Broken: The Story of Marion Motley*, PBS Western Reserve, documentary, 2021.

CHAPTER 24: FINDING MEANING AFTER FOOTBALL

Interviews with Bill Willis Jr., Clem Willis, Mike Brown, Harry Carson, John Wooten, Joe Horrigan, Larry Phillips; Bill Willis, Pro Football Hall of Fame Enshrinement Speech, July 30, 1977; Paul Brown, Pro Football Hall of Fame Presentation Speech for Bill Willis, July 30, 1977; *Expanding Your Horizons: Collegiate Football's Greatest Team* by Donald Steinberg, 1992; "Hall of Famer Helped Break Color Barrier in Pro Football," *Los Angeles Times*, Nov. 29, 2007.

CHAPTER 25: GONE TOO SOON

Interviews with Jim Tunney, Kraig Washington, Marvel Washington, Kenny Norwood, Willard Love, Pamela Larson Strode; "Kenny Washington Called 'The Best I Ever Saw' by Bob Waterfield," *Los Angeles Times*, May 17, 1970; "Kenny Washington Feted," Associated Press, Oct. 4, 1970; "Integrators of College Baseball—Kenny Washington," Blackcollegenines.com, Feb. 23, 2019; "UCLA's Washington: A Pioneer," *Los Angeles Sentinel*, Feb. 6, 1986; "Robinson, Washington on Bruin 11," *Los Angeles Sentinel*, Feb. 23, 1950; "The Strange Tale of Kenny Washington: Almost over the Hill at 31, Kenny Washington Fights to Crash Majors," *Michigan Chronicle*, March 18, 1950; "UCLA's Washington: A Pioneer," *Los Angeles Sentinel*, Feb. 6, 1986.

INDEX

ABOUT THE AUTHORS

Keyshawn Johnson was the first overall pick of the New York Jets in 1996 after a stellar career at USC, where he led the Trojans to victory in the 1996 Rose Bowl. He played 11 seasons in the NFL with the Jets, Tampa Bay Buccaneers, and Dallas Cowboys, and won a Super Bowl with the Bucs after the 2002 season. He was recently named the co-host of a nationally broadcast ESPN morning radio show and makes regular appearances on the network's *NFL Live, First Take,* and *Get Up*, as well as guest appearances on a variety of other media platforms.

Bob Glauber is the NFL columnist for New York's *Newsday* and has covered the NFL since 1985. A two-time winner of the New York State Sportswriter of the Year by the National Sports Media Association, as well as a first-place honoree of the Associated Press Sports Editors, Glauber has served as president of the Professional Football Writers of America since 2018, and in 2021 the PFWA awarded him its Career Achievement Award..